A Modern Heretic and a Traditional Community

A Modern Heretic and a Traditional Community

Mordecai M. Kaplan,
Orthodoxy, and
American Judaism

JEFFREY S. GUROCK AND

JACOB J. SCHACTER

COLUMBIA   UNIVERSITY   PRESS   •   NEW YORK

Columbia University Press
Publishers since 1893
New York   Chichester, West Sussex
Copyright © 1997 Columbia University Press

Library of Congress Cataloging-in-
Publication Data
Gurock, Jeffrey S.
A modern heretic and a traditional
community / Mordecai M. Kaplan,
Orthodoxy, and American Judaism /
Jeffrey S. Gurock and Jacob J. Schacter.
p.   cm
Includes bibliographical references and index.
ISBN 0-231-10626-2
1. Kaplan, Mordecai Menahem, 1881–   .
2. Rabbis—United States—Biography.
3. Reconstructionist Judaism.
4. Orthodox Judaism—New York (State)—
New York—Relations—Nontraditional Jews.
I. Schacter, Jacob J. II. Title
BM755.K289G87   1996
296.8'344'092—dc20
[B]   96-32329
          CIP

Casebound editions of Columbia University
Press books are printed on permanent and
durable acid-free paper.

Printed in the United States of America
Designed by Linda Secondari

c 10 9 8 7 6 5 4 3 2 1

For Leah, Jon, and Sarah

Eli, Rosie, and Michael

CONTENTS •

ACKNOWLEDGMENTS ·

We gratefully acknowledge the many groups and individuals who have assisted us in the research and writing of this book.

All research on Mordecai M. Kaplan begins with his invaluable journal, which he kept from 1914 to 1972. We are extremely grateful to Dr. Ismar Schorsch, chancellor of the Jewish Theological Seminary of America, for granting us permission to examine, refer to, and cite excerpts from these essential writings. We also want to thank Dr. Mayer Rabinowitz and Rabbi Zechariah Schwarzbard of the Jewish Theological Seminary Library for their assistance in facilitating our research.

Uncommon among American rabbis, Mordecai Kaplan maintained many of his own personal papers, early diaries, sermon texts, notebooks, and other materials that document his life. These invaluable sources and records are now on file at the Reconstructionist Rabbinical College in Wyncote, Pennsylvania. We are very grateful to that college's former president, Dr. Arthur Green, and to its librarian, Mr. Eli Wise, for their kind and gracious assistance.

We were very fortunate that the two Orthodox congregations Kaplan served had a strong sense of their own history and preserved many of their early twentieth-century documents. We thank Mr. Robert J. Leifert and Mrs. Florence Cohen, of Congregation Kehilath Jeshurun, who made the synagogue's earliest minute book and other records available to us. And we acknowledge with gratitude Rabbi Irving Wietschner, executive director of the Jewish Center and Mr. Martin Schwarzschild, its former president, for their assistance with materials made available from that synagogue's archives.

The minute book of the Society for the Advancement of Judaism tells us much about Kaplan's institutional disengagement from Orthodoxy in the 1920s. We thank Rabbi Alan W. Miller, former rabbi of the Society for the Advancement of Judaism, and Mrs. Jane Canter for giving us access to these important documents.

We have also benefited from speaking to a number of individuals at the Jewish Center when Mordecai Kaplan served as its rabbi who graciously shared their recollections with us: his four daughters, Mrs. Judith Eisenstein, Mrs. Hadassah Musher, Dr. Naomi Wenner, and Mrs. Selma Jaffee Goldman; also, Mrs. Beatrice Halperin, Mrs. Dorothy Sheldon, Mrs. Rita Bernstein, Mrs. Ruth Oliver, Mr. Jay Harold Garfunkel, Mr. Clarence Horwitz, and Dr. Eli Ginzberg. We also benefited from conversations with Dr. Malcolm Cohen, Mr. Elias Cohen, Mrs. Hinda Neufeld, Mr. Albert Bernstein, Dr. Mel Scult, and Dr. Jenna W. Joselit. A number of other individuals, whose names are scattered through the notes of this work, also assisted us in our research, and to them we also extend out thanks. We would also like to acknowledge the assistance of Mrs. Gertrude Welkes, who has graciously supported our research in memory of her late brother, Rabbi Harold Goldfarb.

As with all our scholarly endeavors, we are very fortunate that our home institutions, Yeshiva University and the Jewish Center, led by their respective presidents, Dr. Norman Lamm and Mr. Arthur G. Degen, appreciate our efforts and have encouraged us to avidly pursue them. We are also appreciative of the efforts of Dr. Benjamin R. Gampel of the Jewish Theological Seminary, near and dear to both of us, in reading early drafts of this work.

Finally, we are grateful for the unceasing daily support Pamela Gurock and Yocheved Schacter have given to our work. We also hope that our children, Leah and Jonathan Knapp, Sarah Schacter, and Eli, Rosie, and Michael Gurock, to whom this work is dedicated, will read and appreciate this book.

New York City and Lake Waubeeka, Connecticut
February 1996

A Modern Heretic and a Traditional Community

INTRODUCTION •

In the mid 1970s a creative publicist at Yeshiva University conceived of an intriguing gimmick to advertise the school's forthcoming ninetieth anniversary celebration in 1976. His idea was for Yeshiva to search for, identify, and honor the institution's oldest former student. The project moved along until it was determined who, in fact, the earliest alumnus was. Mordecai M. Kaplan was the oldest surviving pupil from Yeshiva Etz Chaim, that small boys' *cheder* (religious primary school) on the Lower East Side from which Yeshiva University ultimately would emerge. The publicist's plan was quickly abandoned. A decade later, when Yeshiva celebrated its centennial, the search was revived. Ultimately a retired foreman who had worked in New York's garment industry—a member of an Orthodox synagogue in the Bronx—was singled out for special mention. Mordecai Kaplan had died some three years earlier, in November 1983, at the age of 102.[1]

It is quite understandable that the educational flagship of American Orthodoxy chose not to honor Kaplan. By the 1970s the founder of the Reconstructionist movement had been, for more than half a century, an outspoken critic of Orthodox Judaism and an expositor of theological views opposing the very fundamentals of traditional faith. Kaplan would not have questioned this characterization either. Although he had, only a few years earlier, publicly referred to himself as "one of the oldest alumni of the Yeshiva University,"[2] he also asserted unabashedly that, almost from the turn of the century, he had not subscribed to Orthodox teachings or been a loyal member of that community.

As each approached the end of their tenth decade, Kaplan and Yeshiva had little use for or connection with one another. But mutual disinterest— even antipathy—did not always characterize the relationship between the critic and his erstwhile yeshiva, between this dissenter and the myriad of Orthodox individuals and institutions with whom he had long interacted. To begin with, for the first twenty years of Kaplan's life he was an Orthodox Jew who believed in the truths and conformed to the statutes of traditional Orthodoxy. He was, in fact, an outstanding member of that community who dedicated himself, onward from his teen years, to helping his generation of American Jews gain greater comfort with a Jewish tradition existing in consonance with American values.

During his next score of years, Kaplan began, privately and then publicly, to question and criticize Orthodox traditions and practices. In the 1910s, he also affiliated with the then incipient Conservative movement's rabbinical school, teachers' institute, and congregational association. However, as late as 1920 nothing he had yet said or done substantially altered Orthodox attitudes toward Kaplan or his relationships with most members of that community. Kaplan remained someone to whom the most traditional American Jews turned for assistance and guidance in reaching the youth of their community. He participated in the founding of the Orthodox Young Israel movement and helped Orthodox Jews modernize their talmud torah system. The leaders of the Rabbi Isaac Elchanan Theological Seminary (RIETS), another forerunner of Yeshiva University, gave their own, numerous indications that neither his statements nor his new affiliations had made him a threat to or an enemy of Orthodoxy. Most significantly, in 1917 a group of Orthodox Jews on the Upper West Side of Manhattan in New York City engaged him as leader and rabbi of their neighborhood's new Jewish Center.

Kaplan accepted these calls because long after the rabbi stopped walking with God, in the traditional sense of the phrase, he still enjoyed strolling with and influencing those who believed in Orthodoxy. More important, in his most optimistic moments Kaplan firmly believed he would eventually convince this mass of Jews of his own East European heritage that he had the only viable approach and program for preserving twentieth-century Judaism from dissolution through assimilation and disaffection.

It was only at the end of 1920 that Kaplan began to hear the rhetoric of antipathy that would follow him for the rest of his life. The heretic was separated from the community when he, for the first time, launched two highly provocative attacks against the tradition. He expanded on his earlier theoretical swipes against Orthodoxy and proceeded to enumerate those basic Orthodox rituals and observances he considered to be outmoded and untenable, also announcing that he was prepared to head a new society or expression of Judaism that would enthusiastically propagate his radical approaches. At that point Orthodox leaders both in New York and nationwide responded indignantly to a man who was now called a heretic, an *apikorus*, and a sworn enemy of Judaism. The firestorm of protest eventually led to his removal from the Jewish Center after a year-and-a-half-long battle.

In the subsequent six decades of Kaplan's very long life the Reconstructionist rabbi would have no further formal affiliation with any Orthodox institution. The Young Israel movement, the Orthodox talmud torah system, and, certainly, the Rabbi Isaac Elchanan Theological Seminary, which was soon to add on a Yeshiva College and ultimately become, in 1946, an Orthodox university, were among those traditional groups that could not abide his deviant theological views. The angriest of Kaplan's Orthodox enemies were heard from whenever the Reconstructionist published major statements that defined what his movement stood for and how it would reorder Jewish religious life. In 1934 the publication of Kaplan's *Judaism as a Civilization* occasioned highly antagonistic responses in Orthodox Jewish newspapers. In 1945, upon the appearance of the Reconstructionist *Sabbath Prayer Book*, the Agudath ha-Rabbanim (Union of Orthodox Rabbis of the United States and Canada) gestured dramatically against Kaplan. They excommunicated their enemy, designating him the arch-heretic of their time.

Orthodox Jews all agreed, from the 1920s on, that Kaplan's views on the Torah, God, and His commandments should be condemned. But antipathy toward Kaplan was mitigated, in some Orthodox circles, by a recognition that this expert pedagogue could offer useful practical advice in meeting their own communal needs. Among New York's Orthodox Jews the issue of the "usable" Kaplan provoked debates and, sometimes, personalized disagreements. Elsewhere, particularly in parts of America that were remote from New York, Kaplan's influence was a recognized and even welcomed part of Orthodox life.

Kaplan had nothing but disdain for those Orthodox Jews who publicly reviled his life's work. He also had no interest in acknowledging those who made their own distinctions—for their own purposes—between his theo-logical approaches and his practical prescriptions for promoting Jewish survival. At the same time, Kaplan never stopped enjoying his interaction with Orthodoxy's rank and file. In the period after 1920 he found them primarily in communities far west of the Hudson River. He continued to believe that these Jews would ultimately accept the enduring truths of his Reconstructionist creed and, for more than half a century, continued to maintain relationships with them.

A Modern Heretic and a Traditional Community follows the course of this complex relationship for what it tells both about the dissenter and his for-mer community. As a biography of a modern heretic, this book reveals not only when Kaplan's own thinking, studying, and emotions moved him away from Orthodoxy but also identifies the fears, interests, and concerns that constrained him from immediately articulating his views and publicly projecting their implications. Our work shows that while a youthful Kaplan already differed fundamentally with many of the teachings of tra-ditional Judaism, he was slow to disavow Orthodoxy publicly and reluc-tant to separate himself from those with whom he had theological differ-ences. His caution was predicated, in part, upon his perception that even in voluntaristic America, where no Jew could officially enforce sanctions against another, some Orthodox leaders still had the capacity to isolate him from the mass of potential constituents whom he desired to influ-ence. Kaplan the heretic projected a degree of residual strength and power on traditional religious authorities that, in reality, they did not possess in this most modern of times and countries. So disposed, the optimist in Kaplan believed he could, in time, bring to his side many of those who struggled with the demands of traditional faith in twentieth-century America. Meanwhile, the pessimist in the Reconstructionist sometimes felt that if he did not tread gingerly toward those with whom he differed they might use their power against him. He actually worried, in one par-ticular instance, that Orthodox zealots might even be able to deny him gainful employment, a punitive measure that their powerful premodern predecessors would surely have imposed on him.

All told, while Kaplan's dissent from traditional Jewish teachings was early and always sincere, he long remained, for personal, professional, and strategic reasons, very concerned with Orthodox sensibilities and closely tied to Orthodox Jews of many social, behavioral, and ideological stripes.

Indeed, that Kaplan alternately courted and was apprehensive about various groups of Orthodox Jews at different times and places underscores a basic truth about his erstwhile community fully evidenced in this social history. Orthodox Jewish religious attitudes, identities, and self-definitions were greatly variegated throughout late nineteenth- and twentieth-century America. In following Kaplan through his century of life among American Jews, almost every conceivable type of Orthodox opinion, point of view, and lifestyle is encountered. On the Lower East Side there were members of Chief Rabbi Jacob Joseph's court who aggressively resisted Americanization and others, within that same small religious circle, who wanted a different American Jewish future for themselves and their children. Mordecai Kaplan's own parents held to this modern Orthodox point of view. Kaplan's early efforts as an advocate of aesthetic and social change within Orthodoxy, demonstrates, similarly, that immigrant Orthodox synagogue members were of several minds over the appropriateness of such modifications.

Kaplan's initial experiences at the Jewish Center expose any number of Orthodox Jewish attitudes toward having a critic of traditional Judaism lead that congregation. There, initially, within the center, even the most religiously committed Jews were totally prepared to work with this dissenter, so impressed were they with Kaplan's proven ability to reach out to the disaffected within their community. Their only substantial fears were that Kaplan would aggressively espouse his unorthodox views in the congregation, openly object to the traditional rites that would be used in the center, and, in so doing, deeply embarrass them among other segments of this country's Orthodox community who might take a more jaundiced view toward a dissenter in their midst. Of course, situated as they all were in a voluntary American religious context where no authoritative voice could hold sway, from the first time Kaplan went public with his criticisms each Orthodox group was permitted to, and did, decide for itself what constituted heresy and what, if anything, should be done about this former Orthodox rabbi.

The reactions within the West Side congregation when Kaplan ultimately showed himself incapable of following the Jewish Center leadership's implicit commands to keep his views largely to himself speaks even further about Orthodoxy's multiple identities among second-generation Jews. When those leaders who first engaged him moved for his removal, they found others in that same Orthodox synagogue who did not care at all about his heresies. In some instances their absence of concern correlated with their own lack of punctilious observance of Orthodox traditions, reflecting an American Jewish relationship with Orthodoxy that was emotional, historical, or sentimental. These individuals might have been taken with Reconstructionist creeds even as they maintained formal Orthodox affiliations. Indeed, when the Kaplan-Jewish Center relationship unraveled, these Jews, who had previously adhered unqualifiedly to Orthodox teachings only within the confines of the synagogue's sanctuary, helped Kaplan found his new Society for the Advancement of Judaism (SAJ).

Finally, as we have noted earlier, in the period after 1920, when the practical implications of his dissent were well known, Orthodox Jews were divided in their approaches toward interacting with and learning from Mordecai Kaplan. Again, variegated Orthodox opinions ranged from those who were almost ready to accept parts of Kaplan's new religious message to other, implacable, foes, who opposed everything for which he stood. In many instances feelings for this arch-dissenter reflected larger Orthodox communal disagreements over the appropriateness of cooperation with Jews who belonged to other denominations on communitywide issues that were not strictly religious. All told, the saga of Mordecai Kaplan's encounter with American Orthodoxy illuminates not only a significant aspect in the life of this influential and controversial figure but also highlights the varying shades assumed by American Orthodoxy in this last century.

CHAPTER 1 • *An Orthodox Rabbi's Son on the Lower East Side*

The leaders of the Association of the American Orthodox Hebrew Congregations prayed that they would be given the strength to "preserve . . . the knowledge and practice of the Law (Torah), Worship (Avodah) and Charity (Gemilut Hasadim)" among American Jews in a manner "not inconsistent with the Laws of Moses, the usages of the Talmud, and the ecclesiastical authorities." Formed in 1887, the association, composed of representatives from some fifteen of the largest congregations on the Lower East Side of New York, had set out to recreate in America, against all odds, the civilization they remembered from Eastern Europe. America, they thought, had the potential to be a great Torah center with the "liberty [they enjoyed] to observe our religion, to study, teach, observe, perform and establish our Law." But, to their dismay, they observed that Judaism was "neglected and our Law held in light esteem [by] . . . they who stray like sheep, listening to shepherds who bid them to drink from broken cisterns that hold not the true water of life" or who "have been brought up in ignorance of our Holy Faith."[1]

In their view the tide of disaffection and assimilation could not be stemmed solely by heartfelt commitment. Unity, organization, and leadership were desperately needed "to correct abuses . . . which have been a reproach for us, and a weapon for the enemies of Judaism." Association leaders realized that before they could hope to influence others to adhere to Judaism's old world teachings, Orthodoxy in America had to put its own house in order. The constant squabbling over who controlled kashruth regulation had to end. Insufficiently trained or outright impostor rabbis, who made a mockery of the holy regulations of matrimony and divorce, had to be put out of business. And the "brazen outlaws," as one contemporary put it, the unobservant laymen who sometimes dominated synagogue life and politics, had to be upbraided and removed. A man of unquestioned rabbinic pedigree and personal charisma—a chief rabbi— had to be appointed to remedy such intolerable situations, all wrought by the libertine and voluntaristic American world within which they now found themselves.[2]

The association did anticipate, however, that once this envisioned chief rabbi was effectively ensconced, accepted by, and in control of all pious Jews in New York and their synagogues and activities, the crusade could then commence to "keep the next generation faithful to Judaism in spite of educational, social, and business influences which, in America, are so powerful to make our sons and daughters forget their duty to the religion in which their ancestors lived, and for which those ancestors died." For the association, the spiritual return of immigrant Jewry to the ways of their ancestral past was to begin with the selection of that eminent East European rabbi who would preside over their community. Thus, with no small measure of pride and hopeful expectation, the association announced in April 1888 that Rabbi Jacob Joseph of Vilna, a renowned preacher and religious judge, a student of the famed Rabbi Naftali Zevi Yehudah Berlin (the Netziv) and Rabbi Israel Salanter, had accepted their invitation.[3]

In the association's scheme of things, immigrant boys like Mordecai Kaplan who were the sons of rabbis from Russia, part of the pious minority of downtown Jews, were essential to the mission of transplanting European Judaism to American soil. If properly trained in the ways of the yeshiva world of Russia, these youngsters could be projected to their larger Jewish community as a learned religious elite, living proof of what religious Jews could achieve in the unholy land of America. They would be role models to those who wavered from adherence to their ancestral faith and would demonstrate that young Jews could become, under the conditions of freedom, "zealous followers" of the sacred past despite all the lures of the world around them. It was thus another moment of great consequence for the association when, in 1886, several of its members helped found America's first yeshiva, Etz Chaim, which promised to train these exceptional boys as they would have been educated back home in Russia.[4]

Rabbi Moses Weinberger, a Hungarian rabbi who lived then in New York and loyally supported the association, spoke for many when he ecstatically reflected on how a center for the study of Torah had been planted amidst the aridity that was American Jewish religious life. "Hurrah! What pleasant news! How lovely! How dear!" he wrote.

> A yeshiva for Mishna and Gemara! How much good is hidden in these words. . . . Now if we can only see that it is not established on a false foundation . . . to add to the amount of jealousy, hatred, and disagreement among us. . . . May it [be] . . . established for the sake of God and his teachings, to ascertain truth, to spread Torah in Israel, to strengthen the faith.[5]

Great expectations were placed upon the rabbis and students who would enroll in this fledgling institution.

Mordecai M. Kaplan suffered the burden of these communal expectations as keenly as did any religious youngster of his time. After all, his father was, for a while, an employee of the association and a colleague of Rabbi Joseph on the latter's rabbinical court. But, although Kaplan did, in fact, study for a time at Etz Chaim, neither he nor his parents conformed to the association's fondest hopes and dreams. They deviated because their worldview varied from their fellow downtown contemporaries in subtle but essential ways. Despite the fact that Israel Kaplan (1848–1917) looked, spoke, and acted much like "an old-time Rov [rabbi]"[6]—he, for example, never really did learn to speak English—this elder Kaplan and, to a lesser extent, his wife were also influenced by, if not representative of, newer Orthodox attitudes then evolving in a Jewish Eastern Europe that was not religiously monolithic. The Kaplans were products of the modernization and enlightenment ideas that had been slowly changing Russian yeshiva life. They lived in accordance with this different strain of Orthodox life and, when they settled on the Lower East Side of Manhattan in 1889, transmitted its perspective to their son.

To be sure, Mordecai's father was a learned talmudist who studied in a number of Eastern European yeshivas, including Volozhin, the same school that produced Jacob Joseph. Like the chief rabbi, Israel Kaplan also received his rabbinic ordination from the Netziv as well as from Rabbi Yitzchak Elchanan Spektor of Kovno and from Rabbi Yitzchak Reines, the well-known leader of the Mizrachi (Religious Zionist) movement. In 1881 Reines was serving as rabbi in Kaplan's hometown of Swentzian, near

Vilna in Lithuania, and reportedly had a close relationship with his young colleague.[7] After receiving *semichah* (rabbinic ordination), Israel Kaplan continued to study in the Denaburg and Asisok yeshivas, then taught for a while in a town near Vilna before being considered for the post of rosh yeshiva (dean) in Taurogen.[8]

However, the study of the traditional texts, the Talmud, the commentaries, and codes, were not the only intellectual horizons that captivated this young scholar. While still a student in Lithuanian yeshivot, Israel Kaplan displayed "unusual liberal tendencies for a man whose background and training were entirely traditional." He was, to begin with, inquisitive about the world of secular culture outside the yeshiva and persistent enough to earn "privileges [within yeshivas] not accorded to other students. He was permitted to read something of modern Hebrew literature and journalism." It is probable that, while in the Volozhin yeshiva, he joined that circle of students who were attracted to the Haskalah, or Jewish Enlightenment. But, the best early evidence that Israel Kaplan possessed a long-enduring affinity for the Jewish Enlightenment, and a desire to learn more about its disciplines, is that he counted among his friends Samuel Joseph Fuenn, the famous Enlightenment figure, who provided Kaplan, upon his departure to America, with a letter of introduction to Professor Alexander Kohut, care of the Jewish Theological Seminary.[9]

Israel Kaplan also showed himself to be somewhat modern and unconventional when he provided his daughter, Sophie, Mordecai's older sister, with a formal Jewish education. When Sophie was a little girl her father insisted upon her attending cheder with the boys in Swentzian "because that was the only way she would have the opportunity of learning Hebrew and understanding the Bible." It is unknown how the community reacted to his demand. Mordecai Kaplan would later suggest that this "rather remarkable action probably classed father with the *Maskilim* or intelligentsia, who were suspect of heresy." In any event, Israel Kaplan's reputation in the European yeshiva system remained intact. He was protected, his son claimed, by virtue of his association with the town's rabbi, Isaac Reines, which only emphasizes that even if Kaplan behaved somewhat differently than most Orthodox scholars, his attitudes were not completely unique or deemed to be outside the pale of Orthodoxy.[10]

Anna Kaplan did not actively pursue the disciplines of the Haskalah. And it is not known whether she approved of her daughter being educated far differently than she had been as a young girl. Where she differed most from the women of her time and place was in the unusual dreams she harbored for her son. While most Russian rabbi's wives prayed that their boys would grow up to be great Talmudic scholars in the renowned yeshivas, Anna Kaplan's not so secret ambition for Mordecai was that he would become chief rabbi of Great Britain. In the Kaplans' home hung a picture of the great Anglo-Jewish philanthropist, Moses Montefiore. She understood that the educational requirements for this English government post were much broader than any job a Volozhin graduate might normally aspire to occupy. The legally recognized leader of British Jewry, that community's official ambassador to the Gentile world, had to be a skilled speaker of English and conversant with the wisdom of the West. Anna Kaplan understood that, somewhere along the line, her son would have to become expert in the cultures around him. Indeed, Mordecai's mother would make a number of efforts to advance him toward that goal. It was into this kind of family that Mordecai Kaplan was born on June 10, 1881, in Swentzian.[11]

Like most shtetl youths of his time, Mordecai Kaplan's "Jewish training [began] the moment I began to speak." He would remember many years later that as a lad of no more than four he sat on his father's knee and was "asked by him to spell out the Hebrew alphabet with the aid of matches." When he performed this somewhat precocious intellectual feat, young Mordecai was rewarded with "a whistle in the form of a leaden bird."[12] At the age of five he began his cheder education in Swentzian. His first lessons "consisted of nothing but learning to read the prayers." From there he was taught to read "the Pentateuch and to translate it into Yiddish, the vernacular of all the Jews in town."[13] Of course, living, as he recalled, in a homogeneous Jewish social environment, he had "no conflicts, no adjustments" to make. In his "little town . . . eight versts (which is about five miles) from a railroad station," Kaplan had almost no contact with Gentiles, save with Pavlova "who scrubbed our floors" and with a Polish policeman who frequented his mother's small store. For the young boy "the idea of being a Jew was natural, normal and complete." He experienced the Jewish holidays, customs and traditions as a matter of life's course long before he formally explored the niceties of their legal details in the study hall.[14] Had Mordecai Kaplan remained in Russia, the next step in his traditional training would have been his attendance at one or more of the advanced yeshivas in Lithuania where he would have immersed himself full-time and long-term in Torah study. When Israel

Kaplan planned on first exposing his young son to the wider worlds of Jewish and general knowledge is not known.

Mordecai Kaplan's early Jewish life and basic Jewish education terminated, however, at the age of seven when, in 1888, the family was forced to leave Russia for America.[15] As was the case with so many Jewish families at the time, economic deprivation led the father to trek off to America with the plan of bringing over his family once he established himself in New York. In the Kaplans' case "Polish boycott methods" put the "little store which was the family's source of livelihood" out of business.[16] And Israel Kaplan, who, until then, had been permitted, through his wife's mercantile labors, to travel, learn, and grow as a scholar, had to assume "the bread winner's" role. The Kaplans' migration differed only slightly from the norm in that Mordecai, Anna, and Sophie stopped in Paris, where they stayed with two of Anna's brothers and waited for more than a year to receive the good news that their husband and father was settled in America.[17] On the road to Western Europe the family stopped in Kovno where, in a great expression of respect for the tradition, young Mordecai received the blessing of Rabbi Yitzchak Elchanan Spektor. This leading Torah authority, who never discouraged his disciples from migrating to the United States despite its earned reputation as a land inhospitable to Orthodox observance, must have felt that, in the Kaplan family's case, Russian Jewry's loss was American Jewry's gain. A father and a son committed to Jewish learning could only elevate Jewish life in that religiously barren land.[18]

Arriving in New York, Israel Kaplan linked up with the religious establishment that was forming around the chief rabbi. Rabbi Spektor had recommended Rabbi Joseph for his job and Israel Kaplan, as we have just seen, revered Russia's senior rabbi; it made sense that the new arrival would seek out those who shared his background and many of his sensibilities. Indeed, Israel Kaplan's first home in America was in the residence of his fellow Volozhiner, Rabbi Jacob Joseph, where "he was given food and lodging and some pocket money for services he rendered in the way of deciding upon ritual questions and entertaining scholarly visitors with discussions on talmudic lore." Soon, Israel Kaplan received formal recognition as a *dayyan* (judge) in Rabbi Joseph's court, where he "answer[ed] questions of halachah and arbitrat[ed] in cases of litigation." No questions were asked or eyebrows raised about Israel Kaplan's other wider-ranging interests.[19]

By the summer of 1889 Israel Kaplan was well enough established in New York—he was earning $12.00 a week—to send for his wife and children. On Saturday morning, July 8, 1889, the three Kaplans set sail from Le Havre on *La Bourgoyne* for New York. They arrived at Ellis Island eight days later, on Sunday, July 16. After passing through immigration, they boarded a small boat to the tip of Manhattan, Castle Garden, where they were met by Israel Kaplan and one of Mrs. Kaplan's brothers, Mendel Krizansky. They took the Second Avenue elevated train to the Lower East Side and, for a few days, stayed in Krizansky's apartment on the fourth floor of a tenement house at 49 Eldridge Street. They then moved into their own two-and-a-half room apartment on the ground floor at 32 Suffolk Street, corner of Grand Street, which they rented for $10.00 a month.[20]

Once settled, Israel and Anna Kaplan turned their attention, among their many other concerns, to the schooling of their two children. Given who Rabbi Kaplan was, and the association for which he labored, it was expected that his young Mordecai would be immediately enrolled at Etz Chaim. He would study Torah in New York just like the boys in Swentzian and, hopefully, become part of Etz Chaim's elite cadre of American Torah scholars who were to uphold American Orthodoxy. Downtown cheder students rigorously learned traditional subjects from nine in the morning until mid-afternoon. General studies were offered grudgingly and haphazardly after 3 P.M.[21] Sophie Kaplan, like all girls from religious families of the time, would be educated in the city's public schools. Her religious training could only come through private tutoring. In the late 1880s there were no Orthodox Jewish schools available in the ghetto of the Lower East Side for immigrant girls.[22]

However, given their orientation and the ambitions they entertained for their son, the Kaplans were not completely sold on the values of an Etz Chaim education, and young Mordecai was not immediately enrolled at the small yeshiva. "On the advice of friends I was taken by my mother to public school," wrote Kaplan many years later.[23] Months earlier, while awaiting word from America, Anna Kaplan had enrolled Mordecai in Parisian public schools.[24] To be sure, Kaplan did not stay long at first in this highly secular environment. But his removal from New York's "Temple of Americanization" was not due to either Mordecai's or his parents' abhorrence of what was being taught there. Rather, Kaplan's parents withdrew him because, as he later remembered it, "after staying there a few days, I said I was not learning anything there and was wasting my time. I was bored."[25]

Ultimately, young Kaplan did attend Etz Chaim for a while.[26] And when enrolled at the association's flagship educational institution, the young rabbi's son displayed some of the attributes hallowed by the school. Admitted to the second class, he and his twenty classmates studied "about half a folio page of Talmud each week with Rashi's commentary" under the supervision of a Rabbi Elias Ratkowsky.[27] There, at Etz Chaim, he also did more than just comform to the yeshiva's separatist credo. On at least one occasion he advocated an old world lifestyle, arguing that New York's young Torah scholars should study the traditional texts in Yiddish like the Russian yeshiva boys did. Many years later Kaplan would recall that when he once encountered his Etz Chaim classmates speaking English in the "Bet-Hamidrash of the Eldridge Street Synagogue . . . I was such a zealot that I would plant myself in front of them and denounce them for acting so goyishly. 'Is it not disgraceful, is it not a *cherpah* [shame] for us Jewish boys to be talking in *shul* a language other than Yiddish?' "[28] Notwithstanding this momentary gallantry for past ways from the polyglot Kaplan, by the time he was ten and a half he was already back in New York's public schools, receiving his Torah education from his father and a private tutor.

When Israel Kaplan determined that his son could be exposed to Jewish wisdom from unconventional sources, he distanced himself further from the association's norms. As it was, the eminent biblical scholar, Arnold B. Ehrlich (1848–1919), a former apostate from Judaism who, before his return, had assisted his German colleague, Franz Delitzsch, both in his Hebrew translation of the New Testament (1877) and in his missionary newspaper, was a frequent guest in Kaplan's New York home. There they would discuss the sources of various rabbinic passages relevant to Ehrlich's work well within earshot of the bar mitzvah-aged Mordecai, who was just beginning his student career at the Jewish Theological Seminary. In their volatile intellectual encounters, "[Ehrlich] would have occasion to pour scorn upon traditional commentators or to express some of his heretical views about the Bible."[29]

Israel Kaplan's belief that he had much to discuss with all types of Jews—including the religiously radical—did not sit well with Anna Kaplan, particularly as it involved her son. Mordecai Kaplan would later reminisce that "after [Ehrlich] left the house, she [would] rebuke father for having anything to do with him." She did not want her son exposed to his heresy and was concerned about the mixed messages emitting from young Mordecai when she observed him reading Ehrlich's manuscripts "in the mornings, for a half hour each day," albeit "with his *tefillin* on."[30] A future chief rabbi of England[31] could be worldly enough without having to experience an Ehrlich.[32]

To counteract the heretical influences of Ehrlich, and to keep peace at home, Israel Kaplan arranged for Mordecai to study with another scholar, Rabbi Joseph Sossnitz. But, in keeping with the senior Kaplan's views of what he wanted his son to know, he did not simply hire a typical old-time *rebbe* (teacher). Although Sossnitz was the first principal of the fledgling Uptown Talmud Torah of Harlem—then little more than a cheder—and, according to Kaplan's recollections, "a *Hasid* in the fullest sense of the term, though he refused to wear the hasidic garb," this tutor was also "a mathematician and a physicist." Like Israel Kaplan, he too had some discernible affinities for the Haskalah.[33]

It is not clear whether Israel Kaplan's unusual views and friendships were widely known within downtown's Orthodox community. It is possible that the educational choices Israel and Anna made for their son troubled some association leaders. But, in the end, nothing that the Kaplans said or did really separated them from those who full-heartedly supported the thrust of the chief rabbi initiative.[34] Anna and Israel were deemed neither outcasts nor notorious dissenters because they were, to begin with, far from the only immigrant rabbinical family to reject Etz Chaim in a move to expose their son to broad worldly horizons.

For example, the parents of young Solomon Theodore Hurwitz shared the Kaplans' attitudes toward their own son attending public school. Solomon's father, Rabbi Nathan (Noteh) Hurwitz, was, like Israel Kaplan, a learned Russian-trained rabbi who migrated to America in the late 1880s. Rabbi Hurwitz, too, secured a position in New York as a dayyan, although, in his case, the title was wholly honorific. The actual occupation of this "short, stocky, white-bearded, old world scholar who knew no English" was to deliver "complex Yiddish *droshoth* [homiletical discourses] on Sabbaths and some weekdays between afternoon and evening services for the more foreign and erudite worshippers" in a congregation located outside of the downtown immigrant enclave. When his son was brought over, or came over with him, at age nine, "possessed of a good beginner's knowledge of Hebrew," he too was a likely candidate for Etz Chaim, where he could have been an active participant in the recreation of European Judaism in America. Nonetheless, Solomon was enrolled in the public schools, where, to his parent's apparent delight, "he always managed to keep at the head of his class." The elder Hurwitzes were content with the fact that their intellectually precocious son "devoted most of his time to the study of the Talmud and the Hebrew commentaries" only "after school hours."[35]

Moreover, even those families and youngsters who initially heeded the association's and chief rabbi's call had their own substantial doubts about whether the Orthodox life that was marked out for them in America was, in fact, precisely to their liking. Indeed, the beginning of the end of this early attempt to recreate unchanged the Russian yeshiva world of the nineteenth century in America may be dated from the moment when Etz Chaim students, boys Kaplan knew quite well, also from the most religious of homes, demanded that their school provide them with systematic exposure to American education. In time the school leaders felt compelled to acquiesce.[36]

Currents of thought that were moving slowly through Orthodox communities in Russia ran deep in America even among its most pious Jews. And, in a sense, the Kaplans were just slightly ahead of the norm. In any case, to maintain good standing within the Orthodox community on the Lower East Side did not require rejection of all aspects of modernity and Americanization. Almost every Orthodox immigrant family wanted its boys to possess the skills to advance in this country that their friends were obtaining in the public schools. That the public schools would educate and acculturate the ghetto's Orthodox girls went without saying. If anything, although the Kaplans' views of modernity and Americanization were somewhat more positive than those of families that kept their boys in the yeshiva until graduation, their opinions were probably more representative of Orthodox views in that community than the most unwavering of association members. All told, the Kaplans were quiet exponents of an alternate shade of immigrant Orthodoxy on the Lower East Side. We will later see that, in time, many of those who actively supported the chief rabbinate initiative came to share this incipient American Orthodox point of view.

In the meantime, for all their interests in modern Jewish disciplines and their resultant differences with the association over how Orthodox youngsters should be trained, the Kaplans still possessed a commitment to the advancement of religious learning and the perpetuation of traditional

Judaism in America that they communicated to their son. Thus, while most Etz Chaim graduates might have remained personally religious, it was the Kaplans' boy who would end up working to advance Jewish identification. The same could be said about the Hurwitzes and their very bright youngster. Solomon Theodore Hurwitz, as we will later detail, went on to earn advanced academic degrees in linguistics. While still in his twenties he became librarian in the Department of Jewish Literature at the New York Public Library, teaching courses in his field at Columbia University. This fully Americanized Jew secured these achievements while maintaining an enduring allegiance to Orthodox Judaism. And, in the last years of his all-too-short life, he turned his attention to advancing Orthodox *Wissenschaft* scholarship and secondary Orthodox Jewish education. Mordecai Kaplan fulfilled his parents' wish that he become an Orthodox rabbi, maybe toward the day when he might be appointed chief rabbi of the British Empire. And, for training in his calling, he went off, in 1893, to the Jewish Theological Seminary of America.

CHAPTER 2 • *Training at the Seminary for the*
American Orthodox Rabbinate

Israel and Anna Kaplan's social circle
of friends, associates, and acquaintances within downtown's Orthodox
community of the 1890s were of several minds over their decision to enroll
young Mordecai at the Jewish Theological Seminary (JTS). Some contemporaries wondered how the Kaplans expected their son to learn enough at
this New York-based institution to become an Orthodox rabbi.

After all, in curriculum, staffing, or outlook the seminary hardly resem-
bled the citadels of Torah learning they remembered from Eastern Europe.
Although this school "for the training of rabbis and cantors" did offer
courses in Bible, Talmud, Midrash, responsa, and codes, it was definitely not
a yeshiva. In Volozhin young Torah scholars studied the Talmud and its
commentaries "for their own sake," for the merit, satisfaction, and intrinsic
intellectual value inherent in religious scholarship. If that yeshiva had a this-
worldly goal, it was the production of scholars who would continue the hallowed traditions of Torah learning of the past. At the seminary, by contrast,
this most traditional of Jewish subjects was balanced by studies in Jewish
history and philosophy, Hebrew literature, voluntary training in *hazzanut*
(cantorial singing) and the "practice of homiletics in German and English,"
disciplines that were unheard of in the world of East European Orthodoxy.
Those religious immigrants populating the Kaplans' world were not yet
attuned to the reality that, in America, talmudic erudition alone could not
garner a rabbi enduring respect and that this country's conditions warranted
that its spiritual leaders be trained and perform differently than did the *rab-
banim* (traditional rabbis) they once revered in the old country. Consequently,
they did not understand what the Kaplans were doing.[1]

Other downtown Orthodox doubters comprehended that since America required an Orthodox rabbi to be widely skilled and multitalented, a seminary could, in theory, provide the Kaplan boy with the training he needed to be successful in this land. Their complaints about the particular school Israel and Anna chose centered around the outlook and questionable orientation of the teachers the young man would encounter there. Although seminary founders like Rabbis Sabato Morais, Henry P. Mendes, Henry W. Schneeberger, and Bernard Drachman established their school in 1886 as an Orthodox answer to the Reform Hebrew Union College for "the purpose of . . . preserv[ing] in America the knowledge and practice of historical Judaism as ordained in the Law of Moses and expounded by the prophets and sages of Israel in Biblical and Talmudical writings," their pursuit of that goal did not preclude them from associating with Jewish scholars who did not share their fidelity to Orthodoxy. By contrast, East European yeshivas never countenanced religiously heterogeneous faculties. The presence of "nontraditional" men like Rabbis Marcus Jastrow, David Davidson, Joshua Joffee, and Alexander Kohut in seminary teaching or advisory positions made it suspect to this segment of Orthodox downtowners. They worried about what would become of young students, like Kaplan, who opted to study with these professors.[2]

Ha-Ivri, one of the early Orthodox periodicals on the Lower East Side, led the chorus of criticism of the seminary's mission and activities. It scoffed at what it characterized as the low level of Torah learning achieved by seminary students. The weekly once claimed that the advanced students had finished but seventeen pages of Talmud and only segments of Rashi's commentary in the course of an entire year of study. Moreover, *Ha-Ivri* asserted that these undereducated rabbinical school graduates who were ostensibly to lead the battle against Reform and assimilation were being taught by professors lacking in commitment to traditional faith.[3]

A reporter for the *Yiddishe Welt*, another organ of downtown Orthodoxy, shared this negative assessment of the seminary's work and people. He was scandalized and outraged that at the seminary's commencement in 1902, "professors of the school sat with uncovered heads . . . and Professor Joffe [the instructor of Talmud] who delivered a major address in Hebrew was also bareheaded and mentioned the name of God without covering his head." For this correspondent, "that there is naturally a great difference between rabbis who graduate from a Volozhin yeshiva and those who graduate from a Jewish Theological Seminary" was an understatement.

This newspaperman unquestionably believed that Israel and Anna Kaplan were exposing their son to the wrong sorts of influences.

But this writer as well as the writers for *Ha-Ivri* were not the only Orthodox voices heard by the Kaplans on the Lower East Side.[4] People like ghetto literati Judah David Eisenstein understood and applauded those families who sent their sons to the seminary to learn how to serve the needs of the next generation of Jews as an American Orthodox rabbi. Eisenstein himself had publicly gone on record as asserting that many of the immigrant Orthodox rabbis were simply not doing the job of reaching the Americanized immigrants and their children. Why, he asked, must we continue to request rabbis from overseas, if we can produce our own here in the United States who understand the environment? The rabbis who do come over, he averred, often do not understand American culture, its language, or the outlooks of native-born Jews. Furthermore, some of these rabbis are corrupt impostors, "evildoers without any traits of decency." Graduates of a seminary, on the other hand, are intimately familiar with American Jewish life and would be known to all for their moral rectitude, having been properly screened from the very start of their rabbinic training.[5]

Turning to the specific seminary, the JTS, Israel and Anna Kaplan had chosen for their son, Eisenstein was much calmer than the correspondent for the *Yiddishe Welt* was about the faculty young Mordecai would encounter there. And he certainly did not question the faith commitments of the Orthodox students who chose to study at that institution. To be sure, this unofficial historian of Norfolk Street's Beth Hamedrosh Hagodol—the seat of Rabbi Jacob Joseph's court—who was a founder of Etz Chaim and secretary of the association,[6] had his difficulties with the seminary's unorthodox faculty members. In 1888, for example, Eisenstein strongly criticized Alexander Kohut. While acknowledging that the professor, who would soon join the seminary faculty, was "a great thinker, a renowned preacher, and an expert in Hebrew literature," Eisenstein was also clear that this "Conservative [rabbi] not unlike the radical [Reformers] lacked [religious] authority because he does not rely on the *Shulchan Aruch* [Code of Jewish Law]." Incidentally, for Eisenstein, there was not much difference between those whom he characterized as "Conservatives" and those who he considered to be "Radicals." For him, Radicals simply wanted to change Judaism quickly while Conservatives were more patient and circumspect. Despite his discomfort with Kohut and with what he called "Conservative Judaism," Eisenstein nonetheless asserted that the seminary could be "good, useful and warranted" for American Jewry.[7]

However, for the seminary to truly fulfill its warranted functions, Eisenstein argued that "many changes had to be made." The school had to be certain "not to admit Radical congregations to its association because if their numbers increased over the course of time, they would overturn" the seminary's mission. The faculty had to be faithful to Orthodox tradition, being careful to "observe the conservative faith[8] and be sure not to break with even the most minor mitzvah of the commandments of the Torah." These teachers had to instruct "with their heads covered and in all their teachings never to deviate from the strictures of the *Shulchan Aruch*." So disposed, Eisenstein shared the *Yiddishe Welt*'s condemnation of Professor Joffe's 1902 commencement performance but retained a sense that the seminary, if it followed his strictures, had the potential to do good in the community. Indeed, Eisenstein even suggested that JTS would remain useful and legitimate even if it ended up producing *Conservative* rabbis in addition to the best type of American Orthodox rabbi.[9]

Israel and Anna Kaplan harbored no qualms about their Mordecai attending the seminary the way it was in 1893. Although, many decades later, their son would recall that "by the time I was twelve I was already eager to serve the cause of our people," it is clear that Kaplan's parents were the driving forces behind his enrollment at JTS. Kaplan himself allowed that, if not for them, he "might have gone into the study of law or medicine or worked my way up in business, but my parents' heart, especially mother's, was set upon my becoming a rabbi because in that calling I would be leading a Jewish life, and furthering the spiritual welfare of my people."[10] And while Israel Kaplan may, at one point, have thought about sending Mordecai back to Eastern Europe for the most rigorous of Talmudic training, in the end both he and his wife understood what it meant to be an American rabbi and wanted that form of useful education for their son.[11] Moreover, they had no second thoughts about him studying with the likes of Rabbis Kohut and Joffe. After all, the elder Kaplan had carried with him from Russia a letter of introduction to the former. And, as far the bareheaded talmudist Rabbi Joffee was concerned, the tolerant Israel may have been a friend or an acquaintance of this fellow Volozhiner who had received semichah from Rabbi Reines in 1881 before moving on to the modern Berlin-based Hochshule in 1888.[12] And whatever Joffe's deviations were from tradition, they were not nearly as profound as had been those of Kaplan's household friend, Arnold Ehrlich.

Eliezer Robison, principal of the Machzike Talmud Torah, Kasriel Sarasohn, editor of the Yiddish weekly, the *Yiddishe Gazetten*, and the daily, *Yiddishes Tageblatt*, and a number of important lay leaders of the Kaplans' own home congregation, Kehal Adath Jeshurun of Eldridge Street, had no problem understanding Israel and Anna's decision. Each of these people, in his own way, supported the seminary endeavor, demonstrating again that even if the Kaplans' views differed from those of the most unyielding association leaders, young Mordecai's mother and father were not unique within the variegated downtown religious community.

For example, by the time Kaplan attended JTS, Robison was on record as stating that the seminary was "the only seat of learning in this country whose graduates are looked upon as worthy of occupying the high position of orthodox rabbi."[13] In other words, the head of downtown Orthodoxy's most established afternoon school, an institution close to the heart of the Orthodox association—second only to Etz Chaim—unqualifiably saw the seminary as a legitimate trainer of American Orthodox rabbis.[14]

Kasriel Sarasohn seconded the Kaplans' views on the value and quality of a JTS education. Although Sarasohn, like his literary colleague Eisenstein, was a founder of Etz Chaim, he was also quick to call upon immigrant congregations in 1888 to support the uptown Orthodox effort.[15] Eight years later Sarasohn even more strongly charged "all Russian rabbis . . . to support this important institution [Jewish Theological Seminary] . . . and to encourage their congregations to support the building, where pure American Judaism, the Judaism which has not denied the Sabbath, holidays and kashruth is being taught and strengthened."[16] During the time Kaplan attended the seminary Sarasohn also characterized that school as a "Pumbeditha [a prominent early medieval Babylonian academy] of the twentieth century that might yet produce geonim [great rabbinic scholars]." Speaking to the more acculturated readers of his papers—those who might peruse the daily English back page of the *Tageblatt*—Sarasohn would later urge downtowners "to become acquainted with this *Yeshiva* because orthodox rabbis are coming forth from the Jewish Theological Seminary" (emphasis added).[17]

Immigrant banker Sender Jarmalowski was not as articulate about his views on the legitimacy of the seminary's Orthodoxy. But he undeniably applauded the Kaplans' career plans for their son. The presence of Jarmalowski, president of Eldridge Street's Kehal Adath Jeshurun, on the seminary's founding board of trustees spoke loudly about his positive appreciation of JTS's role in the religious lives of his own and of future generations.[18] It also suggested that a leader of a substantial downtown synagogue could both revere past ways—he and his synagogue were constituent members of the Association of the American Orthodox Hebrew Congregations[19]—and still make allowances to meet America's new religious demands.[20]

Jarmalowski was not the only Lower East Side lay leader to support or be linked to both the association activities and the seminary initiative. Indeed, there was a community of interest of which they and the Kaplans were a part that, once again, constituted a different strain within a variegated immigrant Orthodox community. For example, Nathan Levin of East Broadway was both an association vice president and a founding trustee of JTS.[21] Harry Fischel, a founder of the Machzike Talmud Torah, and an individual destined to play a major role in Kaplan's activities as an Orthodox rabbi, was listed in 1900 as a "Subscriber" to the seminary.[22] So were Asher Germansky and Moses Bernstein, who, most significantly, were also among the founding trustees of the Rabbi Isaac Elchanan Theological Seminary (RIETS).[23] This latter school was established in 1897 to continue Etz Chaim's type of education on a more advanced level. At its inception RIETS was literally an East European yeshiva on American soil, with a curriculum and outlook comparable to Volozhin. In time, and after significant changes of its own, RIETS would become a competitor to the seminary.[24] But, for now, RIETS and JTS operated in different worlds. These astute lay leaders understood those differences and once again showed the capacity to support and pay homage to the hallowed East European past while looking favorably upon the seminary's championing of a new approach to the American future.[25]

Given what Jarmalowski and his fellows had come to believe, it was a moment of shared joy for the family and congregation when, at his bar mitzvah on June 16, 1894, seminary student Mordecai Kaplan ascended the Kehal Adath Jeshurun pulpit and offered a learned rabbinic discourse in Yiddish. Congregants knew young Mordecai well. He was the lad who attended services daily, sat "near the ark and . . . engage[d]" his father "in involved Talmudic discussions." Almost seventy years later Kaplan would recall that his discourse was based on a text that his father provided him from the Tractate Shabbat 49a "concerning the saint Elisha of the Wings, who lived during the Hadrianic persecutions." At that auspicious moment this rabbi's son stated to his proud audience that

> the reason given in the Talmud for the tefillin having turned into the wings of a dove is that the dove is the emblem of the Jewish People, as the eagle is of other peoples. Moreover as the dove is able to use its wings in a way that saves it from its enemies so does the Jewish People use its *mitzvot* as a means of saving its life. We use our religious practices—tefillin, talit, mezuzah, Sabbaths and festivals, kashrut, etc.—not to win God's favor but to manifest our love, loyalty and devotion toward our Jewish people.[26]

Those in the congregational family and the Kaplans' social circle who saw real value in the seminary were reassured that their faith was well placed. It was apparent that Mordecai's father, who was then giving talmud classes in their congregation, had raised his son well and that the boy had not been ruined by attending JTS. A year later a second boy from Israel Kaplan's informal Talmud circle went off to study at the seminary. Mordecai's study partner in the Eldridge Street synagogue, Alter (Isaac) Abelson, who began his own Torah studies in the Lithuanian yeshiva at Lomzhe, now joined his friend at this new modern institution.[27]

Indeed, Abelson was but one of possibly several dozen young men from the downtown community who studied at JTS. They included, to begin with, scions of Eastern European Orthodox families who wanted to learn how to be American rabbis after having received traditional training in Russian yeshivas. There was Alexander Basel, who received his earliest training in Talmud at the Telshe yeshiva in Lithuania and who joined Kaplan in JTS's senior class. Julius Greenstone, who could also boast of Russian "cheder and Talmudical College" training, progressed very quickly through his seminary studies. He arrived in this country in 1894 as a young adult of twenty-one, was already in the Junior class of the seminary with Mordecai Kaplan in 1896, and was ordained in 1900. Menahem Max Eichler and Henry M. Speaker were two other contemporaries of Kaplan with extensive old world training in rabbinics.[28]

Then, of course, there was young Mordecai's group of four friends from the old Lower East Side neighborhood. Charles Kauvar, Herman Abramowitz, Elias L. Solomon, and Phineas Israeli were to be Kaplan's schoolmates throughout his educational career. These four boys, like Kaplan, were born in Lithuania and brought as children to the United

States. They met up with Mordecai in Public School No. 2 on the Lower East Side and continued to study together and with him at City College of New York, where Kaplan first matriculated in 1895 at age fourteen into the "subfreshman class," and at the seminary.[29] Kaplan, retrospectively, would credit Kauvar with having informed him and his family about the school "uptown" that trained young men "for the rabbinate," though it is clear that the Kaplans already knew about JTS from the Kohut connection.[30] In any event, many years later Kaplan would recall that, during the 1897–1898 school year, he and Solomon "moved away from our parents' homes and lived in the seminary dormitory. Ten students were then housed" there, "of whom four were Elias Solomon, Phineas Israeli, Herman Abramowitz and Charles Kauvar."[31] Ultimately, Kaplan had the closest ongoing relationship with Israeli, who married Kaplan's sister, Sophie. And, as we will later see, Kaplan was intimately involved in Israeli's own endeavors to meet the religious needs of their fellow second-generation American Jews, the essential goal of JTS's training.[32]

While at the seminary, Kaplan and his cohorts lived up to the expectations of their parents and the downtowners who saluted their enrollment there. These serious and religiously observant rabbinical students followed a very strict academic and religious regimen. "Every morning," Kaplan once reminisced, "the students would hold services beginning at 8:00 and go down to the basement for breakfast at 8:45. At 9:00, we would start walking to City College . . . then located on Lexington Avenue corner 23rd Street." Kaplan's only reported bout with youthful frivolity would take place sometime between 1900–1902 at the close of his studies at the JTS, while he was taking his M.A. at Columbia's Teacher's College after having earned a B.A. from CCNY in 1900.[33] Another classmate of his, Benjamin Aaron Tintner, whom Kaplan once described as "a marginal student with considerably less Jewish background than I had," interested Mordecai in taking up the sport of boxing. Kaplan would later admit that he was drawn to Tintner because "he was sufficiently athletic to be on the [Columbia University] scrub football team, on which it was my desire to get . . . but I had too much work to do to carry out my ambition." In any event, Kaplan's athletic career was short-lived. He sparred with Tintner, who "managed to break the edges of two of my front teeth."[34]

Otherwise Kaplan and his friends walked both a straight social and, more important, religious path. Their only documented departure from strict Orthodox behavior was their frequent attendance on Friday night at "services in what was then the Rodef Sholom Temple" just a few blocks from their dormitory. The boys, taken with "the beauty and comfort of the Temple [which] was originally a church," probably attended the Reform service as a field trip to learn more about the social world of the American synagogue, including the pulpit style of a modern spiritual leader and preacher. There is no indication that, at this time, Kaplan and the others shared the theological perspectives of that congregation's rabbi, the Rev. Dr. Rudolph Grossman.[35]

Although Kaplan understood what his parents and their segment of the downtown community wanted him to learn in order to become a successful American Orthodox rabbi, it is not certain what the young teenager himself wanted most out of his education at JTS. Indeed, there is some evidence to suggest that, for all the modern ideas and talk about Mordecai's career that swirled around the Kaplan home, traditional subjects, the bedrock of Talmud that his father taught him, long intrigued and impressed the youngster. And when he did not find that sort of learning at JTS, he became unhappy and was openly critical of the institution and its faculty.

If Kaplan's reminsicences accurately depict his mood—they are the only extant sources we have on his mind-set during his student days[36]—the young man first become acutely aware and disappointed that JTS was in no way a yeshiva when he took the school's standard admissions test. Kaplan did not know that JTS was not overly concerned that its candidates for the preparatory class possess the strongest of Judaic backgrounds. It wanted bright young gentlemen whom they would provide with the appropriate ministerial training. The most that was required was that an applicant "be able to translate easy passages in the Bible and Talmud [and] possess some knowledge of Jewish history." The seminary administration was more anxious that prospective rabbis coming uptown "be able to speak the English language" than reflect a facility in Hebrew and Judaic texts. From Kaplan's account of the oral examination he took, it is clear that he was not overwhelmed by the depth of his questioner's inquiries. As he remembered many years later: "I had been studying Talmud in its most advanced and difficult sections [for three years], and all [they] . . . examined me in was the reading of the Commentary by Rashi."[37]

Once enrolled, Kaplan became keenly aware that although "we were Orthodox at the Seminary . . . there certainly were no *lamdanim* [first-rate Talmud scholars] there. I suffered very much in that Seminary."[38] In this vein Kaplan recalled his utter contempt for Professor Joffe who, in his estimation, did not compare well to his old-time teachers at Etz Chaim. Joffe, Kaplan said, was "a very poor teacher of Talmud . . . more or less a moron [from whom I] learned practically nothing." As Kaplan crassly put it, he "distinctly felt" that, under Joffe's tutelage, he "forg[ot] the little knowledge of Talmud and Bible I had come with. The former I had acquired from father and the Yeshiva Etz Chaim."[39]

Interestingly enough, this same Professor Joffe was one of his classmate's favorite teachers. Charles Kauvar perceived Joffe as "not only a teacher but also . . . [as a] guide, mentor and friend." Young Charles was extremely taken with the "intimate Friday night gatherings at his [professor's] home where they read Hebrew literature, ancient and modern, and discussed the passing panorama." Kauvar was also grateful for Joffe's special class in codes, where he "prepared us in the practical *luah* [calendar] regulations as well as in the intricate legal decisions of the *Yoreh Deah* [a portion of the *Code of Jewish Law*]."[40] However, none of these testimonials about Joffe, some of which might have been articulated within Kaplan's earshot in the seminary dormitory, made much of an impact upon the unhappy student. Indeed, it was a frustrated Mordecai who complained to Israel Kaplan about his lack of growth in Talmud at JTS. Acting totally in character, but in his own idiosyncractic way, Kaplan's father hastened to remedy this situation. He turned once again to Rabbi Sossnitz, who not only tutored Kaplan in "Talmud [but also] read . . . some of the Jewish philosophical works . . . to supplement . . . studies at the Seminary." At this point Israel Kaplan's desire for Mordecai to be a well-rounded Jewish scholar may have exceeded his son's own interest in a more diversified Judaica curriculum.[41]

In retrospect Kaplan also suggested that during his "miserable years" at JTS he also learned next to nothing from, among others, Bernard Drachman, his professor of Bible, history, philosophy, and homiletics. Kaplan would once write conclusively that "the only training I ever obtained at the Seminary was not in any of the classrooms but in the discussions I carried on with my fellow students Greenstone, Eichler, Solomon, Kauvar and Abramowitz."[42] However, an early bad experience with Drachman, and subsequent confrontations with that senior rabbi in the 1920s, may have clouded or skewered Kaplan's account of his student days and of the rabbinic role model who provided him with practical training and on-the-job experience that he needed to become a functioning and successful American Orthodox rabbi.

For many decades Kaplan walked around with considerable emotional scar tissue from one of his earliest encounters with Drachman. Sixty years or more after the incident Kaplan would recall,

> Not long after I was admitted to the Seminary he [i.e., Drachman] upbraided me in class for not having come better dressed. My parents could not afford then to buy me a white collar shirt, so I tried to use a fancy scarf in place of a white collar. That offended his taste and he criticized my getup in front of the class. That so embittered me that I was ready to leave the Seminary.[43]

Still annoyed in 1956, Kaplan would then characterize his teacher as a vacuous pseudointellectual with a "high pitched voice that lacked masculinity . . . a tongue that was glib with platitudes . . . with not an original idea in his head . . . who taught . . . Bible, History, Jewish Philosophy and Homiletics of which he had only a superficial grasp."[44] But, in fact, Kaplan learned much from Drachman. As a leader of the Jewish Endeavor Society (JES), Kaplan acquired the skills, experiences, and sensitivities that helped him become an effective Orthodox rabbi in the years after he was graduated from the seminary in 1902. And it was Drachman who founded that group in 1900.

His target audience then was the Jewish adolescents and young adults of downtown who were increasingly uncomfortable with the style of Judaism practiced in their neighborhood's synagogues. They were the so-called rising generation in Israel who felt little of the nostalgia for East European Orthodox ways that energized their parents' informal, non-decorous, and Yiddish-speaking *landsmanshaft* synagogue services. They were also unmoved by the strides some of the more established synagogues downtown—like the Eldridge Street Synagogue, for example—were making in the 1890s to modernize their services.[45] Efforts to bring greater order to the rituals and/or the hiring of highly trained cantors to lead the devotions did not captivate them. And when they thought of Jewish education, they were not impressed that special youngsters like a Kaplan or an Abelson received advanced Talmud training. They were more concerned by the fact that even the best of such synagogues did not provide them with adequate educational training or appropriate social activities. These youngsters complained, for example, that congregations like Kehal Adath Jeshurun reserved too much time and money for itinerant preachers, whose Saturday afternoon histrionics educated and entertained some old-timers, expending too little effort on programs and personalities of relevance to them. So estranged from the religious civilization of the Lower East Side, these second-generation Jews stayed away from the synagogue in droves and sought out nonreligious (oftentimes radical), non-Jewish (sometimes missionary), and unsavory venues for their social edification.

Bernard Drachman believed that he was up to this early antiassimilation challenge and he felt that in Kaplan and his circle, who knew this potential clientele from the old neighborhood so well, he had the foot soldiers for his campaign to lead the second generation back to synagogue life. The plan was, to begin with, to inaugurate "prayer gatherings or meetings . . . bring[ing] the message of Judaism to the rising generation in strict conformity with the traditional rules . . . in a refined and decorous manner that appealed to their esthetic taste as young Americans who possessed American culture."[46]

Practically speaking, beginning in 1900, services with men and women separated by a *mechitzah* (partition) were held "usually on Sabbath afternoons" and often in the vestry rooms of the larger Orthodox congregations. Recognizing the growing unfamiliarity of potential worshipers with the Hebrew siddur, the Endeavorers instituted supplementary English readings and considered substituting English-language translations for the traditional prayers. A weekly sermon in English on topics related to the American Jewish experience became standard, with Drachman and several other American Orthodox rabbis associated with the seminary often serving as guest preachers. More important, student rabbis like Abramowitz, Solomon, and Kaplan got their chance to preach and conduct these American Orthodox services. Congregational singing was encouraged, Yiddish played no role in rabbinic discourse or lay discussion, and all overt signs of commercialism were eliminated.

Concomitant with the start of these services, the Endeavorers instituted educational, social, and cultural programs with American values and influences in mind. They ran a small talmud torah (religious school) that offered a varied curriculum of Bible, history, religion, Hebrew spelling, and grammar taught by volunteers after public school hours and on Sundays. In 1902 Drachman would articulate a comprehensive understanding of the value of such an educational system within Orthodox Judaism. That same year Kaplan, Abelson, and Solomon taught Endeavorer Bible and history classes on East Broadway and Clinton Street. Altogether, the seminary students who interned through Endeavorer activities were afforded invaluable field work experience that they would ultimately bring to life-long careers of ministry to second-generation American Jews.[47]

For Kaplan, Endeavorer activities exposed or alerted him to two other essential realities about American Orthodox life that would hold him in good stead in the future. The first was that there were within the downtown community newly affluent and Americanized immigrant laymen—people of his father's generation—who approved of and were willing to back modern Orthodox efforts. There were men like Jarmalowski and Fischel, who had already supported the seminary's founding, and others of similar sentiments, like businessman Jonas Weil, who readily joined with Drachman and the aforementioned Rabbis Mendes, Morais, and Henry W. Schneeberger in founding the Orthodox Union in 1898. Based originally at JTS itself, the goals of the organization were to "protest against the declarations of Reform rabbis not in accord with the teachings of our Torah"—clearly a view in consonance with the seminary's own mission—and to "defend Orthodox Judaism whenever occasions arise in civic and social matters"—part of the Endeavorers' own raison d'être. Indeed, with this type of support, the JES became the earliest youth wing of the Orthodox Union. Kaplan, who knew of some of these lay leaders when he lived downtown and was backed by them when he worked in the old neighborhood as an Endeavorer, would have frequent occasion to turn to and to minister to these worthies and their families when he became an uptown American Orthodox rabbi a decade later.[48]

The other reality of which Kaplan's Endeavorer experience made him highly aware was that, for all of American Orthodoxy's efforts to stay within religious legal bounds in making synagogue life more attractive to Americanized youth, there were many within the older generation who saw their social adaptations as halakhic deviations. Some fifty years after he preached in the Henry Street Synagogue "at a mincha service . . . conducted by the Jewish Endeavor League [sic]," Kaplan would recall that the father of one of his youthful congregants was highly distressed "when [he] learned where [his son] was that Sabbath afternoon. He said to him: 'You are a shaigetz [lit. non-Jew] and Kaplan's a bigger shaigetz.' Henry Street synagogue was regarded as tref because the services were conducted in an orderly fashion." The father, Kaplan explained, "was a hasid to whom the use of English in the pulpit was abhorrent."[49] Kaplan would meet up with this type of American Orthodox opinion, too, when he graduated from the seminary and, in 1903, was called to the pulpit at Yorkville's Kehilath Jeshurun, in the first decade of the twentieth century one of Orthodoxy's most prominent congregations.

Mordecai M. Kaplan. *Courtesy of the Ratner Center for the Study of Conservative Judaism, Jewish Theological Seminary.*

Professor Joshua Joffe with his students, ca. 1900. Mordecai M. Kaplan is seated to his left. Phineas Israeli is seated to Joffe's right. Behind Kaplan stand Herman Abramowitz and Charles Kauvar. *Courtesy of the Ratner Center for the Study of Conservative Judaism, Jewish Theological Seminary.*

The Reverend Doctor Bernard Drachman
Member of Seminary Faculty —
1886 — 1908

Rabbi Bernard Drachman, Orthodox rabbi and faculty member of the Jewish Theological Seminary, 1886–1908. *Courtesy of the Ratner Center for the Study of Conservative Judaism, Jewish Theological Seminary.*

Rabbi Jacob Joseph. *Courtesy of the American Jewish Archives, Cincinnati Campus, Hebrew Union College-Jewish Institute of Religion.*

READING FROM THE SCROLL.

Services at Kehal Adath Jeshurun at the time of Mordecai M. Kaplan's bar mitzvah, ca. 1894. From Richard Wheatley, "The Jews in New York," *Century Magazine*, January 1892. *Courtesy of the Eldridge Street Project.*

Rabbi Moses Sebulun Margolies. *Courtesy of the Department of Public Relations, Yeshiva University.*

Harry Fischel. *Courtesy of the Department of Public Relations, Yeshiva University.*

Rabbi Jacob David Willowski. *Courtesy of Dr. Milton R. Konvitz.*

Joseph H. Cohen. *Courtesy of the Jewish Center.*

William Fischman. *Courtesy of the Jewish Center.*

The Jewish Center synagogue, 1937. *Courtesy of the Jewish Center.*

N.Y. Nov. 16, 1903

Mr. M. Davis,
  President, Congregation Kehilath Jeshurun
    Dear Sir:—
          I herewith apply for
the position of preacher and superintendent of your school, which position,
to my knowledge, has not yet been
filled. I was graduated from
the Jewish Theological Seminary of
New York in 1902, and have since
then been taking courses under Prof.
Schechter in the Jewish Theol. Seminary
of America. My secular education
I acquired for the most part in the
College City of N.Y. where I obtained
the degree of A.B. in 1900 and in
Columbia University which conferred
upon me the degree of Master of Arts
in 1902. As to what other essentials

which qualify one for the position I pray
kindly consult the authorities of the
Seminary.

          Yours respectfully
          Mordecai M Kaplan

328 E. 52nd St.

Mordecai M. Kaplan's letter of application for the position of preacher and school
superintendent at Congregation Kehilath Jeshurun, November 16, 1903.

N. Y. Nov. 26, 1903

My dear Dr. Joffé,

Your efforts on my behalf have already begun to show results. I have been appointed superintendent of the school of the 85th St. Congregation till the next general meeting which will take place some time after Pesach. In the meantime I will have to preach at least once a month and do all I can to make myself indispensable to the congregation.

Thanking you for all that you have done on my behalf,

I am

Your loving pupil

Mordecai M. Kaplan

328 E 52nd St.

A grateful student, Mordecai M. Kaplan, thanks his professor of Talmud, Dr. Joshua Joffe, for his help in securing his first pulpit, November 26, 1903. Years later Kaplan would recall Joffe in less glowing terms.

CONTRACT. No. 81.

W. Reid Gould, Law Blank Publisher and Stationer,
120 Nassau Street, and 120 Broadway, N. Y.

Contract, Made and concluded the *Thirtieth* day of *April* one thousand nine hundred *and four* by and between *Congregation Kehilath Jeshurun of the City of New York, party of the first part and Mordecai M. Kaplan, party of the second part in manner following;*

of the second part, in these words: The said part of the second part covenant and agree to and with the said party of the first party, to

The said party of the first part engages the party of the second part to act as Minister at the Synagogue building of the party of the first part on the northerly side of eighty fifth Street in the Borough of Manhattan for the term of two (2) years beginning on the first day of May one thousand nine hundred and four and to end on the thirtieth day of April, one thousand nine hundred and six.

The said party of the second part hereby agrees covenants and promises to attend at all divine services of the Congregation, superintend and attend at each

And the said party of the first part covenant and agree to pay unto the said part of the second part, for the same, the sum of

lawful money of the United States, as follows ; the sum of

session of the religious school, perform that part of the wedding ceremony usually allotted to the Rabbi, (Birchas Eirusin) deliver sermons at such times as shall be prescribed by the Board of Trustees, attend and officiate at the funeral of a member of a member's wife and follow the remains to the grave, if, for that purpose, furnished with a seat in a carriage

and for the true and faithful performance of all and every of the covenants and agreements above mentioned, the parties to these presents bind themselves each unto the other in the penal sum of ———— dollars, as fixed and settled damages to be paid by the failing party.

In witness whereof, the parties to these presents have hereunto set their hands and seals the day and year first above written.

Sealed and delivered in the presence of

and perform all other duties appertaining to his office in accordance with the customs and regulations of this Congregation.

over.

In consideration of such services, so to be performed the party of the first part promises and agrees to pay to the party of the second part the sum of One Hundred and Twenty five Dollars monthly.

And it is expressly covenanted, agreed and understood by the parties hereto that the said party of the second part must lead an upright life and comply with all the laws compiled in the Shulchan Aruch.

In witness whereof the said party of the second part has hereunto set his hand and seal and the said party of the first part has caused these presents to be subscribed by its President and the seal of the Corporation to be affixed the day and year first above written.

Signed Mordecai Menahem Kaplan

Contract between Congregation Kehilath Jeshurun and Mordecai M. Kaplan specifying the traditional religious duties of the synagogue's "minister," April 30, 1904.

Congregation
Kehilath
Jeshurun

TO

Mordecai M. Kaplan

CONTRACT.

Dated Apr 30 1904

The Journal of the Jewish Center

A WEEKLY BULLETIN OF ACTIVITIES

MAY 10, 1918   VOLUME ONE—NUMBER SIX   כ״ח אייר תרע״ח

RABBI KAPLAN'S INAUGURATION
Next Sabbath—Second Day Sh'vuoth

The day toward which our hearts are turned is Sabbath, the Second Day of Sh'vuoth, May 18, 1918.

On that day we, the congregation of the Jewish Center, will formally accept the leadership of Professor Mordecai M. Kaplan, as our Rabbi and teacher.

Although we have in many ways enjoyed the fruits of his thoughts, and of his labors on our behalf, we have never before this day been privileged to express the joy we feel at being the community he has chosen, of all Israel, to dwell amongst and inspire by his daily teachings.

We realize, too, that the Jewish Center may become, through our Rabbi, the pulpit from which many messages may be sent to the larger community about us, to help build and strengthen the new idealism of American Jewish life.

Next Sabbath, therefore,—the first occasion on which the Jewish world will hear Rabbi Kaplan as our leader—is to be a memorable day. Be ready for it.

The Jewish Center inaugurates its leader, Mordecai M. Kaplan, May 10, 1918.

The Journal of the Jewish Center

A WEEKLY BULLETIN OF ACTIVITIES

Friday, November 12, 1920   Vol. IV.—No. 10   א' כסלו, תרפ״א

DISCUSSION, QUESTIONS, CRITICISM

The Sabbath afternoon meetings have spontaneously developed of late into interesting open forums. Topics of Center interest and policy were openly discussed, criticised and reviewed. Already many of the ideas expressed at these meetings are being put into practice.

And now comes another attractive plan. Why not make the Saturday afternoon tea a live wire substitute for the quiescent, innocuous courtesy box?

Informally, frankly, intimately, we will discuss the sermon. Perhaps we disagree or misunderstand or are perplexed. No time like the present to begin things. Come then, this Saturday afternoon at 3:30 o'clock to the afternoon tea and open forum.

? ? ?

Have you played a game of billiards on the seventh floor?

Have you wrestled on the fifth floor?

Have you selected your locker on the eighth floor?

Have you lounged luxuriously in that wonder room on the tenth floor?

Did you have a great time Election Night on the first, fifth and tenth floors?

Are you planning to have an even finer time this Sunday night?

EARLY WEDNESDAY MORNING

Added zest has been given to the plans for the work and entertainment of the Intermediate Group. At a meeting held in the early hours of Wednesday morning, Mrs. Morgenroth was assured of the cooperation and helpful guidance of the mothers in the important work of making the Center a means for a richer, happier, more cultured life for their children.

CONGRATULATIONS

To Mr. & Mrs. Henry Witty on the marriage of their daughter, Ethel, to Mr. Joseph Dorf, Tuesday night, November 9th.

The Jewish Center promotes a series of open forums and discussions in November 1920, a month before the battle over Kaplan's views took center stage.

THE JEWISH CENTER
131-135 WEST 86TH STREET
NEW YORK

PHONE SCHUYLER {1641
{10482

February 4, 1921.

Dear Mr. and Mrs.

A number of members have approached me with the request to set them
right with regard to certain views that I have had occasion to give expression
to in writing and by word of mouth.   I have ~~therefore~~ decided to invite all
of our members to a heart to heart talk, in order that the atmosphere might
be cleared of all false rumors and misunderstandings.   I have set aside next
Wednesday, February 9 for this purpose.   This is a matter between the members
and myself, and I would not like to have any outsiders present.

May I ask you kindly to make every effort to be present at the gathering
which will take place at the Center on Wednesday evening at 8:15 promptly, even
if it involve setting aside some other engagement.

Very sincerely yours,

Kaplan attempts to explain his views and answer his critics within the Jewish Center,
February 4, 1921.

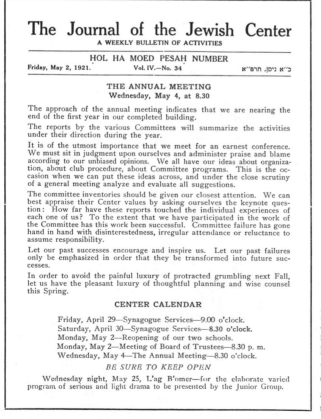

The Journal of the Jewish Center
A WEEKLY BULLETIN OF ACTIVITIES

HOL HA MOED PESAH NUMBER
Friday, May 2, 1921.   Vol. IV.—No. 34   כ"א ניסן, תרפ"א

THE ANNUAL MEETING
Wednesday, May 4, at 8.30

The approach of the annual meeting indicates that we are nearing the
end of the first year in our completed building.

The reports by the various Committees will summarize the activities
under their direction during the year.

It is of the utmost importance that we meet for an earnest conference.
We must sit in judgment upon ourselves and administer praise and blame
according to our unbiased opinions. We all have our ideas about organization, about club procedure, about Committee programs. This is the occasion when we can put these ideas across, and under the close scrutiny
of a general meeting analyze and evaluate all suggestions.

The committee inventories should be given our closest attention. We can
best appraise their Center values by asking ourselves the keynote question: How far have these reports touched the individual experiences of
each one of us? To the extent that we have participated in the work of
the Committee has this work been successful. Committee failure has gone
hand in hand with disinterestedness, irregular attendance or reluctance to
assume responsibility.

Let our past successes encourage and inspire us. Let our past failures
only be emphasized in order that they be transformed into future successes.

In order to avoid the painful luxury of protracted grumbling next Fall,
let us have the pleasant luxury of thoughtful planning and wise counsel
this Spring.

CENTER CALENDAR

Friday, April 29—Synagogue Services—9.00 o'clock.
Saturday, April 30—Synagogue Services—8.30 o'clock.
Monday, May 2—Reopening of our two schools.
Monday, May 2—Meeting of Board of Trustees—8.30 p. m.
Wednesday, May 4—The Annual Meeting—8.30 o'clock.

BE SURE TO KEEP OPEN

Wednesday night, May 25, L'ag B'omer—for the elaborate varied
program of serious and light drama to be presented by the Junior Group.

Announcement of the
Jewish Center's annual
meeting during the
height of the contro-
versy over Kaplan.
Only veiled references
are made to the battle
then raging.

THE JEWISH THEOLOGICAL SEMINARY OF AMERICA
531-535 WEST ONE HUNDRED AND TWENTY-THIRD STREET
NEW YORK CITY

January 16,1922.

Mr. William Fischman,

President,Jewish Center,

New York,City.

Dear Mr. Fischman,

I herewith tender to you my resignation as rabbi of the Jewish Center.
I could hardly have dreamt ten or twelve years ago,when I first suggested the conception
of a Jewish center to Mr. Joseph H. Cohen,that it would come to this. I then confided to
him not only my ideas on Jewish life and organization,but also my interpretation of the
fundamental truths of Judaism. He knew me as well as I knew myself. When,therefore,about
six years ago the first steps toward the establishment of the present Center were taken,
I greeted with joy the opportunity of collaborating with him in the founding of an institution that I had hoped would serve as a model to the Jews of America. Ever since the first
" Family Gathering"which took place on November 12,1916,I have written,preached,lectured and
planned for the Jewish Center,so that the very term "Jewish Center" has become an integral
part of the vocabulary of American Jewish life. I refused to be recompensed,either directly
or indirectly,because I wanted my contribution to the Center to be a whole-offering to God.
In attempting,however,to carry into effect my ideals of Jewish life and thought as I had
originally planned and explained to Mr.Joseph H.Cohen and some of his co-workers,I found
myself hampered at every step by the Board of Trustees. I find it,therefore,necessary to
discontinue my services at the Center,and to ask you to accept my resignation forthwith.

Yours truly,

Mordecai M. Kaplan

Kaplan's letter of resignation as rabbi of the Jewish Center, January 16, 1922.

THE JEWISH CENTER
131-135 WEST 86th STREET
NEW YORK

PHONE SCHUYLER {1041
              {10482

January 19, 1922.

Dear Doctor Kaplan,

Your letter of January 16 in which you tender your
resignation as Rabbi of the Jewish Center, was presented
by me to the Board of Trustees at its meeting on Wednesday
night, January 18.

I quote the following excerpt from the minutes of the
meeting:

"Mr. Fischman presented a communication from
Dr. Kaplan which was read by the Executive
Secretary. Upon motion duly made, seconded
and unanimously carried, the resignation of
Dr. Kaplan was accepted."

Very truly yours

President

Doctor M M Kaplan
1 West 89 Street
New York City

Letter informing
Kaplan that his resig-
nation has been
accepted by the Jewish
Center's Board of
Trustees, January 19,
1922.

CHAPTER 3 • *Promoting American Orthodoxy*
While Beset by Doubts in a
Yorkville Pulpit

Sometime between Kaplan's concluding years as a seminary student and the end of his career at the Orthodox Congregation Kehilath Jeshurun in 1909 the young rabbi began to have serious reservations about the teachings and truths of Orthodox Judaism and no longer defined himself as an Orthodox Jew. Many years later, looking back on his personal break with traditional faith, Kaplan offered several approximate dates and a number of varying scenarios to describe how and when he started to move philosophically out of Orthodoxy's orbit. Some of these sources identify the crushing impact that philosopher Matthew Arnold's *Literature and Dogma* had on Kaplan's faith in a divinely revealed Torah. Those same references also offer some idea of how Ahad Ha-Am's conception of Spiritual Zionism came to replace Orthodoxy as a faith in which Kaplan could believe. We also can derive from Kaplan's memoirs a sense of how deeply the young man ultimately felt Arnold Ehrlich's critical influence. However, none of these accounts permits us to definitively ascertain when this confluence of thoughts, along with the other ideas he was exposed to at CCNY, Columbia, and through his wide-ranging readings, combined to lead him away from Orthodoxy forever.[1]

In 1952, for example, Kaplan recalled that while *still a student at JTS* he was "tossed by doubts and questionings concerning the tradition which I would soon be expected to teach to others." Kaplan recounted that he "had a hard time maintaining my equilibrium during those storm and stress years of my life." And, in dating his first "experience [of] pangs of inner conflict" to his student years, Kaplan allowed that "the study of the Jewish medieval philosophers . . . did not help to bridge the gap that divided the thought world of the Bible and Talmud from the thought world I lived in." He recalled that "it was in this state of mind that I was graduated from the Seminary . . . [and soon] accepted a call to an Orthodox pulpit."[2]

In 1951 Kaplan had suggested a somewhat later date for the beginnings of his emergence out of Orthodoxy. In this version Kaplan recalled that *in 1909* he read a paper at the seminary "in which I frankly stated *my newly acquired views*" (emphasis added). This account is very close to the story Kaplan offered in 1942, in which he dated the fissure as beginning sometime before 1909 but certainly after he came to the pulpit at Kehilath Jeshurun. Then he remembered that his being offered the principalship of jts's Teachers Institute immediately after his speech was "a redemption from . . . spiritual plight, especially in view of the fact that Dr. [Solomon] Schechter was fully aware of my break with Orthodoxy." But when did this "spiritual plight " begin? In the 1942 account Kaplan alleged that his discomfort clearly began after he left the halls of jts. When he graduated from jts he "had reached a solution of my philosophical doubts which on the whole belonged to the kind for which one finds an answer in the writings of medieval philosophers" and thus "felt strong enough to grapple with the problem of religion as I then understood it [and could] accept without hesitation the offer of the pulpit at Kehilath Jeshurun." Only at the end of this century's first decade did he "realize that [he] could not remain in the Kehilath Jeshurun pulpit."[3]

In other words, in the 1942 version, we have the story of a young rabbi who, in 1902, successfully dealt with his theological questions and was quite comfortable as an American Orthodox rabbi. Later on he lost his way. If this understanding is true, then Kaplan's initial breaks must have taken place between 1902 and 1909.

A vision of Mordecai Kaplan moving away from Orthodoxy while at Kehilath Jeshurun is also forthcoming from four other autobiographical reflections. In the preface to his classic *Judaism as a Civilization*, published in 1933, he described himself as "naive" when he assumed the Yorkville pulpit. But, when he "found himself drifting away from the traditional interpretation of Judaism," he made up his mind to leave the rabbinate.[4] Some twenty years later, writing in his own *Reconstructionist* magazine, Kaplan would recall that, while at Kehilath Jeshurun,

the Zionist movement and particularly the Ahad Ha-Amist conception of the Jewish people as a living organism, animated by an irresistible will to live, enabled me to find spiritual anchorage. Moreover, I had by that time done considerable study and thinking in the field of anthropology and sociology. Though those studies undermined the conception of religion as a supernatural intervention in human life, they prepared the way for evaluating religion as a normal and indispensable expression of human nature.[5]

Similarly, in a speech he gave at the Society for the Advancement of Judaism on Purim 1957, in which he referred to himself in the third person, Kaplan stated that "it was during the six years of his first ministry (between 1903 and 1909) that he arrived at a realization of what was wrong with contemporary Judaism and the beginning of an understanding of what was needed to set it right."[6] And, finally, in 1959 Kaplan allowed that "by the time" he was at Kehilath Jeshurun he

> had become disqualified, in my own mind and conscience, to function as an orthodox rabbi. The informal instruction which I had been receiving from the late Arnold B. Ehrlich (the greatest modern Jewish exegete of the Bible) ever since I was fifteen years old, finally shattered my belief in *Torah min Ha-Shamayim*. The traditional outlook which I had acquired from my Jewish Seminary, was entirely dispelled. Simultaneously, however, with the loss of my Orthodox perspective on Judaism, there was forming in my mind, with the aid of what I learned from Ahad ha-Am, on the one hand, and from Matthew Arnold on the other, together with the aid of my post-graduate studies in philosophy, sociology and education, a new perspective on Judaism.[7]

There is even a Kaplan autobiographical sketch suggesting that the rabbi's break with Orthodoxy postdates his Kehilath Jeshurun years. In 1951 Kaplan described his first pulpit experience as basically without spiritual turmoil. In this self-profile he spoke of the opportunities Kehilath Jeshurun afforded him to study traditional texts, as any good American Orthodox rabbi would do. Kaplan also noted his effort to obtain Orthodox ordination and his chance to teach Mishnah on a daily basis as well as the opportunity he had to run a Hebrew school. Most important, in this account Kaplan did not speak at all of his moving on to JTS's Teachers Institute as a redemption from Orthodoxy. As simply told here, Schechter invited the young rabbi to head up this new pedagogic endeavor because

Henrietta Szold "by sheer coincidence happened to hear" of Kaplan's successes in organizing a modern talmud torah at Kehilath Jeshurun and suggested his name to the head of JTS.[8]

It remains for Kaplan's own contemporaneous diary to provide us with the earliest specific and unquestionable date for his first personal breaks and initial theological departure from Orthodoxy. On the basis of this document it is clear that by the fall of 1904 Kaplan was privately harboring serious misgivings about traditional Judaism. Writing first in "Communings with the Spirit," the young rabbi's earliest extant journal, Kaplan strongly critiqued Orthodoxy both for its unwillingness to adjust to the modern needs of the Jewish community and, even more profoundly, for its inability to satisfy his own personal spiritual quest.[9]

Kaplan felt, for example, that traditional prayers and ceremonies were empty rituals, devoid of meaning and relevance to the contemporary Jew. "There is no doubt," he wrote in 1906, "as to the deeply religious character which the rites and ceremonies had for our fathers. But on the other hand, there is equally no doubt as to the failure on the part of these same rites and ceremonies to call forth any deep religious response in us." He was convinced that modern Jews now recognized "that rites and ceremonies are of human origin . . . and if a ceremony is human, it follows that once such ceremony is emptied of its soul it is a sheer waste of energy to attempt to revive it."[10]

Writing in 1907, Kaplan argued that Judaism had to confront this spiritual malaise head on, but "an exaggerated conservatism [i.e., Orthodoxy] . . . so blind and stupid sometimes that we do not realize what is going on before us . . . has made us stiff so that we can not bend and we snap under the strain." He scoffed at the idea that traditional prayers can remain unaltered and their outdated statements explained away as somehow speaking to contemporary experiences. "We will be uttering prayers," he chided,

> for Babylonian academies fifteen hundred years after all traces of
> them is gone. We will be uttering curses against sectaries whose
> very names have been forgotten. Of course we can bend and twist
> and wriggle words till they can be made to mean anything under
> the sun; we can be praying for Babylonian academies and mean
> Russian, we can be cursing sectaries and mean present day black-
> mailers, but then why not say so and be done with it.

Indeed, on another occasion, Kaplan stated that he would have been much happier if "somebody would make a suggestion that a man like Bialik or Tchernochowsky write some Piutim [liturgical poems] in place of the ones we have now." But, to his consternation, no such creativity was readily apparent.[11]

But what about the argument he imagined "the religious quarters" might make: "It is this conservatism, which you [Kaplan] call exaggerated, that saved us from being swamped and flooded by the dominant religions?" To this imagined interlocutor Kaplan replied: "Saved us for what . . . for tragedy of death and ignominy of suicide? What have all these years of arid existence brought to us or to the world?"[12]

Kaplan would find that writing about his personal religious feelings and beliefs was more spiritually edifying than reciting the words of the siddur. In "Communings with the Spirit" he once mused, "These ramblings are more . . . truly prayer and confession than the infinite repetition of the daily prayers in our ritual, from which I find it necessary to desist occasionally in order to be able to recite it at all without getting the nausea."[13]

Kaplan also faced a daily personal crisis with rabbinic traditions when, as an Orthodox rabbi, he had "to spend time upon those ridiculous laws," to which he referred as "the cobweb intricacies of the *posekim* [rabbinic decisors]," in order "to be more effective in preaching religion to my brethren." The Talmud, he decided for himself,

> is tolerable, considering the age they lived in and at times there
> really sparkles some germ of thought or morality, but the *posekim*.
> . . . Their modes of thought, their narrowness, their absolute
> slavery to the past . . . are below criticism. . . . I find that "Julius
> Caesar" and "Hamlet" wield more influence over my true inner life
> than the 4 vols. of the Shulchan Aruch; there is certainly more
> divinity and inspiration in them than in the latter.[14]

Kaplan was apparently in the same frame of mind when he wrote in his diary in August 1905, "An essay which I recently read with much zest is [Matthew] Arnold's Literature & Dogma. It did a great deal more to stimulate my Jewish self-consciousness than anything I have ever read in English or in Hebrew except the Bible."[15]

So conflicted, an anguished Kaplan questioned his choice of calling. Just three years after earning ordination, Kaplan said to himself: "I little thought that at this time of life I will find myself so aimless. In the way of the personal ambition which the particular training I have had might enable me to entertain, stand my altered religious beliefs . . . . I find a perfect photograph of my mental life in the book of Koheleth [Ecclesiastes], in its skepticism, in its fear of God, in its worldliness and in its threadbare spirituality."[16]

The distressed young rabbi cried out in his diary:

> Oh God, what anguish of soul! How doubt tortures me! It sometimes seems to me as if the whole thing were a mere cobweb. It's all a terrible phantasmagoria. But again in case it is all true and real I dread to think of the extent of my sin in doubting . . . these moods which come over me, moods of melancholy. . . . It is then that the possibility of it all being a show and a figment agitates my whole being.[17]

Within the privacy of his journal Kaplan blamed both his parents and himself for his predicament. They had wanted him so much to be a spiritual leader for his generation, and he had acquiesced. But now, to his own shame, he was nothing less than an Orthodox rabbi who preached about and supported traditional teachings and ideas to which he personally no longer subscribed. He prayed that his parents would release him—as it were—from his vows. But they did not appear to understand the pain he experienced. Kaplan summed up his feelings in 1906 when he wrote, at age twenty-five:

> O God! What an inveterate hypocrite I have become! My sin weighs me down. My heart is torn by the conflict, and all for the sake of my parents! . . . I ask not for riches, I ask not for fame, only that God should open the eyes of my parents to see how they are slowly permitting my soul and spirit to die within me. . . . [My parents] believe that my ideas will change . . . but I tell [them] that ideas are as subject to natural law as bodies , and it is by the fatality of things that I believe as I do, and can never change. But yet they hearkened not, and I still go on my weary way.[18]

In other words, by mid-decade Kaplan had lost faith in the origins and meaning of the ceremonies and prayers held sacred by Orthodox Jews. He defined accepted rites and rituals as being of human invention and not divinely inspired. When he was spiritually moved, it was due solely to the impact of secular Jewish or non-Jewish voices and ideas. Moreover, the young rabbi no longer saw himself as a staunch link in the chain of divinely revealed rabbinic tradition that undergirded Orthodox theology and practice. Disturbed as he was, Kaplan found his publicly perceived role as an advocate of a modern version of the old faith to be a source of enduring pain and shame.

Notwithstanding these emerging theological doubts, which pained Kaplan in private and often made his life on the pulpit an unbearable ordeal, the young rabbi remained, almost until the end of the first decade of the twentieth century, fully identified and firmly identifiable—in his public position, words, and deeds—with the Orthodox Jewish community. Kaplan's parents may have known that their son no longer saw himself as an Orthodox Jew,[19] but nobody else did. Kaplan was aware of how hidden from view his heterodoxies were. He once wondered to himself, "What would Kehilath Jeshurun say" if they knew that "I find it necessary to desist occasionally [from the course of daily prayers] in order to be able to recite it at all without getting the nausea."[20] To the Jewish general public, Kaplan was, rather, the paradigmatic young American Orthodox rabbi of his day.

To the outside world, he was a bright young man who was living up to his family's career aspirations. Kaplan was also making those within the downtown Orthodox community who supported the seminary feel good about their investment as he tried to apply what he had learned there to meet the needs of the newly acculturated, religiously confused young people of his day. To those not privy to his innermost thoughts, Kaplan's major battles seemed not to be with his own soul but with old-fashioned congregants, who did not appreciate the aesthetic and social changes he advocated in synagogue life, and with residual elements of the transplanted East European rabbinate in America who did not accept him as an Orthodox rabbi. The latter challenged the religious authority and authenticity of any rabbi trained at the seminary, regardless of his fidelity to Jewish law. In response, during these times of personal "storm and stress," Kaplan presented himself consistently to the community as a devotee of the traditional faith. Indeed, he went so far in proving his authenticity that he traveled back to Russia to secure Orthodox semichah from a leading contemporary Torah sage. Through it all, his heterodox views were wholly concealed. Indeed, when some members of his synagogue raised eyebrows about what was truly behind the procedural modifications Kaplan wanted in Kehilath Jeshurun's service, a congregational committee determined that the rabbi's intentions were purely Orthodox.

The young Kaplan and the maturing Congregation Kehilath Jeshurun were seemingly a perfect match. When the seminary graduate applied for the position of its spiritual leader in 1903, the synagogue was just coming into its own as a commodious synagogue attractive both to Yorkville's long-time German and East-Central European Jews and to the newly affluent and acculturating immigrants and their youngsters who had more recently moved into the neighborhood. And the candidate was, like most of his seminary teachers and classmates, anxious to show "young men and women" that they need not attend "reform temples in order to hear a sermon in the vernacular," [that] "an enlightened orthodoxy, with a clean decorous services [and with] rabbis and ministers who will ever keep in touch with the young . . . must ultimately survive."[21]

Kehilath Jeshurun had been founded in 1873 at a time when New York's German and East-Central European Jewish communities were beginning to relocate out of the Lower East Side to Yorkville, that neighborhood of "better-class tenement buildings" and factories situated in the upper reaches of Manhattan, south of Harlem and east of Park Avenue. The hard-working Jewish burghers who moved to this section of uptown had none of the great wealth of their Fifth Avenue "Our Crowd" cousins. They merely had the economic wherewithal and the job opportunities available to move out of their former Delancey, Norfolk, and Grand Street tenements before neighborhood overcrowding and deterioration reached their peaks with the arrival of the East European Jewish masses beginning in the 1880s.[22]

Nor was this class of uptown Jews necessarily or uniformly enamored or attuned to the Reform Judaism that reigned supreme among the Schiff, Sulzberger, and Lewisohn crowd. Indeed, two of the congregations established on the Upper East Side in the 1870s—Kehilath Jeshurun and Orach Chaim—were strictly Orthodox in their ritual and less than fully American in their social orientation. Orach Chaim, founded in 1879, and initially situated in rented quarters on 54th Street and First Avenue, followed the "German Ashkenazic custom" and earned the praise of one downtown Hungarian-born rabbi as "a congregation . . . whose members are enormously wealthy [?] and completely German—that is from Germany and Prussia—and who gather daily after the afternoon prayers to enjoy Torah study."[23]

Kehilath Jeshurun, too, started out in humble quarters. From the 1870s to the early 1880s it had any number of temporary homes, including rooms above a beer garden known as the *Schwartze Adler* on East 86th Street. There and elsewhere, no matter the ambience, devotions were offered in the most traditional style. It differed only from Orach Chaim in that "Anshe Yeshurun," as it was first called, early on attracted the neighborhood's first East European elements. Indeed, one family tradition has it that three members of a single Polish Jewish family were among the founders and first trustees of this synagogue. Abbe Baum, Jacob Webster, and Theodore Crohn all arrived in this country before 1850. Behaving much like most Central and East-Central European Jewish immigrants of the time, they first sought their fortunes out West, only to settle after 1850 on the Lower East Side of New York, which was then predominately German Jewish. By 1870, and after a short sojourn in a Western Pennsylvanian oil town, these families were again ready to follow their German Jewish brethren out of the New York ghetto and up to Yorkville. They transferred their synagogue allegiance from Norfolk Street's Beth Hamedrosh Hagodol to Kehilath Jeshurun. In any event, by the time the fledgling congregation was able to engage as rabbi the Yiddish-speaking Rev. Meyer Peikes in 1885, Kehilath Jeshurun was well on the way to becoming a multiethnic synagogue within which the East Europeans predominated.[24]

The 1880s and 1890s brought a new Jewish element into Yorkville, which transformed the social base and cultural orientation of its synagogue life. Newly affluent and acculturating Russian Jews—those who arrived in 1881, if not before, and who had quickly advanced economically—were moving uptown for the same reasons that had driven Yorkville's first Jewish settlers to the neighborhood. They too did not want to live among the latest arrivals in a ghetto. And assuming that they maintained an interest in traditional synagogue life—they could, of course, attempt to gain membership in one of the elite Reform temples—they wanted to affiliate with an Orthodox synagogue that reflected their advancement beyond new immigrant status. So disposed, they either transported their synagogues from the Lower East Side to Yorkville, joined with the more Americanized segments of the indigenous congregations in that neighborhood, or created new synagogues uptown with their own social interests fully in mind.

For the members of Congregation Beth Israel Bikkur Cholim, an English-speaking rabbi was essential to their identity as American Jews. This synagogue "of Americanized Jews of Polish origin and their American-born posterity" traced its origins to downtown's Chrystie Street in 1847.

When the congregation was moved, in 1887, to Yorkville's 72d Street and Lexington Avenue, it turned to a young American-born Orthodox rabbi possessed of a Ph.D. from a German university to be its spiritual leader. Bernard Drachman accepted that call and was prayerfully confident that, given "the history and composition of the congregation . . . it would be naturally receptive to . . . the union of loyal adherence to the precepts of historic faith with modern culture and demeanor." Unfortunately for Drachman, he was soon to find that his laity's definition of modern demeanor in synagogue life included family pews with men and women sitting together, in clear violation of Orthodox strictures. Shocked and dismayed, Drachman quickly resigned his post.[25]

Soon, however, Drachman was to find in Yorkville other upwardly mobile German American and East European Jews who wanted a modern rabbi and respected his and the traditional Jewish ritual perspective. In 1889, with the considerable support of his father-in-law, real estate magnate Jonas Weil, Drachman founded Congregation Zichron Ephraim, named in memory of Weil's father, on 67th Street and Lexington Avenue. That synagogue, in Drachman's words, was a truly multiethnic, acculturated Orthodox synagogue. To his mind, "the best Orthodox elements of the city were represented . . . not of one class or national origin . . . among them Jews of Russian, Polish, Hungarian, German and other ancestry. The Congregation was . . . of broadly representative character and could be correctly designated as a genuine American Orthodox Jewish group."[26]

The East European Jews who settled near Kehilath Jeshurun shared many of the same hopes that those who affiliated with Zichron Ephraim held for theirs. Solomon Bachrach, who "owned a jewelry and silverware store on Grand corner of Norfolk Street," wanted Kehilath Jeshurun to exceed in beauty and in modern tenor Kehal Adath Jeshurun, where he previously had been a member. He saw how his acquaintance from Eldridge Street, Sender Jarmulowsky, had also moved uptown and linked himself with Zichron Ephraim. Jarmulowsky's brother, Meyer, did likewise and became a member of Orach Chaim. So influenced, Bachrach became chairman of a building committee that, in 1902, erected Kehilath Jeshurun's magnificent permanent home, a nine-hundred seat capacity building in mixed Byzantine-Romanesque style on 85th Street off Park Avenue. Once ensconced, he and so many others—including Harry Fischel, who moved up to Yorkville in 1902, and "the rising next generation," who were beginning to live in the neighborhood in growing numbers—wanted "a real modern Orthodox congregation." Specifically, they required "a rabbi who would raise the congregation to the level of the fashionable ones which boast of English speaking modern rabbis."[27]

At this point Reverend Peikes simply would not do. This old world rabbi understood the shifting sentiments within his congregation and tried to accommodate its members by reading a prepared English sermon once a month. But when mischievous youngsters, one Sabbath morning, stole his text, leaving him embarrassed and humiliated, the synagogue's leaders realized they needed to hire an English-speaking rabbi "who would be on preaching terms with the young people."[28]

Peikes's fate was sealed and his departure made imminent when the congregational board revised Kehilath Jeshurun's constitution and bylaws in 1903 to include a clause explicitly stipulating that "a Rabbi candidate for election must possess the necessary certificate of Hatoras Horaah [Orthodox ordination], from the proper authorities, and must be able to deliver sermons and discourses in the English language." To add insult to injury this Americanized congregation reminded the incumbent rabbi and cantor of their specific terms of office and that, when their contracts expired, "they must send in their application to the Annual Meeting if they wish to retain their positions." Since Rabbi Peikes's contract expired on Rosh Hodesh Iyyar of that year (April 15, 1903), the board of trustees, in a meeting on April 6, authorized the secretary to notify the rabbi to submit an application, should he desire to continue in that capacity.[29]

The rabbi did not immediately recognize the right of his laymen to dictate terms, procedures, and new requirements to their spiritual leader. Defining himself in traditional rabbinical terms as a religious leader whose authority could not be questioned, Peikes wrote back to his unruly flock that "he cannot make a direct application for the position of Rabbi, which he now holds, claiming that when a Congregation once elects a Rabbi, he holds the position for life." Rabbi Peikes's stance only momentarily stymied the insistent congregational leaders. At the synagogue's annual meeting of April 15, 1903, some outspoken members decided to "construe" the rabbi's protest letter as "an application for election to the office of Rabbi of our Congregation." This variant reading of the true intentions of Peikes's letter forced the European-trained rabbi to face the reality of who governed synagogue life in America. The congregation's minute book records that "during this discussion [over what Peikes meant in his letter] a regular application was received from Dr. Peikes applying to be elected." Indeed, one wonders whether Peikes was standing in the ante-room, calculating his support and awaiting the decision. In all events, it was soon made clear that the majority of Kehilath Jeshurun's membership wanted a new spiritual leader. Rabbi Peikes's application for reelection was defeated at that same meeting by a vote of nineteen to sixteen, although the membership did agree to allow him to continue in his position "tem-porarily for a term not exceeding four months."[30]

Twelve days later, however, Kehilath Jeshurun members made it clear that they did not want to wait for that time to elapse before removing the old-timer from the pulpit. On April 27, 1903, the membership decided at a special meeting to rescind the severance period tendered Rabbi Peikes. But, in order to soften the blow, they authorized a gift of five hundred dol-lars "to show our good feeling toward him." And, in a final backhanded tribute to the rabbi, a committee was appointed "to arrange for a banquet to be tendered to Mr. Peikes, our retiring Rabbi; at which time and place the $500 should be presented to him with suitable resolutions."[31]

The congregation's search for an Orthodox rabbi and fluent English preacher began with advertisements "in the Jewish papers" and private consultations with Dr. Joseph Asher, a professor of homiletics at the sem-inary,[32] "in reference to engaging a Rabbi in England." The public press initiative quickly yielded an inquiry "from Herman J. Elkin of Newburgh NY who wishes to know whether we are looking for a reformed or an orthodox rabbi. The secretary was instructed to write to him that we are looking for a strictly orthodox Rabbi." Soon thereafter, other "letters [were] received from Rabbis and Chasonim [cantors] in answer to the advertisements," but apparently none of them caught the fancy of the Kehilath Jeshurun leadership. One aspirant was a Rabbi A. Brande who wished "to lecture on Rosh Hashona and Yom Kipur [sic]." It is not known what Brande's qualifications and experience were. He might well have been one of the many itinerant preachers, possessed of little or no rabbinic training or certification, who lived in and around the Jewish communities of this country.[33] In any event, Kehilath Jeshurun had no interest in his services, even for a temporary stint.[34]

Applications from Asher's students, recent graduates of the seminary, were considered more seriously. While none of these men possessed the Hatarat Horaah mandated by the newly adopted bylaws, for most con-gregants this criterion was not a compelling consideration. These

Yorkville Jews were primarily looking for young ministers who spoke English with ease and proficiency. Rev. David Levine, JTS class of 1900 and holder of a freshly minted Ph.D. from Columbia University, was invited on June 15, 1903, to deliver a guest sermon "on either next Saturday or the Saturday next." His candidacy apparently remained current through the summer of 1903 because, in September, congregational leaders discussed "whether to allow . . . [him] to lecture on Kol Nidre night." Ultimately, "a vote was taken resulting in a tie" and it "was left to the President to decide if [Levine] would be asked to speak." President Moses Davis ruled against Levine and in favor of his classmate, Rev. Julius Greenstone (JTS, 1900) of Philadelphia, who was invited to lecture on that occasion.[35]

Ultimately, Mordecai Kaplan, then twenty-two years of age, emerged as the most attractive candidate. While at the seminary he had become an accomplished public speaker. He had delivered sermons, taken part in student debates, led services and, in March 1902, had represented his classmates at the seminary's memorial service for its deceased lay leader President Joseph Blumenthal. Those Kehilath Jeshurun leaders who looked carefully at press reports about the seminary that appeared between 1900–1902 in the *American Hebrew*, an important local Anglo-Jewish weekly of the time, knew of Kaplan's school activities. The candidate's name appeared no fewer than thirteen times as a leader or participant in the school's public events. What is more, the daughter of Moses Davis heard him preach at Congregation Beth Israel Bikur Cholim during the fall of 1903 and alerted her father that young Mordecai was a compelling orator. And the young man was clearly looking for a job. Years later Kaplan would credit the intercession of Davis's daughter to explain "how I came to be invited to give a trial sermon on Shabbat Vayeshev [November 1903]." And when the candidate performed on that occasion synagogue officials were impressed with the manner in which he expressed himself in English fluently and extemporaneously. From an embarrassing experience as a student, he had learned never to "memorize a public address." And he certainly did not read from a prepared text, which, as already noted, served as the undoing of Rev. Peikes.[36]

The most traditional members of the congregation—those who were as concerned with the Orthodox religious content of Kaplan's message as they were impressed by his smooth style of delivery—were surely additionally pleased with his choice of themes on that occasion and his use of Torah and midrashic texts to make his point. Fifty-four years after he delivered that fateful sermon, Kaplan recalled how he had commented on the Midrashic statement, about the biblical Joseph, *ve-nireh mah yihiyeh chalmotov* ("we will see what becomes of his dreams"), "which has the Shekinah [the Divine presence] saying that. I applied the text to what the nations taunt Israel with and to the divine reaction to that taunt."[37]

Of course, for the Bachrach family and for others who once prayed at Kehal Adath Jeshurun—and may even have remembered Kaplan's Yiddish bar-mitzvah address—seeing their young man from Eldridge Street perform so well was a source of personal pride and joy. In a sense, Kaplan's own maturation and emergence as a fully capable American Orthodox rabbi reflected their own story of acculturation in this country.[38]

In imagining Kaplan as a possible spiritual leader who could "keep in touch with the young," synagogue leaders noted that Kaplan's qualifications went well beyond his obvious formal homiletical abilities. The candidate had significant recent field experience as an Endeavorer; moreover, his resume indicated that, in 1895–1896, he had had the opportunity to teach Hebrew school in the Bronx and, most recently, from 1900–1902, he had taught in the Polonies Talmud Torah School of Congregation Shearith Israel of Manhattan.[39]

In fact, when the trustees of Kehilath Jeshurun tendered an offer to Kaplan on November 24, 1903, it was originally "as superintendent of the religious school at $60.00 per month" with the proviso that "he is also to deliver lectures in the synagogue as often as called upon by the President" and with the explicit understanding that, if his work "proved satisfactory," he would then "be elected rabbi of the congregation."[40] In the succeeding four months Kaplan answered all questions about his qualifications as a preacher, teacher, and mentor.[41] And, on April 3, 1904, he was routinely elected spiritual leader of the congregation at an annual salary of $1,500.[42] Significantly, the title conferred upon him was not *rabbi* but *minister* of Kehilath Jeshurun. The withholding of the more traditional designation reflected some congregants' or trustees' discomfort with the one glaring lacuna in Kaplan's curriculum vitae. He had his college degrees and was working toward a Columbia Ph.D. He had abundant internships and was surely very talented. But for some members—maybe those who had voted to retain Rev. Peikes in the first place[43]—that Kaplan did not possess the requisite Hatarat Horaah was problematic. Possibly to head off tensions within synagogue ranks—after all, appointment of a rabbi without this degree was in violation of the congregation's own bylaws—Kaplan would only carry the modern clerical designation.

At that moment Kaplan was unperturbed that he was not immediately called rabbi. In fact, when he formally applied for the Yorkville post in April 1904 he explicitly stated that as "Superintendent of the religious school," he had "carri[ed] through [his] work successfully" and was now prepared to be "elected *minister* (emphasis added) at the general meeting." He clearly understood what the designations meant, was attuned to the nuances of the synagogue's politics, and was not offended. If anything, in seeking election, Kaplan readily acknowledged the formal deficiency in his training and made every effort to mollify any potential critics. He was quick to inform his potential congregants of his traditional learning, first at Etz Chaim and then with "my father [who] has been giving me instruction in Talmudic lore right along," and of his "hope within a year or two to obtain S'micha from universally recognized Rabbis." Moreover, he made a point of his record in "organizing a class for young men for the study of Mishnayoth and History of Tradition."[44] The class met twice a week, with a steady attendance of ten, studying the first four chapters of the tractate Berachot together. Whatever the theological rumblings that coursed through his soul, in 1904 Mordecai Kaplan gave every indication that he very much wanted a clerical post—as rabbi or "minister"—in this prestigious Yorkville Orthodox synagogue.

Indeed, just a month before his Kehilath Jeshurun trial sermon Kaplan had applied for Bikur Cholim's pulpit—even though it had mixed seating during services—and had placed second to his seminary classmate Aaron Eiseman. We can readily surmise that the prideful Kaplan was less than satisfied when his "competitor" whom he described as "good looking but with a very limited knowledge of Judaism" captured that uptown post.[45] What is certain is that the young rabbi was ebullient when he received Kehilath Jeshurun's call and pledged himself to "do all I can to make myself indispensable to the Congregation."[46] No one would have then suspected that Kaplan was unsure of his calling or his faith.

Though Kehilath Jeshurun's members were clearly pleased with their choice of a seminary man, elements within the downtown community were not. Two months after Kaplan's election as minister the Agudath ha-Rabbanim, an organization of rabbis from Eastern Europe founded in 1902 to transplant East European Judaism to this country and to resist Americanization, issued a strongly worded condemnation of the seminary faculty, its graduates, and the Orthodox congregations that might employ its rabbis. At that moment this union of rabbis was in the midst of a multipronged campaign to delegitimize JTS in the eyes of the immigrant Jewish population. Clearly the antipathy harbored, as early as 1887, by these rabbis and some of their earlier arriving colleagues toward the mission and personnel of the seminary had not dissipated. Indeed, as the JTS began, after 1900, to further modernize its own orientation, the union's discomfort and fear of the seminary increased considerably.[47]

Rabbis like Bernard Levinthal of Philadelphia, an outspoken member of the Agudath ha-Rabbanim's presidium, were unhappy with the school's emphasis on teaching and preaching in English. And, now, they were scandalized that, with the reorientation of JTS in 1902, professors like Orientalist Solomon Schechter and Talmudist Louis Ginzberg, who were "expounders of the Higher Criticism which is anything but Orthodox," had assumed control of this training institution for American rabbis. Leaders of the Agudath ha-Rabbanim had only to look at the writings of Schechter and Ginzberg in the recently published *Jewish Encyclopedia* and know of Schechter's advocacy of "Catholic Israel"—a basic theological building block of Conservative Judaism—to resolve that "it is high time to organize a 'Protestant Israel' to protest against such rot and decay in Judaism." They determined that all Jews had to stay clear of those whom they "classed with the apostate and . . . deserter of Judaism." And this condemnation extended to loyal Orthodox students like Mordecai Kaplan and other senior colleagues of his who were graduating even as Schechter and Ginzberg were arriving and who never really studied with those who, they claimed, would not have "a share in the world to come."[48]

Since Kaplan had just been appointed "to one of the most prominent Orthodox congregations in the city," he was a particular focus of attack. One New York Jewish weekly reported that "all the fury of these Orthodox rabbis has been directed against this synagogue and its leaders."[49] Many years later Kaplan would recall how they "distributed handbills signed by Rabbi Levinthal denouncing the Seminary and the Congregation, the one for designating me 'rabbi,' the other for accepting me as such." Kaplan, who never had anything good to say about the Agudath ha-Rabbanim, subsequently thought that it was this "violent protest" that "deterred [the congregation] from entrusting its spiritual destiny into the hands of a Seminary graduate." He felt that Levinthal's actions had "fright[ened]" Kehilath Jeshurun away from calling him "rabbi," even though the record shows that the congregation named him "minister" months before the condemnations were announced.[50] In any event, Kaplan would continue at Kehilath Jeshurun to have his difficulties with these East European naysayers. But his personal doubts and theological misgivings remained his own private business. They were never the subject of public scrutiny and debate.

Minister Kaplan's most vexing early encounter with the continued power of old world influences and personalities within his congregation took place during the next High Holiday season when the "President and one or two of the trustees" invited Rabbi Jacob David Willowski (the Ridbaz) to preach at Kehilath Jeshurun. The Ridbaz was decidedly not the kind of rabbi a congregation that said it was dedicated to modern practices within Orthodoxy wanted as spiritual guide for its young people. Yet some synagogue officials felt that the "presence of the Rav would add to the impressiveness of the Holy Day services."[51]

The Ridbaz was, after all, an outstanding rabbinic scholar who, as early as 1881, had published his first volume of responsa, *She'elot u-Teshuvot Bet Ridbaz*. In 1890, after having served as rabbi in a number of small communities, he was chosen rabbi of the Russian Jewish community of Slutsk where, in 1899, he devoted himself to publishing a new edition of the Palestinian Talmud with his own commentary. His presence in America, and ultimately at Kehilath Jeshurun, was solely and specifically to raise money for his Torah project. It was clearly not to settle there because, to his mind, America was no place for Jews. His most telling epigram was that "America is a *treif* land where even the stones are impure."[52]

Given the Ridbaz's orientation, Kehilath Jeshurun members could have anticipated that their guest, in the tradition of the great itinerant preachers of the past, would strongly upbraid them for their residence in this ungodly country. What they might not have expected was Rabbi Willowski's demand that the congregation's young, recently appointed spiritual leader not be allowed to preach in English if he were to preach there at all. He felt that sermons in English were a grave danger to Judaism.[53]

It is, of course, remarkable that, given the Agudath ha-Rabbanim's campaign of just a year earlier, Rabbi Willowski did not object to the very presence of a seminary graduate with him on the pulpit. Still, that most minimal form of recognition was of little consolation to Kaplan when he watched Kehilath Jeshurun's leadership capitulate to the Russian rabbi's demands, in clear violation of the congregation's revised bylaws. Although one contemporary observer of congregational activities reported that "the young minister . . . imbued with the love for learning that the seminary and the traditions in which he had been reared have instilled in him, was among the first to insist that the . . . proper mood of reverence be accorded the visiting Rav," Kaplan was troubled with the Ridbaz's demand and the congregation's acquiescence. Responding as a principled Americanized Orthodox rabbi would, Kaplan "sought to counter his [the Ridbaz's] agitation by sending a mimeographed letter to the members of the congregation pointing out the need for reckoning with the use of the vernacular as a medium of Jewish teaching and preaching." In that missive Kaplan candidly declared "that Judaism need not and must not be afraid to meet and absorb all that is good in modern culture. I believe that the manners and the jargons which are the accretions of the Ghetto must be cast off." Taken aback by this turn of events, Kaplan concluded: "I have faith and confidence in Judaism. You have no faith in Judaism's strength nor confidence in me." When the controversy was discussed in the Anglo-Jewish press and the *American Hebrew* publicly attacked the synagogue for its lack of courage, Kehilath Jeshurun trustees considered whether, since "in a recent issue of the American Hebrew our synagogue was attacked and the Slutzka rabbi was assailed . . . [Kaplan] be requested to write an article in refutation thereto." Mordecai Kaplan conveniently ignored the request.[54]

This disturbing development caused Kaplan to question whether most of his congregants truly wanted the "enlightened Orthodox" services that he was ostensibly hired to provide. A letter to the *American Hebrew* alleging that "not over 10 per cent. of them [members of Kehilath Jeshurun] understand the English preacher" and that Kaplan was hired "to satisfy the prevailing style of rich congregants" did not please him at all. Putting aside the rabbi-minister question, Kaplan wondered whether his "business was to be entirely with the children and young people," while "the elders . . . would not think of deriving . . . spiritual authority . . . from me." It may also have troubled Kaplan that Judah David Eisenstein was the author of the letter. The young rabbi might have wondered whether this influential figure had backed away from his belief that American Jewry needed rabbis who understood American culture and preached in English.[55]

A response in the *American Hebrew* from "A Woman of the Synagogue" reassured Kaplan only slightly about the direction Orthodoxy was taking in his new synagogue and in America in general. She wrote that "the ten percent figure represents those who were *not* familiar with English" and she argued that her rabbi was "a man of broad, liberal culture" with a "loyal, well meaning and sincere heart" who enjoyed the respect of all factions within the congregation.[56] But, notwithstanding this endorsement, it remained clear to all that residual allegiances to old world practices still obtained strongly within this modernizing synagogue. As an American Orthodox rabbi, Minister Kaplan had much work to do.

Kaplan again felt marginalized when in the fall of 1904, concurrent with the Ridbaz's visit to Kehilath Jeshurun, a decision was made "for the interest of the Congregation to have a Rabbi and that we advertise for same." There was a perceived need within this Americanizing synagogue, as Kaplan would later characterize it, to give "the illusion that it was maintaining the East European type of rabbinate." And the person the congregation had in mind for this position, Rabbi Moses Sebulun Margolies (the Ramaz, an acronym of his name), surely "filled . . . the effect of Rav." This distinguished old-world rabbi had been trained in Bialystok and Kovno and had served as rabbi in Slabodka before assuming the position of chief rabbi of Boston in 1899. The Yiddish-speaking Ramaz had never been the recipient of any formal secular education.[57]

A series of rhetorical, symbolic, and financial gestures from congregational leaders reassured Kaplan that, in spite of this effort, he was and would remain their primary spiritual leader. Certainly, no one at Kehilath Jeshurun suggested that they could do without their young minister. The original motion in 1905 authorizing this search expressly stated that "the duties and powers of such Rabbi are not to conflict with our Minister, Mr M M Kaplan." When negotiations became serious, a committee met with Kaplan "in relation to engaging Rabbi Margolies of Boston or any other Rabbi as associate with Dr Kaplan." Kaplan told the committee that he would not object to Kehilath Jeshurun hiring an *associate Rabbi*. And, apparently, the synagogue's leaders acquiesced, at least formally, on this point. Upon Ramaz's induction as the "rabbi," Kaplan remained the "minister," but the official congregational minute book always referred to Ramaz as Kaplan's associate. Furthermore, once the new rabbi's arrival was assured, the board explicated "the respective duties of Dr Kaplan and Rabbi Margolies" and made it abundantly clear that "the status of Dr Kaplan be the same as heretofore." Years later Kaplan would further define the responsibilities of the two when he wrote that Ramaz's "function was to preach in Yiddish on Sabbath and Holiday afternoons, while I would not only preach in English on these mornings, but also headed a five day a week afternoon Hebrew School and met regularly a young men's group once a week in the study of Judaism, and led daily an elderly group . . . . I managed to cover the entire Mishna with the main commentary, and Ramaz delivered the *hadran* when I concluded it." In other words, at least in theory, Ramaz's appointment and presence did not isolate Kaplan from the more mature and traditional elements in the synagogue.[58]

Kaplan also felt good about the salary differentials that kept him above the older rabbi from Europe. For example, in April 1906 they both received a one-year contract renewal; Ramaz being paid $1,000, and Kaplan $1,800. In April 1907 they were both reelected for a three-year period; Ramaz at $1200 per annum and Kaplan at $2500, which was more than double his senior colleague's salary.[59]

Still, the presence in Kehilath Jeshurun's pulpit of a man who personified the past—and who may have been the candidate of his enemy, the Ridbaz[60]—had the potential to undermine the seminary graduate's position and his plans for changes within Orthodoxy. What neither Kaplan nor Willowski could have anticipated was that Ramaz not only turned out to be respectful of Kaplan's training and degree but was also supportive of Americanized Orthodoxy within and without the congregation. Many years later Kaplan wrote that he and Ramaz "functioned in a very friendly fashion with each other."[61] Indeed, Ramaz was more sympathetic than some of Kehilath Jeshurun's lay leaders toward the modifications in procedure and ritual that Kaplan defended as permissible within Orthodox teachings.[62] In fact, the minister and the rabbi worked well together as public advocates of American Orthodoxy and humanitarian causes in general,[63] even as Kaplan was privately drifting further and further away from his faith in the tradition that spawned them both.

Nonetheless, Kaplan found that, even with Ramaz's public recognition of his authenticity, there remained constant problems to overcome in moving the congregation to accept the changes he had in mind. As Kaplan remembered one particular situation fifty years later, his "first run in with Orthodoxy . . . as rabbi of the Kehilath Jeshurun congregation" had nothing to do with ideology or philosophy. Rather, when he "suggested that the 'schnoddering' be abolished, I was at once misunderstood as wishing to abolish the ritual of the mi-sheberach." To Kaplan's mind, the often unruly practice of publicly announcing one's donation when being called to the Torah was an unseemly carryover from immigrant congregations that had no place in a modern Orthodox synagogue. That opinion was not new or unique to Kaplan nor in any way contrary to Orthodox Jewish law. The goal of a more decorous and, ultimately, more attractive prayer service had been high on the Endeavorers' agenda. When a man was honored by being called to the Torah in their services, the prayer blessing him and his family (*mi-sheberach*) was recited without any attendant solicitation of funds, which was precisely what Kaplan wanted to institute at Kehilath Jeshurun.[64]

Synagogue leader Harry Fischel was one of those who at first misunderstood Kaplan's intentions. He initially feared the "reform" implications of the abolition of "schnoddering." However, when he clarified this issue with the accommodating Ramaz, the layman became convinced that "it is a benefit to Orthodoxy instead of a step towards Reform." Fischel was also not immediately comfortable with the recitation of some prayers in English, even if the use of the vernacular was surely permissible within the law. "I must admit," acknowledged the longtime Kehilath Jeshurun member, "that at the beginning [English prayer] was a great hardship to me and probably to a few more of the old school." But, understanding that vernacular recitations, like the English-language sermon, could attract the youth to the sanctuary, "not only did I decide to put up with it, but I even gave [it] my entire approval."[65]

Other congregants had their own problems with what Kaplan thought were merely more innocuous changes in the atmosphere of his Orthodox congregation. He wanted it understood that "speaking during the reading of the Torah should not be countenanced" and requested that "during the sermon no person should be permitted to enter the Synagogue or leave the same." Additionally, he thought that the stationing of ushers at strategic posts in both the men's and women's sections would discourage noise and idle gossip. All these modifications were surely within Jewish religious tradition, or so he thought. They were, at most, only small first steps toward the congregation facing its major future challenges, like getting "members sons [to] attend school, their wives and children to attend services on the Sabbath," and "getting members to show more interest in the work and progress of the Congregation."[66]

But, once again, Kaplan's suggestions were neither immediately nor universally accepted. Although Kaplan had been hired to promote American Orthodoxy in their midst, the trustees still waffled over whether they should have ushers and, if so, who they should be. Others whispered that these changes—instituted by the JES and destined to be the hallmarks of many American Orthodox congregations—were the first steps in the imposition of Reform Judaism upon the congregation. Everyone drew their own personal line between what they liked about the new and what they were still comfortable with about the old ritual of Orthodoxy. Ultimately, endemic congregational inattentiveness, inactivity, and opposition frustrated Mordecai Kaplan so much that, in November 1906, the twenty-five-year-old minister tendered his resignation. What then ensued within the congregation's leadership must have bitterly amused the rabbi who, as we have noted, had already made his own private break with Orthodoxy. A committee that "deliberat[ed] on all matters" concerning "the resignation of Rev. M. Kaplan . . . came to the conclusion that not in any way, shape or manner do the propositions made by Dr. Kaplan involve reform measures." The incipient heretic was exonerated, and, ultimately, his most modest proposals for the promotion of Americanized Orthodoxy were implemented. Although this decision did nothing to address or change Kaplan's innermost feelings about Orthodoxy, it did permit him to practically continue as its public advocate in Kehilath Jeshurun's pulpit. In December 1906 Kaplan acknowledged the committee's efforts, agreed to rescind his resignation, and continued as minister.[67]

Over the next three years Kaplan continued to work hard for his synagogue programs and for himself to be accorded communitywide approbation as an Orthodox rabbi. Indeed, as he continued his talmudic studies toward the traditional ordination he promised Moses Davis and his committee he would earn, he was extending himself to answer the ever-critical Agudath ha-Rabbanim and to silence the skeptical within his own congregation. He labored persistently toward achieving a goal worthy of any committed American Orthodox rabbi, even as he harbored heretical thoughts within his soul. Kaplan studied with his father and a Rabbi Ebin whom Israel Kaplan "had gotten to study with [him] *Yoreh Deah* [the portion of the *Shulchan Aruch* that has to be mastered for semichah] for Hatarat Haraah."[68] Tutoring continued until Kaplan's marriage to Lena Rubin on June 2, 1908. One week later Kaplan left for Europe on his honeymoon and, during that summer of travel, presented himself to Rabbi Yitzchak Reines, his father's old friend, who, after a cursory examination, conferred rabbinic ordination upon the American minister. Rabbi Reines did not ask the candidate about his innermost religious views and, for his part, Kaplan did not volunteer any damning information. In any event, Kaplan returned to the United States with Hatarat Horaah in hand and was elected rabbi of Kehilath Jeshurun in the fall of that year. His supporters within the congregation had no reason to believe that Kaplan would do anything other than continue to establish himself as a leading spokesman for "Enlightened Orthodoxy" in New York City and across the nation.[69]

Such proved not to be the case. Kaplan did not last more than another year in the Orthodox pulpit. Whatever his personal or professional reasons for wanting to study for and earn traditional ordination, by 1909 Kaplan no longer wanted to serve as an Orthodox rabbi. His own growing religious misgivings coupled with continuing frustrations in getting American Orthodoxy's message across convinced him that he had to move on. Increasingly, Kaplan sermons were for him "mental torture," as he had "to wriggle so as not to offend" and, as a result, could not express what was really on his mind. "The lie which I live," he once cried to himself, "is so clear and palpable to me." And endemic congregational apathy to his innovative efforts more than offset every programmatic success he had achieved in working with the congregation's youth.[70]

So afflicted, Kaplan considered alternative career opportunities. He thought about selling insurance and entertained notions about becoming a businessman. Maybe he would study the law. But he decided that he was not suited for any of these callings. While pondering his future, he was fortuitously invited, in June 1909, to speak before the JTS alumni organization. There, as we have noted, Kaplan was publicly critical of Orthodoxy for the first time. As fate would have it, after the presentation an impressed Schechter offered Kaplan the principalship of the newly established Teachers Institute of that institution. Decades later Kaplan would recall that, as a troubled spiritual leader, "the post offered . . . redemption from . . . spiritual plight. . . . So anxious was I to get away from Orthodoxy that I was glad to do anything for a living." He soon resigned from his Yorkville pulpit and ultimately determined that accepting this new position at the seminary had "emancipated me from Orthodoxy."[71]

But those sentiments, articulated long after he had arrived at the seminary, were neither generally known nor appreciated at the time. Kaplan's people in Yorkville saw their friend as a frustrated American Orthodox rabbi who left the pulpit in order to be more fulfilled in an academic setting teaching others how to be educational leaders. One contemporary newspaper closed the story of his Kehilath Jeshurun career on an upbeat note, declaring that "he was the first English-speaking minister that that congregation had had and is leaving his charge with a feeling of mutual affection and good will." Kaplan's public emergence out of Orthodoxy had surely begun, but his dissent was not recognized or understood by anyone within his congregational circle. Indeed, as the next decade unfolded, and even as Kaplan became more explicit in what he thought about the tradition, he continued to interact with and was largely considered to be a leader of the Orthodox community in America.[72]

CHAPTER 4 • *An Unrecognized Opponent*

In the years between 1909 and 1917 Mordecai Kaplan publicly articulated a series of pointed criticisms of Orthodoxy, serving notice that in his view the traditional faith and its practices were not responsive to the great spiritual needs of contemporary Jews. Although none of his speeches and writings reflected the depth of emotional and intellectual estrangement he expressed in his diaries, his remarks, which became more definitive over time, were far from those of an advocate for American Jewish Orthodoxy.

Kaplan's open criticism of Orthodoxy was initially contained in his June 1909 paper entitled "Nationalism as a Religious Dogma," which he delivered before his fellow seminary alumni. This wide-ranging speech was published two months later in the August edition of the *Maccabaean*, the organ of the Federation of American Zionists. Showing himself to be a true disciple of Ahad Ha-Am's Spiritual Zionism, Kaplan declared that nationalism was the only contemporary Jewish expression that allowed "the Jew to adapt himself completely to the culture of the day without surrendering one iota of his self-hood," the key to Jewish survival in modern times. As he explained it, no other Jewish group or ideology truly comprehended that "the future of Judaism demanded that all Jewish teaching and practical activity be based on the proposition that the Jewish religion existed for the Jewish people and not the Jewish people for the Jewish religion." Indeed, in his view, neither Orthodoxy nor Reform had shown to date the capacity to halt disaffection from Judaism. With specific reference to Orthodoxy, he pointed to the irony that Zionism has been more successful than Orthodox Judaism in preserving the greater part of traditional customs. It has done what Orthodox Judaism would never have done nowadays, and that is actually to induce Jews who are remote from traditional Jewish practices as they were from Hinduism to return to them once again.[1]

Kaplan reiterated these themes several years later when he spoke before the Society of the Jewish Institute at Kessler's Second Avenue Theater on the Lower East Side. In a public lecture entitled "What Zionism Has Done" he told a large Sunday morning gathering of young downtown Jews that it was Jewish nationalists, and not Jewish denominational thinkers and leaders, who understood the keys to Jewish survival. When he turned to upbraid Orthodoxy specifically, he asserted that

Orthodoxy knows [only] . . . to maintain traditional beliefs and practices at all costs. The demands of reason and comfort must be suppressed as illegitimate. Loyalty to the past is exalted as the chief virtue. The fact is, however, that this uncompromising attitude is nothing less than suicidal, for the result of this stubbornness is continued loss of numbers and constant thinning of the ranks of loyal adherents to Judaism.

For Kaplan, the contrast with Zionism was striking and compelling. "Zionism," he asserted, "calls upon us to become thoroughly involved with the principle and workings of the soul of the Jewish people."[2]

By that time Kaplan had also begun to speak out publicly against what he considered to be Orthodoxy's wrongheaded response to the challenge to traditional faith wrought by what he believed was widespread Jewish belief in the truths of modern biblical scholarship. In 1912, speaking again before his fellow JTS alumni, and possibly projecting his own inner conflicts on the community around him, Kaplan argued that modern biblical scholarship had shattered the modern Jew's belief that the Pentateuch was revealed to Moses at one time and in one form. (We know that such scholarship, particularly the work of Arnold and the teachings of Ehrlich, had certainly destroyed his own faith.) His subtle point and larger concern was that if rabbis and teachers continued to project these texts as divinely given, they would find their communities increasingly estranged from Judaism.[3] How then, he asked, could the "Supremacy of the Torah," be reestablished among Jews? That was the title the speech carried when it was published in 1914.[4]

Kaplan's answer for the Jewish community and, arguably, for himself was that educators should not attempt to uphold the traditional understanding of biblical sources at all costs. "Much more will be gained for the cause of Judaism," he contended, "if the pre-eminence of the Torah can be shown in no way to depend upon the outcome of the conflict between Tradition and Biblical Criticism." Kaplan asserted that "the evaluation of the Torah has nothing to do with theories as to date, composition and historic background of the various writings of the Bible. . . . The Torah," he continued, "can be maintained as supreme on the basis of a conception of revelation, which the modern mind can subscribe to, no less than the ancient one did to its own." For Kaplan, the key to restoring the Torah's place in the minds and lives of Jews was to "uphold the Torah as supreme in Jewish life, since more than any other agency it has been the cause of Israel living and exerting influence upon the world as an instrument of divine revelation."[5]

It remained for Kaplan, in two *Menorah Journal* articles published in 1916, not only to state that the presentation of a Judaism predicated upon mere unquestioned acceptance of ancient traditions would destine it to extinction—a stance that an overly pessimistic but still loyal Orthodox observer could take—but also to identify himself as being among those modern Jews who questioned the very truths of those traditions. In that latter stance he projected himself as a critic who stood outside of Orthodoxy's fold. Addressing himself to second-generation American Jewish intellectuals, the rabbi declared that "there can be no question that the sacred writings in which Judaism has found expression imply to some extent, at least, an outlook upon life and the world that has long been found untenable. The average person is repelled by statements which he finds irreconcilable with his own experience."[6] Kaplan saw, for example, that "a rational interpretation of Judaism," an approach to the faith that so many young people demanded, was "irreconcilable with the kind of belief in the supernatural which involves accepting unquestioningly the traditions concerning the frequent suspension of the laws of nature in the past and entertaining absolute faith in the recurrence of miracles in the future."[7]

This malaise of nonbelief, Kaplan contended, affected Jewish young people of all backgrounds. Writing in almost an autobiographical vein, Kaplan observed:

In New York there have been in existence a number of Jewish schools where hundreds of boys are taught to read fluently both the Bible and the Talmud before they are far in their teens. Many of them are highly gifted and in time achieve great careers. But despite the facility with which they can read the ancient lore, they begin to lose interest in Judaism as soon as they find that what they have learned about it does not harmonize with the entire spirit of modern thought.

For Kaplan, it was clear that "not by suppressing the intellect but by pointing out how one may use it in the service of religion can Judaism hope to win adherents among the strong-minded who can think for themselves."[8]

During these same years Kaplan also let it be known in semipublic forums that he was in favor of Jews taking a long, hard look at reassessing the viability of even the most basic Jewish traditions. Once, for example, when he spoke to a Sabbath afternoon study group that kept him in contact with some of the young people who were attracted to him during his tenure at Kehilath Jeshurun, Kaplan threw out the idea that a Jewish synod or religious congress might be formed that would consider whether Jews "in certain nations [should be] exempt from the strictness of the Sabbath laws, because conditions were such as to make it impossible for the Jews in those nations to observe them."[9] And it was at one of these informal gatherings of people close to Kaplan, those, he said, who were committed to "an examination of Judaism and Jewish life [not as] dilettantes but as Jews vitally interested in the preservation of Judaism," that the former Orthodox rabbi made clear that "one of the facts that we have to reckon with is that the people no longer recognize external authority. You cannot force people to observe the thing that you want."[10]

Through all these years, however, only Kaplan's closest family and friends were privy to the fact that his public utterances were but pale reflections of the unqualified heretical views that he shared most often with his diary. In July 1916, for example, Kaplan wrote in his journal that he did not accept that "God actually spoke in an audible voice to the Israelites at Sinai." And, several weeks later, he explicitly questioned the most basic Orthodox teaching "that the revelation took place as it is described in the Torah."[11]

This same time period also saw Kaplan cast his lot publicly with two major American Jewish religious organizations that were not Orthodox. Although the seminary valued its Orthodox faculty and while the school drew many of its students from Orthodox homes, JTS's mission after 1902 was the promotion and propagation of what its president called "Conservative Judaism . . . the uniting of what is desirable in modern life with the precious heritage of our faith . . . that has come down to us from ancient times." Thus, when Kaplan returned to his alma mater in 1909, he became part of a religious community that, in the majority, advocated continued observance of most of the laws and customs of the past. But their rationale for maintaining even the old ways that they did support was not necessarily the Orthodox belief in divine revelation and one unbroken authoritative tradition. Rather, the faith of these Conservatives was rooted ultimately in the power of the "people's will" or "Catholic Israel," the ongoing reinterpretation or evaluation of all past ways in the light of contemporary thought, science, and surroundings.[12] In 1910 Kaplan broadened his professional association with the Conservatives when he succeeded Rabbi Joseph Asher as professor of homiletics at the seminary. Soon he would also be teaching midrash to rabbinical students, a position that would project his influence on a substantial segment of American Jewry in the years to come.[13]

In 1913 Kaplan helped found the United Synagogue of America (USA). At its inception he served as a vice president and as a member of its executive council. Kaplan was also the first chairman of the United Synagogue's education committee and occupied a position on its committee on propaganda. In these capacities he worked with some twenty-two ritually diverse congregations to put an end to what one early Conservative rabbi called their era of "gropings and wanderings and even of disorder and chaos" as they sought to create for themselves an institutional locus and alternative to the Reform Union of American Hebrew Congregations and the Orthodox Union. Kaplan was closely involved, as were his friends Kauvar, Solomon, and Abramowitz, with the movement that was to bring Catholic Israel and Conservative Judaism into the American congregational field.[14]

Although Kaplan had now, by word and deed, distanced himself from Orthodoxy's teachings and community, he was neither recognized nor treated by its supporters as an outsider, dissenter, or opponent. Americanized Orthodox leaders, in particular, and the congregations and schools they represented, did not perceive their relationship with Kaplan as having come to an end. Though no longer a full-time, pulpit-occupying Orthodox rabbi, Kaplan continued to be someone to whom traditional Jews turned for help, counsel, and leadership. Kaplan remained a thinker whom Orthodox intellectuals actively sought out in their quest to advance traditional ideology. Only one American Orthodox rabbi of the era took public exception to what Kaplan preached about the faith.

Kaplan's formal alignment with Schechter's seminary and the nascent Conservative movement also failed to raise the eyebrows of most Orthodox leaders. Ironically, Kaplan, who was privately so disgusted with traditional faith and was then beginning to attack Orthodoxy in public, was frequently perceived and treated as the JTS faculty member most sympathetic to Orthodoxy. And, when it came to essential practical matters, those leaders of the Orthodox Union who were concerned with the modernization of Jewish education found common cause with Kaplan, who, as the Teachers Institute's principal, was one of the Jewish community's resident experts. Indeed, in one interesting case, as we shall see, a prominent lay leader of the Orthodox Union personally backed Kaplan's own efforts at the Conservative seminary.

Several factors contributed to American Orthodox Jews continuing to see Mordecai Kaplan as one of their own. To begin with, although Kaplan remembered his 1909 speech as being a defining moment in his life and Kaplan lore has his audience and his future colleague Solomon Schechter grasping the momentous implications of his speech, this presentation, where, for the first time, "I frankly stated my newly acquired views," did not command the compelling attention of contemporary Jewish media. Many years later Kaplan would remember that the thesis he offered "marked a Copernican revolution in my thinking." And he would recall that Solomon Schechter told him point blank when he articulated these heretical views, "Kaplan, you are walking on eggs."[15] But the truth is that Kaplan's public contrast of Zionism with religion did not catch the interest or strike the fancy of the Jewish newspaper correspondent assigned to cover the Seminary convention. The *American Hebrew*, the organ closest to JTS, neither headlined nor spoke in detail about Kaplan's views. Rather, it reported that Schechter's paper on "Recent Hebrew Literature" and Cyrus Adler's address on "The Part of the Alumni Association in the Promotion of Judaism in America" were "the principal features" of the session Kaplan addressed. Kaplan's paper was noted along with a talk by Dr. Morris D. Waldman of the United Hebrew Charities who advocated "the necessity of the Rabbi giving more of his time to charitable institutions." As far as audience reaction to the thought-provoking presentations was concerned, much was said in the *American Hebrew* about Rabbi Nathan Blechman's report on "Judaism in the Smaller Communities" and on Charles Kauvar's public urging of the formation of a National Organization to Promote the Observance of the Sabbath.[16] And, when Kaplan's paper was subsequently published in the *Maccabaean*, it again failed to engender any public discussion or debate.

The young rabbi's 1912 statement to seminary alumni that addressed the challenge of biblical criticism to traditional faith garnered only a bit more immediate attention in the Jewish media. Rabbi Charles I. Hoffman's presidential message was the featured talk of that year's convention reported in the July 12, 1912 edition of the *American Hebrew*. That story took detailed note of his discussion of the roles of "tradition . . . and authority in Judaism." It quoted liberally from a presentation that asserted, "Authority cannot be gain-said, and it must be strong, efficient and binding" [and] "Tradition is absolutely authoritative [even as] there is still much room for discussion as to the nature of tradition, as to its product in the past, its affiliation in the present and its probable tendency in the future." Meanwhile, Kaplan's speech, which suggested that Jews did not have to believe in the divine origins of the Torah in order to appreciate its importance in Jewish life, was described only as "an interesting paper . . . which gave rise to considerable discussion."[17]

One plausible reason why Kaplan's seminary alumni speeches failed to capture headlines and did not stir Orthodox reaction is that the rabbi stopped well short of telling his audience what he fully felt about the tradition. For example, there was enough left unsaid in his 1909 speech for a charitable Orthodox listener or reader to surmise that Kaplan was but a critic within their camp who chafed mightily at their movement's inability to stop assimilation. After all, he never said explicitly that Orthodoxy was intrinsically and fundamentally incapable of meeting modernity's challenges. And, as far as his 1912 address about the crises wrought by biblical criticism was concerned, he did not state in that presentation that he was personally a devotee of modern scholarship. Accordingly, it was possible for his contemporaries to construe his remarks as simply asserting that teachers, like himself, could no longer rely solely on old-time belief in divine revelation to keep Jews faithful to the Torah's teachings.

Kaplan's former classmate, Julius Greenstone, was one such individual who read Kaplan's 1912 speech but did not comprehend or believe that his friend had personally moved far from traditional thought. Otherwise, Greenstone would not have written to his colleague:

> In general, I wish to say, with your permission, that the secondary position given in your article to the idea of revelation as to the basis and the sanction for the supremacy of the Torah is open to misinterpretation and may become a dangerous weapon in less skilled hands. . . . The supremacy of the Torah must be made dependent on the supremacy of God, and not on the good sense of Israel in making it supreme. . . . I fear that your manner of expression may mislead others who are not familiar with your personality and your mode of thought.[18]

It remained for Kaplan to spell out more precisely for his friend where he stood on some essential points. "Personally," he responded to Greenstone, "I cannot conceive of a theophany as a historical event." He continued:

> I believe—yea, and am quite convinced—that the Israelites were at Sinai, that a Covenant was made there, symbolic of an alliance with God, but that there was a voice that spoke out of the sky, or that there were tablets of the Law miraculously inscribed, these are beliefs to which I cannot get myself to assent.[19]

However, Kaplan was not always as forthright as he was with Greenstone. Indeed, he frankly admitted to his dairy, in more than one case, that he coyly avoided answering interlocutors who pointedly questioned his faith commitments. Kaplan himself contributed more than his share to this continued lack of clarity because he was repeatedly oblique or disingenuous by intention. Though willing to write and lecture about his new approaches to Judaism, he habitually shied away from outright disputation and direct personal confrontation.

Another related factor that led to Orthodox communal uncertainty about Kaplan was the reality that he occasionally posed or acted as an Orthodox rabbi. Even if Kaplan no longer walked with God in the traditional sense of the word, he clearly liked strolling among and interacting with Orthodox Jews, particularly Americanized and affluent ones. His continued friendship with these Orthodox Jews and their community bespoke a kinship with traditional Judaism that Kaplan, in actuality, no longer possessed. Indeed, as we shall see, for several summers during the 1910s Kaplan, who had told his diary previously that he hated every hypocritical moment in the Kehilath Jeshurun pulpit, served as a rabbi in an Orthodox congregation along the New Jersey shore. There he maintained the respect of several important Orthodox visitors and the approbation of the congregation for his fidelity to the traditional faith. We will also have occasion to note that Kaplan even returned during a number of holidays to officiate at Kehilath Jeshurun and he was several times a guest preacher—today we would call him a "scholar-in-residence"—at a number of other well-known Orthodox congregations. He never used any one of these occasions to challenge Orthodox teachings, stances, or approaches.

Additionally, although Kaplan was clearly associated with the United Synagogue from its start, he did not always come across in his speeches as an advocate of profound change in how religious services ought to be conducted. In at least one noteworthy instance he gave the impression that he was one of those at the USA who wanted the new Conservative Judaism to greatly respect the traditions of the past and to make only the most minimal of changes in the American synagogue. The religious message that he offered on that occasion was worthy of a traditional American Orthodox rabbi, not a radical theologian. All told, Mordecai Kaplan remained for those—maybe the majority of Jews—who chose not to delve into his philosophy of religion very much like the man they had known and respected at Kehilath Jeshurun. He was still a dynamic peripatetic rabbi who was respectful of traditional ways and sensibilities even as he was comfortable with new evolving theologies in a variety of modern synagogue settings.

With the publication of Kaplan's *Menorah Journal* pieces in 1916 it was more difficult for Orthodox Jews to misapprehend what Kaplan believed. In these articles he publicly and unequivocally admitted that he himself questioned the authenticity of ancient beliefs and traditions. Though still not as open to the public as he was to his diaries, Kaplan articulated real personal problems with scriptural accounts of miracles and unnatural occurences. And yet the full import of where Kaplan stood for and against the tradition was still lost on most Orthodox Jews of the time. While he positioned himself outside of Orthodoxy, he certainly had yet to emerge, in their minds, as American Orthodoxy's most nettlesome opponent.

Here again Kaplan's coyness or disingenuity played its role. Moreover, Kaplan still appeared very comfortable and seemed very much at home with Orthodox Jews and their synagogues. He never confronted his audiences nor challenged their commitments. And, once again, even when he preached at United Synagogue congregations he took very traditional positions in his talks, which gave the impression that he was, at least, very respectful of and sensitive to Orthodoxy.

Of course, there were those within the Orthodox community who, by then or from the very beginning, better understood or largely intuited what the rabbi actually believed. But they, for another set of their own reasons, chose to ignore or set aside Kaplan's critical views. These individuals appreciated the rabbi's undeniable abilities as an insightful communal observer, educator, and innovator and decided to work with the dissenter to the extent that they could, avoiding a confrontation with his unacceptable theological stances. The same mind set permitted Orthodox leaders to work with Kaplan in his capacity as a seminary professor in communitywide projects to promote the improvement of pedagogic or educational standards in Orthodox schools.

Dr. Henry Pereira Mendes understood early on that Kaplan was a problem, and this founding president of the Orthodox Union did not like his erstwhile colleague from Kehilath Jeshurun's alignment with the new USA. As a contributing editor of the *Menorah Journal*, he was acquainted with Kaplan's most controversial statements. Yet, Mendes, who knew Kaplan from the time he worked for him in the Hebrew School of Congregation Shearith Israel, still turned to him on October 20, 1915, to inquire whether Kaplan would be interested in joining his old seminary friends Abramowitz, Kauvar, Solomon, and Israeli "in producing an edition of the Pentateuch, as a beginning, with comment in English, that should be strictly and only ethical . . . for homes, schools and ordinary Bible readers."

Mendes perceived that there were few scholars available capable of doing this job. And he was confident that Kaplan, and, for that matter, the four other United Synagogue leaders, would follow their assignment of "taking a verse as a text and . . . bas[ing] upon it an ethical lesson." They were asked only to "cite the central concept of the lesson, as tersely and as tellingly as you can."[20]

Clearly, Mendes surmised that this book, designed to "open the beauties of the Bible to thousands of readers . . . [to] suggest countless sermons for minister's elaborations . . . [and to] elevate our religion in the eyes of all, even Christians," could be written without involving himself in any religious disputation with Kaplan. Biblical criticism would neither be denied nor affirmed in this book, designed for the general and Jewish public. And there was, for certain, no gainsaying the abilities of Kaplan and these other seminary men in reaching "not . . . the first immigrants who came here saturated with religion, but . . . their sons and daughters who are now mothers and fathers and who are bringing up families with the Bible a dead book to all of them," one of the target groups for the project. So disposed, Mendes reached out for Kaplan's assistance.[21]

Dr. Bernard Revel, who was elected president of the Yeshiva Rabbi Isaac Elchanan (then also known as the Rabbinical College of America) in 1915, was one of those Orthodox Jewish leaders who surely read Kaplan's pieces in the *Menorah Journal*. After all, he would contribute his own work to that widely read quarterly two years after Kaplan's criticism appeared there.[22] And he certainly knew that Kaplan, in his role as seminary teacher and USA official, was affiliated with an institutional competitor. Nevertheless, Revel and his colleagues were not immediately or conclusively convinced that Kaplan was an enemy of Orthodoxy. Otherwise, Yeshiva's head and his closest associates would not have asked Kaplan to cooperate with them in the promotion of Orthodoxy and the Yeshiva during the first years of his presidency. If anything, from 1915–1917, the most powerful and influential people at the Yeshiva behaved in deed and in word as if Kaplan was still the devout American Orthodox rabbi he seemed to have been at Kehilath Jeshurun. They actually treated him as if he was one of the most traditional and not the most radical theologian on the seminary's faculty.

For example, on November 15, 1915, Kaplan received an invitation from Harry Fischel, chairman of the Building Committee of Yeshiva, "to deliver an address [at] . . . the dedication of the building of the Rabbinical College to take place during the week of Chanuka."[23] Had Kaplan still been rabbi at Kehilath Jeshurun, this invitation would have made abundant sense and Kaplan would have graciously accepted the call. After all, as a publicly identified Orthodox rabbi, he would have acknowledged that Yeshiva had come a long way since its founding in 1897 as a transplanted East European yeshiva on American soil. At its outset it was a school that provided its students with no secular or English language instruction. And, when the Agudath ha-Rabbanim was founded, it became the most favored institution of those resisters of Americanization. Struggles within and without Yeshiva for close to two decades would transform it into an American Orthodox theological seminary where the highest standards of Judaism would continue but where students would be trained as the type of rabbis who could minister effectively to second-generation American Jews. It developed into the type of school a younger Mordecai Kaplan might himself have attended instead of the old JTS and it showed signs of an ability to compete with Schechter's seminary.[24]

Harry Fischel, Ramaz, and Kehilath Jeshurun played no small role in this transformation. Fischel was consistently supportive of student demands for what the layman would call the "aim . . . to educate and produce Orthodox rabbis who will be able to deliver sermons in English . . . appeal to the hearts of the younger generation" while being "thoroughly qualified" for "congregations demanding conformity with . . . Orthodox Judaism."[25] Between 1906 and 1908 Ramaz served as temporary president of the Yeshiva as the recalcitrant school directors were slowly forced to accommodate student and ultimately community wishes. And Kehilath Jeshurun was the site, in 1908, of a reconciliation meeting between students, directors, community rabbis, and lay leaders that put an end to student strikes against their school and pledged to make the Yeshiva "an institution of Torah and *hakhma*, secular knowledge . . . according to the spirit of the times."[26] If Kaplan had still been Margolies's colleague at Kehilath Jeshurun, the younger rabbi would have been pleased to note his senior associate's role in providing the next generation of rabbis with what he would have considered to be the right type of Orthodox training.

Along these same lines, had Kaplan still been committed to American Orthodoxy, he would have been very happy to speak on behalf of a school that had just appointed Bernard Drachman to its faculty and would soon recruit Henry P. Mendes as an instructor. It was Revel, as part of his modernization of Yeshiva, who had invited Drachman to teach pedagogy, with Mendes hired to teach homiletics. This new post was, for Drachman, an opportunity to once again train young men of Eastern European heritage to be effective Orthodox ministers to the "rising generation in Israel."[27] In fact, these appointments did retroactively bestow a measure of approbation upon the pious early graduates of the seminary, like Kaplan, whom the Agudath ha-Rabbanim did not respect. For now, two of the key seminary people from 1887 were part of what was once the old-line rabbinic organization's favorite institution. In other words, having Drachman and Mendes working at Revel's school was another indication that the American Orthodoxy he advocated was coming of age.

The reality was, though, that Kaplan was no longer affiliated with Kehilath Jeshurun and had no professional association with Ramaz, but was, instead, a proud Schechter seminary employee and a leader of the United Synagogue who did not see himself as an Orthodox rabbi and was publicly critical of Orthodoxy. Yet none of his statements nor any of his Conservative associations was sufficient evidence for Fischel that Kaplan had left Orthodoxy's fold. If anything, in tendering this invitation, Yeshiva officials made, in Kaplan's case, an exception in their policy toward their seminary competitors. For those who would have welcomed the JTS professor to the ceremonies on Montgomery Street included "some who are officially connected with the College [who] have seen fit, on various occasions of a public character, to attack and denounce the Seminary with which [Kaplan was] connected." Ultimately Kaplan did not speak at the dedication, but only because he turned Yeshiva down.[28]

Solomon Travis also acted toward Kaplan as if he was still part of American Orthodoxy's inner circle of friends. In 1917 he disclosed to the rabbi his grandiose plan to return the JTS to its original moorings and to align it with Revel's Yeshiva. Travis, a successful Tulsa, Oklahoma oil man and Revel's brother-in-law, emerged during the transformation of the Yeshiva Rabbi Isaac Elchanan into the Rabbinical College as its most important backer. In 1917, he pledged an annual contribution of five thousand dollars in support of American Orthodoxy's new, incipient flagship school. A few months later, he came to Kaplan with his idea for expanding American Orthodoxy's educational purview even further. "He had in mind," Kaplan confided to his diary, to "subsidize the Seminary in order to swing it over to the Orthodox and incidentally on the same subject, to make his brother-in-law president." Although Travis reportedly did not use the term "merger," he saw, through his plan, the possibility for uniting two schools that served so many of the same people. Indeed, he had already begun "to carry on lengthy negotiations with the directors of the Seminary."[29]

What is, of course, remarkable is that Travis shared these scenarios with, of all people, Mordecai Kaplan. For if there was anyone who might move the Seminary *further away* from Orthodoxy, and whose presence at that school would make a merger most difficult, it was this dissenting rabbi. Indeed, as we will later see, when a second round of more concrete merger talks took place a decade later, Kaplan's continued role at the Seminary emerged as a major stumbling block to fertile negotiations. But, at present, Travis's consultations again evidence the fact that nothing Kaplan had yet said or done had conclusively convinced Yeshiva people that he had no affinity for Orthodoxy. Kaplan again was still perceived as a friend of Orthodoxy within the seminary.

As before, it is likely that Kaplan himself contributed to the ongoing misapprehensions of these Orthodox leaders. In 1911 or 1912, at the very point when the rabbi was just beginning to publicly criticize Orthodoxy, he adroitly avoided the opportunity to set the Yeshiva community straight about his beliefs. About two years after he began teaching at the seminary, Solomon Hurwitz, who would soon become Revel's foremost colleague in modernizing the Yeshiva, sent Kaplan a letter inquiring "whether it was true that [he] taught that the Ten Commandments were not of divine origin." Rumors about what the professor was saying were filtering into the Orthodox community even if his speeches were not front page Jewish news. Apparently there were people who did understand the broader implications of Kaplan's seminary alumni talks. Writing about Hurwitz's missive just a few years later, Kaplan could not recall "exactly what I answered [Hurwitz] but the gist of his message accorded with the verse in Proverbs, 'Answer the fool according to his foolishness.' "[30] In other words, Kaplan again ducked the issue or was disingenuous in his response.[31]

It is not known whether Hurwitz was fully satisfied with Kaplan's answer. What is certain is that, as late as 1916, even after the *Menorah Journal* pieces appeared, both Hurwitz and Revel were still anxious for Kaplan to participate in their plans to expand American Orthodoxy's intellectual scope. And here, once again, they related to Kaplan as if he was more sympathetic to and identifiable with Orthodoxy than most of his JTS colleagues. For Revel, one of the ancillary aspects of his reorganization of the Yeshiva Rabbi Isaac Elchanan was the creation of what we might call today an American Orthodox Jewish think tank. Towards that end, he and Dr. Hurwitz, newly appointed principal of Yeshiva's Talmudical Academy [high school], attempted to create a "Society of Jewish Academicians of America." Under their plan, a highly heterogeneous group of American Jewish intelligensia, including professors at "Jewish or secular higher institutions of learning," men with doctorates in the sciences, arts and theology, physicians and lawyers, among others, would sit together

> to further the ideals of traditional Judaism; to promote, encourage and advance constructive Jewish scholarship; to study current questions and problems from the point of view of traditional Judaism;

to elucidate the truths and principles of Judaism in the light of modern thought; to determine the place of Judaism in modern progress; and to apply the methods and results of modern science towards the solution of ritual problems.

Specifically, they would study "Jewish Science," including "Bible, Archeology, Hebrew Philology, Jewish History, Literature and Philosophy, Ethics and Rabbinics." They would examine "Judaism and Modern Thought," looking at "biology, anthropology, physical sciences and modern philosophy." And they would consider a range of "Modern Jewish Problems" from "Jewish education to Sabbath and religious rites, Jewish immigration," etc.[32]

Most important for us, the "unalterable . . . *sine qua non* for all classes of membership [was] conformity to the usages and practices of Judaism as expressed in the Torah, Talmud and authoritative codes." Such a membership clause should have precluded Mordecai Kaplan's participation; yet Revel and Hurwitz aggressively recruited the seminary professor to their group. Hurwitz went so far as to appear at Kaplan's home to convince him that he had a role to play within this Orthodox circle.[33]

Kaplan's own private and jaundiced explanation of this remarkable move was that Revel and his cohorts were "a new breed" of Orthodox, "namely fanatics with a doubt." He claimed in his journal that they knew his "views were . . . radical and aggressive." But that made no real difference to them because, according to Kaplan, in their own definition of Orthodoxy one reportedly did not have "to subscribe to every one of the traditional tenets or even to the most important ones," so long as one "adhered to the Shulchan Aruch."[34] If Kaplan was right, Revel and Hurwitz in effect accepted as Orthodox anyone who practiced most Orthodox teachings as prescribed in this authoritative code of Jewish law, no matter how extreme their thoughts were about these traditions. Conceivably, then, there could be room within their Orthodoxy even for Kaplan, as long as he "conform[ed] to the *usages* and *practices* of Judaism" (emphasis added). Of course, under this definition of Orthodoxy, Kaplan's colleagues, Louis Ginzberg and Israel Friedlander, who were also ritually observant, should also have been invited and courted. But, they never received an invitation to join, while Kaplan did.

A more likely explanation of Revel and Hurwitz's behavior is that, as late as 1916, no matter what they had read or had heard about Kaplan, they did not really consider him a serious dissenter. None of his writings and statements about contemporary Orthodoxy's weaknesses nor his revelations about his own religious doubts were as important or controversial as, for example, the renowned modern biblical and rabbinic scholarship of Ginzberg, Friedlander, or the late Solomon Schechter, whom the Orthodox viewed as the true champions of a new, dangerous, and competitive Conservative theology and movement.

Meanwhile, if Orthodox community leader Julius Dukas harbored doubts about Mordecai Kaplan, his concerns were not at all reflected in his plan to have Kaplan inspire and work with the Orthodox Jewish youth on the Lower East Side. In 1916 Dukas, who was both "the main pillar of the Orach Chaim Congregation" and the president of the Yeshiva Rabbi Jacob Joseph, a somewhat more modern version of the old Yeshiva Etz Chaim, prevailed upon his former Yorkville neighbor to come back to the Lower East Side to meet "the Alumni of the Yeshiba [sic] or as many [students] as he could get together so as to have them continue their Jewish studies in the Yeshiba [sic]." Dukas hoped that Kaplan would "train them to be teachers," and the uptown businessman was ready to offer these young people all sorts of financial remunerations if they would opt for that calling.[35]

Dukas's perspective was that Kaplan was the ideal role model to project to the downtown youngsters who attended that institution. Kaplan had been one of them, a son of a rabbi, a scion of a family committed to maintaining traditional Jewish life in this country, and a dynamic young thinker who had dedicated his life to Jewish education. Most important, he was clearly a success at his work. He exemplified and demonstrated what these students could do in careers devoted to serving their own generation of young American Jews.

What Kaplan was writing about and against Jewish tradition was not on the mind of Dukas nor of any members of his downtown audience. As far as his seminary connection was concerned, they viewed this uptown professor simply as their resident pedagogic expert on how to teach Judaism to a new American generation and, that evening, Kaplan did nothing to cause them to change their opinion. Indeed, to his diary Kaplan related that when Dukas and he walked into the lecture room "there was a great deal of handclapping." Much of the applause was in honor of the school's lay patron, but Dukas's guest was also warmly received. Kaplan's remarks, which focused on the lofty goal of committing students to studying "Torah for its own sake" engendered no protests from the audience. No one interrogated Kaplan about his fidelity to the faith or raised questions about his fitness to lecture about the value of traditional Torah study. The only criticism of Kaplan's presentation came from the yeshiva's principal, who simply felt the guest lecturer "was not altogether right in expecting the boys to be idealistic." After the speech the major subject of discussion between Kaplan and Dukas was "why Dr. [Moses] Hyamson, his rabbi [at Orach Chaim] did not take more of an interest in the yeshiba [sic]." Dukas replied that his spiritual leader "nowadays is more interested in attending engagements of couples in order to be asked to officiate at their weddings." In other words, on their way back uptown the Orthodox layman and the former Yorkville religious leader did nothing more than engage in the latest gossip of the Orthodox community.[36]

Even as Mendes, Revel, Hurwitz, Travis, Fischel, and Dukas showed that they were not exceedingly exercised over Kaplan's views and professional position, his friends at Kehilath Jeshurun behaved toward him as if he were still a full-fledged American Orthodox rabbi. On more than one occasion they turned to Kaplan with offers that he return to their pulpit.

In some measure Kaplan never completely left Kehilath Jeshurun after his official resignation in 1909 because, for the next three years, he occupied its pulpit on the most important Jewish religious holidays. More important, at a membership meeting in April of 1911 the congregation moved once again to formalize its relationship with him. On that occasion it was "unanimously resolved that a call be extended to Rabbi M M Kaplan requesting him to accept the office of and act as Honorary Rabbi of our English-speaking pulpit without compensation." This resolution was not acted upon and, in the interim, the congregation interviewed other prospective rabbis. But no candidate was found to be acceptable. Finally, over twenty months later, at a trustees' meeting in January 1913 a proposal was made to approach Kaplan with the proposition "whereby a fixed sum is to be given to charity or otherwise placed at his disposal, which amount shall be given by the Congregation in lieu of his services as a lecturer, in place of an English-speaking Rabbi." The synagogue's leadership postponed their search for "an English-speaking minister" for three months awaiting Kaplan's reply. Even when, a few weeks later, he rejected their offer, the membership was not deterred and, in May of 1913, after Rev. Hyamson also declined to serve as their rabbi, they approached Kaplan again to "ascertain if he would consider a call to occupy our pulpit."[37]

Through it all, Kehilath Jeshurun officials were not aware of how unhappy Kaplan had been at their congregation. It took the rabbi's demand that the synagogue affiliate with the new United Synagogue of America, and not the religious stances Kaplan was starting to articulate, to forestall a real drive to bring him back.[38]

While all these Orthodox leaders continued to reach out to Kaplan, the rabbi, for his part, consistently avoided opportunities to put an end to all overtures, to clear up all misconceptions, and to separate himself definitively from the community he once sought to lead. For example, Kaplan did not turn down Dukas's request that he speak at the downtown yeshiva. He avoided simply saying to this lay leader that he was no longer a part of, nor could he relate to, the Orthodox community. He did not remove himself completely from any contract talks with Kehilath Jeshurun and never stated unqualifiedly that he had hated every hypocritical moment in their Orthodox pulpit. Instead, Kaplan repeatedly behaved as he had done when Solomon Hurwitz first questioned him in 1911 or 1912. He did not make the sort of unambiguous gesture or statement that would have convinced one and all that he had broken with Orthodoxy.

Kaplan had his best chance in October 1914 when he debated Rabbi Herbert S. Goldstein on the topic of "Ceremonies: Their Nature and Meaning in Judaism" at Kehilath Jeshurun. But here too Kaplan backed away from a confrontation with a rabbi who was intent on proving to the public that Kaplan was, indeed, an avowed enemy of Orthodoxy.

Kaplan and Goldstein, his former student, did not like each other. Though Goldstein, the new English-speaking rabbi at Kehilath Jeshurun, projected many of the social skills and sensibilities to which his teacher had exposed him while at the seminary, Kaplan was not proud of him. He was unmoved and unimpressed that this young man had followed a career path highly reminiscent of his own early years in the service of the Jewish people. An American-born scion of a devout East European family, Goldstein had attended New York's public schools. He spent a short time at age twelve at Etz Chaim but received most of his early Judaic training from private tutors. As a young adult he enrolled at Columbia for his higher secular education and at the seminary for training as an American rabbi, while he studied for traditional ordination with Rabbi Sholom Jaffe of Norfolk Street's Beth Hamedrosh Hagodol.[39] Rather, Kaplan saw in Goldstein "the embodiment of all that I hate in narrowminded and bigoted Orthodoxy." Simply explained, the widely trained Goldstein had become the type of

American Orthodox rabbi Kaplan had once been but clearly was no more. This forum at his old former synagogue gave Kaplan the platform to expose what he surely considered to be the unworthiness of Goldstein's outdated faith commitments and to explain to all that American Orthodoxy was incapable of really addressing American Jewry's dilemmas. It was an opportunity to tell Kehilath Jeshurun's people precisely why he had left and would not return to their service.

For Goldstein, this debate provided him with the chance to make his mark as a stalwart defender of the faith. A strong showing here would also help Goldstein allay whatever residual disappointments people like Samuel Hyman might have harbored over whether they had settled for the second best available English-speaking rabbi for their congregation.[40] In any event, there had been little love lost between Goldstein and Kaplan since his student days. In fact, Goldstein had already spoken out within the school against Kaplan's "teaching irreligion."[41] Although he did not mention Kaplan by name, during his sophomore sermon, which he delivered at the seminary's synagogue, Goldstein had stated that "he who does not teach that the law was revealed on Mount Sinai is not fit to be a teacher of Israel." And, elsewhere in the sermon, he complained that JTS rabbinical students "were not being taught that the Torah was revealed on Mount Sinai."[42] Now, with Kaplan before him at his home congregation, he had the chance to explicitly identify his opponent as "a disruptive peril" to Judaism and to make everyone aware of how different were their conceptions of Judaism.[43]

As Kaplan described the course of the debate in his diary, aggression was clearly Goldstein's intention when they ascended the pulpit. "He wanted to force me into the admission that I do not accept the traditional conception of revelation and he seemed intent upon proving to his congregation that I am a heretic." But, Kaplan did not accept the challenge. In keeping with what we have seen to be his standard procedure in such circumstances, Kaplan was noncommittal in his response, even as he claimed to have "easily exposed the weakness of [Goldstein's] questioning and arguments."[44]

What Kaplan did say, for example, was that to "the believing Jew the common life that has been handed down from generation to generation of Israel of the past is a divinely constituted life." Speaking not necessarily about his own beliefs but about how Jews traditionally viewed their religious practices, Kaplan continued evocatively that "every time the Jew puts on his tefilin or consecrates the Sabbath by means of the cup of wine or observes a festival, he uses the sign language of the social relation which is considered as divinely ordained." He then moved along in a vein that spoke warmly of the folkways of the Jewish people. Kaplan allowed that "ceremonies such as those that pertain to care of food and person are calculated to give expression to the belief that the bond which holds together all Jews of the same generation is not merely a racial or national one but a spiritual and sacred one that the Jews are still a 'Kingdom of Priests and a Holy Nation.' " In his carefully nuanced words, Kaplan never said that he personally believed the "ceremonies" in the Jewish religion were "commanded by God." And, evidently, Goldstein was unable to pin him down on this most fundamental point.[45]

Emerging from this debate, Kaplan's major complaint about the encounter was that Goldstein showed very little respect for him. Kehilath Jeshurun's former rabbi concluded that "if anyone had treated a friend of mine the way he treated me that night I would looked upon him as incompetent to be a spiritual leader."[46]

Mordecai Kaplan's tendency to steer clear of confrontations when interlocutors pressed him about his true feelings was also apparent early in 1917 when parents of a child being taught by a graduate of the Teachers Institute appeared at the professor's doorstep to complain that their child "was being taught false doctrines." Kaplan was asked "to disavow any such teaching that had been attributed to [him]" by a Teachers Institute instructor. Rather than "giving them a straightforward answer," Kaplan admitted to his diary that he "wagged [his] tongue quite diplomatically and continued to be non-committal during the nearly two hours" of the conversation. The most Kaplan allowed, in a follow-up letter, was that his educational work "was conducted in the most intensely Jewish spirit," a response that was obviously open to a variety of interpretations.[47]

Moreover, Kaplan's willingness during this period to preach in Orthodox synagogues of all sorts did little to clarify, in the public mind, where the rabbi really stood. On these occasions Kaplan invariably spoke very much like the American Orthodox rabbi he once was. Listeners to the traditional messages he offered when he occupied Orthodox pulpits who were not fully up to date with Kaplan's writings had every reason to assume that he was still part of the Orthodox camp. He gave every indication that he was comfortable with Orthodox Jews and their traditions, and they seemed more than content with him.

For example, in the summer of 1914, several months after he had turned down Hyman's Kehilath Jeshurun overture, and even as he confided to himself that the Orthodox rabbinate inhibited him from giving "full vent to my enthusiasm for vital religion on account of the shackles which its outward forms and institutions impose on me," Kaplan agreed to serve as guest preacher in the new, fashionable, American Jewish Orthodox resort community of Arverne, New York. The invitation came from some of his affluent Kehilath Jeshurun friends. Samuel Hyman was among the leaders of its Congregation Derech Emunah, a synagogue demonstrating, in the words of one observer, that "the old-fashioned order of service may go hand in hand with perfect order and decorum." It was, in many ways, Kehilath Jeshurun "by the sea," as "the place was crowded by men and women whose demeanor and faces betokened intelligence and culture. . . . The Redelheim prayerbook [a traditional siddur] was used and strictly adhered to, even to the Anim Zemiroth [a liturgical hymn sung at the end of the services]. The men wearing the Talith supplied by an affable usher, heartily took up the responses and were not bashful in joining even in the singing" led by "the cantor . . . who conducted the service in a most dignified and impressive manner."[48]

Whatever Kaplan thought about the "shackles" that Orthodoxy's "outward forms and institutions impose on me," publicly he appeared very much at home in these traditional religious surroundings.[49] And when he rose to address the congregation he was very much an articulate American Orthodox rabbi. Drawing upon his seminary training and Kehilath Jeshurun experience, Kaplan skillfully integrated biblical sources and modern scholarship to challenge the congregation to actively protest a blatant public descecration of the Sabbath then taking place in their community.

The backdrop to Kaplan's challenge to the community was his understanding that "to feather their pockets . . . characterless [Jewish] men . . . in violation of the Sabbath contemplated holding a carnival in a community that was almost entirely Jewish." For the preacher, fault lay not only with the perpetrators but also with the synagogue for not undermining the profitability of sin. They "failed to cultivate the play instinct," presumably ignoring the needs of the youngsters who, sadly, were attracted to the carnival on the Sabbath.

Drawing upon the thinking of a contemporary philosopher, Richard Cabot, as a good American Orthodox rabbi would be wont to do, Kaplan argued that play "had to be directed with the view that [it might be] rendered fit for worship without which life cannot be complete." It was the job of the synagogue—in this case the Orthodox synagogue—to "foster" the holiness of play and other mundane human activities. Indeed, he argued, referring to a verse included in that Sabbath's Torah portion, that when Jews "cultivate wisdom and character and live a life of service" of that sort, they fulfill, in modern times, the biblical commandment of "not beholding the presence of God empty handed." Practically and immediately, Kaplan "urged that every effort should be made to stop" the carnival, and, at the close of the services, Derech Emunah's president announced that a meeting of protest would be held the following day.[50]

Several weeks later Kaplan and his family spent some time in Long Branch, on the New Jersey shore, and he immediately involved himself with its Orthodox warm weather denizens. As in Arverne, he spoke at a vacation community Saturday morning service. But in New Jersey Kaplan evidently sank deeper roots, choosing to participate in the synagogue's negotiations to buy a Reform congregation's building for their permanent use. Kaplan worked with these Orthodox Jews for more than a year on this project.[51]

The synagogue's president, Aaron Garfunkel, was extremely grateful for Kaplan's efforts "to realize your [Kaplan's] most cherished wish, that Long Branch have a suitable House of Worship, where the devout can commune with their Maker every day whilst on pleasure bent." Garfunkel wrote effusively to Kaplan about how, "owing a great deal to your [Kaplan's] efforts, Long Branch has now a suitable place of worship for our Orthodox brethren." In 1915 the members of this synagogue, which, like its president, perceived Kaplan to be nothing other than the best type of American Orthodox rabbi imaginable, "persistently demanded" that Kaplan "address the congregation."[52]

A year later Kaplan affiliated with the Long Branch Orthodox on a more established basis. And, as their rabbi, he courageously confronted a synagogue architectural problem that did and would confront many American Orthodox leaders of his time. The synagogue had a mechitzah, but "a number of the ultras," as Kaplan described them in his journal account, "claimed that the synagogue was not kosher enough for them because the women were not completely shut out from view." Kaplan took on these critics who were beginning to start their own services, as a good American Orthodox rabbi would, without stepping outside of halakhic boundaries. We will see later on how, in so doing, the nonconfrontational Kaplan actually set aside what he personally thought about this component of the traditional synagogue's architecture. At this point, however, he "maintained that those who found the present construction of the synagogue objectionable [were] entitled to their opinion. But withal . . . it not constitute enough ground for them to break away." Later on, a member of his circle, who was also a friend of Solomon T. H. Hurwitz, informed Kaplan that the "real reason some of the people . . . worshipped [elsewhere] was that they were not given use of the pulpit." In any event, Kaplan's remarks, and maybe his diplomacy, headed off further controversy among the Orthodox of Long Branch. Indeed, Kaplan was very pleased when a highly prominent Orthodox Jew, Rabbi Meyer Berlin, a renowned leader of the Mizrachi movement in Europe and, later, in the United States, "one of the offenders [who would have prayed elsewhere]," attended his services "as he said, to hear him speak [and] he brought along with him a Rabbi Abramowitz of the [Orthodox] Central Relief Committee."[53]

Here, in Long Branch, Kaplan had struck, in the public mind, a positive blow for American Orthodoxy. He had also earned the admiration of a congregation and the approbation of two distinguished Eastern European rabbis. It would have remained for someone who had chosen to closely read Kaplan's *Menorah Journal* essays while on vacation to raise questions about where Kaplan ultimately stood. And no one did. In the meantime, in the Long Branch pulpit and elsewhere Mordecai Kaplan was an Orthodox rabbi.

Back in New York Kaplan was an occasional guest preacher in Yorkville's Orthodox synagogues. In December 1915 Moses Hyamson welcomed him to Congregation Orach Chaim. And, during the High Holiday season of 1917, he returned to Kehilath Jeshurun four times to preach from the pulpit.[54] When Kaplan spoke to Dukas and his friends on the Sabbath of Hanukkah, he used the story of the Maccabaen revolt to emphasize the very basis of Americanized Orthodoxy's creed, the permissibility of the integration of secular culture with Judaism if this synthesis is done with care, thoughtfulness, and control. The Jews' battle against Antiochus, he told the congregation, is only part of the Hanukkah story. "The other half is that which tells of the treacherous efforts of some of our leaders to destroy Judaism." The Syrian Greeks' "evil purposes," Kaplan continued, were only "the climax to the treachery and intrigue in which were engaged those who stood at the helm of Jewish life." The Jewish transgressors were those who blindly rushed to uncritically accept Hellenism and then forced it upon their fellow Jews. They lacked, in Kaplan's analysis, the "self-knowledge, self-respect and self-control" that are the heart of the "soul of Israel."

Expanding in that vein, Kaplan argued further that "the supreme advantage accruing to the possessor of a soul . . . is of being able to differentiate between that in the environment which should be accepted and that which should be rejected, to discriminate between the true and the false, the genuine and the counterfeit." Tragically, the Hellenizing Jews of the second century BCE could not make the right choices. But those who "possessed the main characteristics that go to make up the Jewish soul," like the later philosophers and rabbis, Philo, the family of Rabban Gamliel, and, of course, Maimonides, had the ability to take in the best of Greek culture. Needless to say, the key to success was always fidelity to tradition.

Analogizing to his own contemporary experience, Kaplan argued that American Jews could be like the philosopher-rabbis and not like the Hellenizers if they would only approach American culture with the right measure of "self-knowledge, self-respect and self-control." Implicit in all of these statements was the moderation necessary in accepting the kind of acculturation that American Orthodoxy required. Turning to his audience, the preacher instructed them that

> in giving our child a Jewish training, we should have the rule in mind that the knowledge which we inculcate in him be of the kind that will foster in him both self-respect and self-control. . . . If we will give heed to the message of the Hanukkah lights and walk in the light of the Lord, the words of the prophets will at last be fulfilled, "And the world shall walk by thy light."[55]

It was during this same period, when Kaplan was frequently a guest at American Orthodox institutions and spoke well of their ideas and activities, that he played a role in the emergence of the Young Israel, an Orthodox congregational movement. At its inception, the Young Israel was precisely the type of Jewish religious initiative for which Kaplan had the utmost of sympathies. In 1912 a group of downtown young adults, including at least two seminary students, Moses Rosenthal and Samuel Sachs—Sachs was in the professor's homiletics class—approached Dr. Judah L. Magnes for his support in "an attempt to bring about a revival of Judaism among the thousands of young Jews and Jewesses of this city whose Judaism is dormant."[56] They approached Magnes because he was then the chairman of the newly created New York Kehillah, a communal umbrella organization that attempted to address the many social, economic, political, and religious problems plaguing New York Jewry.[57] Their argument before the communal leader was that too many young downtowners, having broken with the Orthodoxy of their parents, had no appropriate religious guides to which to turn. The Endeavorers were by then a distant memory to downtown's youth. And these religious activists felt that the Jewish services for young people sponsored in the ghetto by Rabbi Stephen S. Wise's [Reform] Free Synagogue were far too removed from tradition to be effective and accepted. They thought that youngsters who regularly attended a synagogue in which the collection plate was passed around on the Sabbath would become more estranged then ever from their parents who frequented old-world style synagogues. And there was always the fear that impressionable youths divorced from synagogue life might fall in with "gangsterism and anti-religious socialism," the Kehillah's greatest fears. In all events, what the Young Israelites proposed was the establishment of an ongoing Friday night lecture forum, with the cooperation of major Orthodox synagogues in the neighborhood, where "our Jewish youth" would be enlightened about "the essential factors that have contributed to the extraordinary stamina of the Jewish people and to its no less remarkable spiritual and intellectual vitality."[58]

Magnes liked their idea and subsequently convened a committee, which included Rabbis Bernard Drachman, Israel Friedlander, and Kaplan, to assist the young people in thinking through their projected program. Drawing upon their Endeavorer experience, Drachman and Kaplan were particularly knowledgeable about ways for the Young Israelites to convince the older generation of their religious sincerity and legitimacy. According to Benjamin Koenigsberg, one of the youngsters who worked with the rabbinical consultants, some of the synagogue leaders to whom they turned "never heard of religious lectures in English." To diminish doubts, the Young Israelites decided to ask their lecturers to "repeat [their] Friday night lecture of English in Jewish [Yiddish] Saturday morning."[59]

What Kaplan liked most about the Young Israel was the methodology they articulated, "to awaken legitimate pride in our storied past, to stimulate and to deepen the historic sentiment of our youth." When the youth group said that "it would be well for [its] lecturers to endeavor to acquaint our youth with the full meaning and import of the Jewish spirit as expressed in the ethical and intellectual life of the Jew" and that speakers had to give "full attention and detailed treatment . . . to the national and universal ideals of the life of the Jew," they were talking Kaplan's language. The professor's rhetoric and implicit influence was also apparent in the Young Israel's goal that "every lecture . . . point out the compatibility of Judaism with modern culture," and that "religious observance should be urged not merely as a matter of faith, but also as a result of rational explanation and logical comparison with the laws of modern nations." Kaplan also was pleased and comfortable with the fact that, although the lectures were to be held in Orthodox synagogues and traditional sensibilities were respected—"suitable accommodations for lodging and meals [would] be provided for speakers who [would] not be able to go home without riding"—the Young Israel movement explicitly stated, in its public broadsides, that their "movement is not Orthodox or Reform. It is not Zionist or Socialistic. [Rather] it intends to awaken Jewish young men and women to their responsibilities as Jews, in whatever form these responsibilities be conceived."[60]

The only conceivable barrier to Kaplan's full participation in the newly established Young Israel movement was the possibility that some of its more traditional members were troubled by his criticisms of Orthodoxy. For, despite the openness of their rhetoric, not everyone who wanted to preach Judaism to Young Israel forums was offered a rostrum. For example, in March 1916 Dr. [Nathan] Krass "offered to give a series of lectures on Jewish educational topics." As "Dr. Krass [was] a reformed Jew, there was therefore extensive discussion" within the Young Israel's board "on the advisability of having him speak under the auspices of the Young Israel." Indeed, when the Educational Committee requested "that a course of lectures . . . be given by Dr. Krass," the Executive Committee rejected that motion.[61] No comparable objections were ever raised about Kaplan.

Treated as one of Orthodoxy's own, Kaplan spoke repeatedly at Friday night forums from 1914 to 1917. And he followed up with a Yiddish oration the following morning, in keeping with Young Israel's deference to the culture of the Orthodox immigrant generation. All told, Kaplan's remarks at these "Friday night revival meetings (not services) after supper" did not make a ripple within American Orthodox circles.[62]

Not long after the inauguration of these Friday night programs, a related group of downtowners, which included some decidedly Orthodox members of the Young Israel, began their own companion initiative to capture the wavering children of immigrants back to Judaism. In 1913 they started the Model Synagogue, first with the assistance and encouragement of a small storefront congregation and then on their own, in rented rooms at the Educational Alliance on the Lower East Side of Manhattan. In this American Orthodox setting all efforts were made, according to movement founder Harry G. Fromberg, to observe

> every atom of our time honored traditions . . . and at the same
> time prove an attraction particularly to the young men and women;
> a synagogue where, with the exception of prayer, English would be
> spoken in delivering sermons and otherwise, complete congrega-
> tional singing instituted, *shnoddering* eliminated and decorum to an
> extent of almost 100 percent maintained.[63]

As these two groups moved toward their final merger, in 1918, as the Orthodox Young Israel movement, Kaplan remained comfortable with those whom he would later call "Jewish fundamentalists" and they articulated no problems with him as well.[64]

Of course, the peripatetic Mordecai Kaplan spoke not only at strictly Orthodox congregations during the mid-1910s. As a founder of the United Synagogue of America, he was frequently called upon to preach at the charter congregations of the Conservative movement. Also, his colleagues and former seminary students in the field often turned to him for advice and inspiration in their spiritual and institutional quests. For many USA congregations, the great question before them was how much of the traditional ritual they should maintain and what of the old services might be abridged in their solemn attempts to speak both to immigrants and to their children. Often, the mixing of the sexes during prayer was the only— albeit a very significant—deviation from Orthodoxy that these synagogues ended up countenancing.[65]

These speaking engagements were an excellent forum for Kaplan to articulate his problems with Orthodoxy and to specify many new ways of attracting Jews to religious life. But the rabbi did not seize the opportunity to spell out his own conception of Judaism at the expense of its more traditional counterpart. Rather, Kaplan behaved and spoke in very traditional ways. Unless his very appearances in these synagogues placed him, in some minds, outside Orthodoxy's pale, one would not immediately have surmised from his words and actions that Kehilath Jeshurun's former rabbi had really left the fold. When Kaplan preached at Roxbury, Massachusetts' Adath Jeshurun congregation in 1914 and in 1917, he was very much an American Orthodox rabbi speaking to two generations of congregants uncertain how traditional they wanted their house of worship to be.

This New England synagogue had some special significance for Kaplan because its history intersected with a number of points in his own life and career. To begin with, some of its founders had been members of the Baldwin Place Shul in the North End of Boston, the seat of Ramaz's chief rabbinate until he was called to New York to work with Kaplan. Indeed, these religious migrants to suburban Roxbury still considered Ramaz their rabbi up until his departure for Kehilath Jeshurun. Kaplan became even more closely related to this synagogue in 1908, when the Americanized element hired his brother-in-law, Phineas Israeli, as their first English-speaking rabbi. Three years after that Kaplan relived, through Israeli, his own most distasteful pulpit experience when Rabbi Gabriel Wolf (Velvele) Margolis challenged Israeli's authenticity as an Orthodox rabbi. In 1911 some of the old-line members of Adath Jeshurun invited Reb Velvele, who was then in town, to speak from their pulpit. Like Kaplan's nemesis Willowski, Margolis was a distinguished East European sage—for a while he too was a chief rabbi of Boston (1907–1910)—who was outspoken in his opposition to modern rabbis. He refused "to speak and present" on both Friday night and Saturday morning and when "introduced by Rabbi Israeli, the visiting rabbi failed to say a word." This embarrassing event convinced one local newspaper editorialist that Adath Jeshurun was "a house divided against itself. At one moment it is more abreast of modern orthodoxy, at another it is used to promote a standpattism, which can be of little use." Committed as Kaplan was to the modern in synagogue life, not to mention his devotion to his brother-in-law, Kaplan, in 1914, felt "in duty bound to strengthen [Israeli] in his position at Roxbury which he has been holding for the last seven years in the face of the most trying odds."[66]

Under Israeli the Roxbury synagogue, though a charter member of the United Synagogue, deviated only slightly from Orthodox practice. The rabbi supplemented the traditional Friday night devotions at sundown with a late evening service which he called his "Junior Congregation." During this service, directed at the "young and middle aged people," men and women sat together "in the main auditorium." The next morning, the shul was completely Orthodox again. The "middle aged and old" men, Kaplan once observed, prayed in the "half filled" auditorium and "a few women of the old fashioned type [were] in the gallery" upstairs. During the work week Adath Jeshurun conducted daily Orthodox services and even sponsored a *chevrah shas* (Talmud study group).[67]

When, in 1914, Kaplan was guest preacher at Adath Jeshurun, he spoke to both groups. He encouraged his after-dinner audience, as a respectful American Orthodox rabbi would, to both "have a strong basis of cooperation with the older men and women" while remaining "nonetheless . . . conscious of their own distinctive needs." He advised them that "while seeking inspiration from their parents, [they] should devise the means of spiritual self-defense [against assimilation] in accordance with their own views." But Kaplan did not tell his audience what were his own attitudes. In addressing his more traditional elders the next morning, Kaplan offered an even more traditional message. While quick to assert, as a proud modern rabbi, that the "East European immigrant community" had erred in "stopping half-way in their efforts to build up Jewish life with the building of synagogues where their own but not their children's spiritual needs were reckoned with," he sounded very much like an old-line—even unacculturated—itinerant preacher when he instructed his audience to "urge their households to cleanse themselves of non-Jewish influences that have contaminated them." It was a statement fully in line with Orthodox teachings.[68]

Returning to Roxbury three years later to help the congregation celebrate ten years in its Blue Hill Avenue building, Kaplan once again spoke before the "Junior Congregation" and continued to encourage them in their work. Interestingly enough, two other noteworthy rabbinical visitors joined in the anniversary commemoration. Rabbi Avraham Yudelewitz, "a former colleague of [Kaplan's] father in his youthful study circles," and Rabbi Joseph Konvitz, who, like Yudelewitz, was a member of the Agudath ha-Rabbanim, both spoke at Israeli's shul—albeit in Yiddish and in the Orthodox minyan. And, sounding very much like Kaplan, Konvitz, the Ridbaz's own son-in-law, "offered words of commendation" for "the incumbent seminary-trained rabbi."[69]

Indeed, what this Roxbury synagogue experience underscores is that, for all the fulminations of the Agudath ha-Rabbanim against the seminary and its products, a rabbi's or a congregation's linkages with JTS or the United Synagogue did not automatically or conclusively remove him or them from Orthodoxy. None other than the son-in-law of Kaplan's former nemesis, the Ridbaz, agreed with this inclusive view. And, once again, as far as attitudes toward Kaplan were concerned, where he worked, and with whom he was formally affiliated, did not set him apart from Orthodoxy or Orthodox Jewish leaders, particularly since he was so circumspect in his public remarks about what his true attitudes were to the tradition.

The involvement of Orthodox leaders with Kaplan's work both at the Teachers Institute and as a consultant to the New York Kehillah further evidences that Kaplan's new formal denominational affiliation was no real barrier to Orthodox interaction with the former Kehilath Jeshurun rabbi. Harry Fischel, for example, tendered tangible support for Kaplan's teacher training work at JTS. He trusted that the seminary could give his Harlem-based Uptown Talmud Torah much needed pedagogic and practical assistance in modernizing Orthodox afternoon school education. Here, once again, Fischel demonstrated that he was far from convinced that Kaplan was an unapproachable opponent of Orthodoxy.

In April 1911 Fischel backed Kaplan's plan to increase Teachers Institute enrollment through organizing special morning classes specifically for teachers at the Orthodox Talmud Torahs who taught in the late afternoon when regular Teachers Institute classes met. The Yorkville philanthropist began his efforts in support of the seminary's school as a member of a Teachers Institute directors' subcommittee consisting of himself, Magnes, and Kaplan. Together they studied "the progress made by the Educational Bureau of the Kehillah"—of which all three were highly placed leaders— "in its efforts to standardize the various Talmud Torahs in the city" with an eye toward ascertaining how this work "might be conducive to the increase of the number of students at the Teachers Institute."[70]

Three weeks later, Fischel proposed to the board that the Teachers Institute organize "supplementary" morning courses "for the purpose of improving the work of the teachers in the various Talmud Torahs and of preparing such applicants for Talmud Torah positions as would benefit by training at the Institute." When this motion was carried, Fischel agreed to serve with prominent Reform Jewish lay leaders Felix Warburg and Irving Lehman on a committee "to secure the necessary funds to carry on the supplementary work at the Institute." Fischel was also instrumental in providing the Teachers Institute with classroom space, free of charge, during its first years of operation. Finally, the Teachers Institute was sufficiently kosher for the Fischel family to allow their daughter, Rebecca, to enroll in its first class. Young Rebecca's parents knew, as Sophie Kaplan's parents understood a generation before her, that there was no comparable Orthodox institution available for her to pursue higher Jewish educational training. Incidentally, a few years later, Miss

Fischel would marry her fellow Orthodox seminary schoolmate, Herbert S. Goldstein.[71]

With all these efforts, Fischel's support for the Jewish Theological Seminary was still far from full-fledged. In June 1911, one month after his intense involvement with the Teachers Institute program, Fischel, respect-fully but conclusively, turned down Louis Marshall's invitation that he become a "subscriber" to the seminary. He cited the multiplicity of insti-tutions that already relied upon him for support, noting specifically his "duty to the Uptown Talmud Torah of which I am president." It is also uncertain whether Fischel ever formally joined the Teachers Institute's own separate board. His activities were noted in the extant minutes discussed above, but the public announcements of Teachers Institute activities did not list him as a board member. It may have been his view that whereas JTS's rabbinical school was problematic, the Teachers Institute was only a school of pedagogy, an institution from which Orthodoxy could certainly benefit and one that it could quietly support. Besides which, the Ortho-dox community had no comparable school of education. And, as far as he was concerned, Kaplan was an ally of Orthodoxy.[72]

The perception that Kaplan had much to offer Jewish education in sup-port of Orthodox needs and that, certainly in this area, his critical views and affiliations did not really matter, also satisfied those within the com-munity who worked with the rabbi on Kehillah educational activities. From its inception Mordecai Kaplan was a major participant in this over-arching communal endeavor. While still at Kehilath Jeshurun, in February 1909, he was that synagogue's delegate to the Kehillah's founding conven-tion. A few months later, when the Kehillah's executive committee was established, Kaplan was appointed acting chairman in his area of prime expertise, Jewish education. And, in one of the first acts of that commit-tee, he and a Jewish public school principal, Bernard Cronson, agreed to conduct a survey of the problems and needs of Jewish education in New York City. The results of this study—the first of its kind in the city's his-tory—were presented to the delegates at the Kehillah's 1910 convention. Kaplan and Cronson's recommendations, which spoke of the need to stan-dardize curriculum, improve classroom conditions, upgrade the caliber of teachers and teaching, and unify the several existing large Talmud Torahs, all within a bureau of education, were uniformly adopted at that plenary meeting. With the establishment of the bureau of education in the fall of 1910, Kaplan became a member of the oversight committee that interacted with the bureau's dynamic director, Dr. Samson Benderly. Needless to say, in fulfilling this communal responsibility, Kaplan also served his own institution's needs. "Benderly needed trained people," Kaplan once recalled, "and the Teachers Institute was looking for students to train."[73]

New York's Orthodox leaders were of several minds over whether to welcome and to support this new educational initiative. For some, there was no gainsaying the much-needed financial support the Kehillah promised to Orthodox schools that would modernize the way they taught Torah. After all, no one could deny the findings of Kaplan's study. Moreover, the Kehillah lay and professional staffs pledged their lack of interest in changing the traditional messages offered by Orthodox schools. Jacob Schiff said as much when he established a large education fund to back the bureau's efforts. For others, however, the issue of trust and reliability precluded any chance of ongoing cooperation with these modernizing American pedagogues. Those who resisted the bureau's activities generally viewed the entire Kehillah educational group as intent on undermining the Orthodox commitments of the youths they sought to serve. The Agudath ha-Rabbanim would have nothing positive to do with Kaplan's leadership, Benderly's initiatives, or Schiff's money.[74]

Harry Fischel, Julius Dukas, Samuel Hyman, and a handful of other acculturated Orthodox leaders, most of them Yorkville dwellers, did not share this perspective. They served as trustees and later as directors of the bureau of education. There they deliberated with Kaplan, Benderly, Magnes, Friedlander, as well as with Louis Marshall and Cyrus Sulzberger.[75] Once again, they only saw, and duly appreciated, the skills and energy that Kaplan and his Kehillah associates could and did bring to improving the education Orthodox Jews could provide for their youngsters.

Harry Fischel was particularly active in the early years of bureau activity. He essentially saw himself as a liaison between the Kehillah, the existing Orthodox talmud torahs, and the rabbis that supported them, striving to convince his colleagues to support Kaplan's plan. In October 1911 for example, this member of the Kehillah executive and president of the Uptown Talmud Torah convened a meeting in his home with the heads of the five largest talmud torahs in Manhattan "to consider the question of joining the system of the Bureau." Some of his colleagues reportedly "fear[ed] that the curriculum which is now proposed may at some future time be so altered as to conflict with Orthodox Jewish beliefs." Although

Fischel said "that he personally was in favor of the methods of the Bureau," he sought to allay the other talmud torah presidents' fears through the passing of a resolution by the Kehillah that no modifications would be made in the traditional curriculum without the approval of representatives of the schools affected. In the months and years that followed Fischel would continue to work to hold his colleagues' interest in what the Kehillah had to offer them and their institutions.[76]

In sum, notwithstanding his critical speeches and writings and his private protestations, for many of the important Orthodox Jews of New York with whom he continued to interact, Mordecai Kaplan remained, in the half-decade or so after he left Kehillath Jeshurun, both an insightful observer of the Orthodox scene and a man with viable solutions for the needs of their group. It was not until 1920, after Kaplan redoubled his public attacks on Orthodoxy, that its defenders spoke out violently and definitively against the heretic. In the meantime (1917–1920), even as most Orthodox Jews did not recognize that Kaplan was an opponent of their faith, one group on New York's Upper West Side who knew full well of Kaplan's attitudes to many of the Torah's fundamental teachings still turned to him to head a new synagogue initiative in their neighborhood. As we will presently see, so impressed were they with Kaplan as an uncommonly talented teacher, preacher, and leader—one who could attract American Jewish youngsters and their parents to synagogues—that these American Orthodox Jews were willing to ignore his theological views, so long as he did not propagate his heresies among congregants and challenge the traditional form of services at their Jewish Center. However, these essential requirements for an ongoing harmonious relationship were not spelled out by the synagogue's builders. And, when the dissident inevitably acted on his own vision of the Jewish Center's mission, a battle ensued. By the time the struggle ended it was clear to all concerned that there was no possible way for Kaplan to again officiate in an Orthodox setting.

CHAPTER 5 • *Hiring a Critic at the Jewish Center*

In the second decade of the twentieth century "everybody then on the East Side who was anybody moved" to the Upper West Side of Manhattan. "Then it looked as though Central Park West would be the center of the local Jewish aristocracy." This was how Mordecai Kaplan remembered the migration of affluent Yorkville Jews to a new neighborhood bounded by Central Park and Broadway roughly from 59th Street to 110th Street. While the Jewish population on the West Side did not exceed fifteen thousand in this still lightly inhabited district, by 1920 West 86th Street was on its way to becoming "the Main Street of the most compact and prosperous Jewish community in the city of New York."[1]

For the entrepreneurs, manufacturers, and real estate owners who headed the "well to do families from the upper East Side" relocating to this community, resettlement on the West Side was the latest step up the American ladder of success that had started a generation earlier on the Lower East Side. People who had once dwelled in downtown hovels and had then succeeded enough to afford apartments in Yorkville's sturdy row houses, boardinghouses, or upgraded tenements were now able to reside in modern West Side luxury apartments that bore "exotic or English or French" names. They exited from a Yorkville confronting its own problems of overcrowding as that uptown neighborhood absorbed increasing numbers of former denizens of the Lower East Side. By the late 1910s in some sections of the Upper East Side, like in the area around Kehilath Jeshurun, the density of population ranged from 700–1,400 persons per square block, a figure comparable to the neighboring poor East Harlem

Jewish community. Yorkville also had little space or inclination for new luxury constructs. Not until 1910 were forty acres of exposed railroad tracks first covered over on stylish Park Avenue.[2]

For the more socially ambitious, a Central Park West address afforded the opportunity to rub shoulders with members of the German Jewish elite. Financier Meyer Guggenheim lived on West 77th Street, right near the Museum of Natural History. Meyer's son, Murray, a financier in his own right, lived around the corner from his father. Isidor Straus, of R. H. Macy fame, resided on 105th Street facing the Hudson River. These notables and their fellow "Our Crowd" compatriots were members of the Progress Club, which was located on the corner of 88th Street and Central Park West. For most former Yorkville residents, a home on the Upper West Side meant the chance to raise their American-born youngsters in a convenient environment where beautiful homes, cultural institutions, grand monuments, and tree-lined streets abounded. Those who had made it to Central Park West could stroll one long block to Columbus Avenue to shop. Walking five additional minutes brought them to the subways, which would rapidly take them to their own stores or factories in midtown or on the Lower East Side. Similar conveniences in this same era had brought upwardly mobile Jews to Central Harlem. In 1904 the underground link between downtown and the northern reaches of Manhattan was complete. But the Upper West Side retained its desirability as a more prestigious place to live and a shorter, quicker commute from the business and trade areas of the inner city.[3]

The Upper West Side also offered an elegant and decorous synagogue where those interested could offer their devotions amid a social atmosphere that agreed with their newly achieved station in life. Congregation Shearith Israel, the Spanish-Portuguese synagogue, ensconced since 1897 on 70th Street and Central Park West, welcomed those new members of East European heritage who were proud to sit among scions of some of New York Jewry's oldest elite families, even if it meant adjusting to the "striking differences between their East European synagogues and the Sephardic tradition" that this oldest American congregation maintained with justifiable pride. Over time those "who had gone from the gangplank to the ghetto . . . to [a] freer life elsewhere in the expanding metropolis" would play an increasingly vital role in the life of that landmark congregation.[4]

Two additional congregations situated in the northern reaches of the Upper West Side, between 95th and 100th Streets, were also available to former Yorkville synagogue-goers. But very few newcomers to the Upper West Side chose to affiliate at either Congregation Agudath Achim on 100th Street, west of Columbus Avenue, or Congregation Pincus Elijah on 95th Street, off Columbus Avenue. As late as 1918 these two *shtibls* (European-style immigrant synagogues) had but forty-five and seventy members, respectively. Most newly well-to-do Jews disdained shuls housed in modest sanctuaries where old world ritual and social practices were doggedly continued and decorum was sorely lacking.[5]

Mordecai Kaplan, who watched many of his neighbors move out of Yorkville in the early 1910s, was keenly aware of the situation, writing: "Among those who joined that exodus [to the west side of the city] was a number of members of the congregation to which I had formerly ministered." Social worker Isaac Berkson, who labored with and taught Jewish youths of the Upper East Side, also cogently noted that it was "the richer portion of" those associated with Kehilath Jeshurun that "has now moved to the west side of Central Park."[6]

Garment manufacturer Joseph H. Cohen was one of the most prominent former Yorkville residents and Kehilath Jeshurun members to settle in the new neighborhood. In his life and career he personified the rising Jewish immigrant, who, within one generation, moved uptown from the Lower East Side and then westward to the Upper West Side. Cohen was born in Russo-Poland in 1864, immigrated as a lad to the United States in 1872, and settled in New York two years later. Beginning work at the age of fourteen, he earned eight dollars a month for seven years, after which, having managed to save four hundred dollars, he went into business on his own. By 1905 he was successful enough to move to Yorkville, where he immediately joined Kehilath Jeshurun. Cohen soon became a leader in the congregation, his name appearing often in the minutes of trustee and membership meetings from 1905 to 1915.[7] In 1915 he and his family relocated again, this time to a luxury building on West 86th Street between Columbus and Amsterdam Avenues, only a brief subway ride from his factory at 33d Street off Fifth Avenue.

Once on the Upper West Side, Cohen sought out a synagogue to his liking. But he found none that met his needs. As an acculturating American, he was impressed with the style and decorum at Shearith Israel, but being an East European Jew at heart, the Sephardic service was culturally foreign to him.[8] Cohen was also not happy with the West Side shtibls. As a longtime member of Kehilath Jeshurun, he had become accustomed to a modern decorous Orthodox synagogue, and he wanted the same type of balance between the traditional and the modern—and, as we have seen, in Boston, Long Branch, Arverne, and on the Lower East Side—to obtain in a congregation in his new neighborhood. So, while he prayed initially at nearby Pincus Elijah and, perhaps, hoped to influence it to change, Cohen quickly became disaffected with a shul that "maintained the traditional ritual" and countenanced no departures from the practices of the past.[9]

William Fischman came from the same background as Cohen, was the same sort of American Jewish success story, and felt similarly about the Upper West Side's religious needs. Arriving from Austria as a young boy, Fischman too became a downtown clothing manufacturer, moved uptown after the turn of the century, and affiliated with Kehilath Jeshurun. Ten years later he settled at 315 Central Park West, at the corner West 91st Street. No less committed than his friend to seeing Orthodoxy practiced and projected in the most modern of ways, Fischman was the longtime president—beginning in 1902—of the Downtown Talmud Torah as that school experimented with modernizing its pedagogic approaches. There he was a close associate of another Kehilath Jeshurun member, Harry Fischel. Fischman was subsequently active in the Jewish Theological Seminary, the United Synagogue of America, and the New York Kehillah, where he served on the powerful executive committee. Thus, it is not surprising that "as soon as [he] began worshiping at the P.E. [Pincus Elijah] synagogue," he "began agitating" for a modern Orthodox alternative to the West Side shtibls.[10]

Cohen and Fischman ultimately wanted the Upper West Side to have an Orthodox synagogue in which both they and the youth of their neighborhood could be comfortable. The reality of their concerns about the next generation was brought home most poignantly one Saturday afternoon in April 1915, after they had discussed their plans for a "West Side Jewish communal center" with their friend and former rabbi, Mordecai Kaplan. Having completed their conversation about the need for parents and children to better express themselves as committed American Jews, the threesome walked a few blocks from Kaplan's Yorkville home to the Orach Chaim synagogue, where "they found a few dozen people some of whom sat in the back saying tehilim [psalms] but most of them listening to Dr. Hyamson reading and translating the Yad Hachazakah [the code of Jewish law authored by Maimonides]." While the old-timers were content with this sort of traditional activity as the Sabbath day came to a close, Fischman was quick to note that "there were no young men among the listeners." Instead, "there were about four or five in the back indulging in pranks." As Cohen, Fischman, and Kaplan exited the synagogue, they "met a number of young fellows, sons of Orach Chaim members, playing ball in the streets." Cohen and Fischman were not happy with the disregard these children from Orthodox families were showing toward Sabbath observance, and this experience further motivated them to create the kind of synagogue that would attract them as well.[11]

For Cohen and Fischman, Mordecai Kaplan had the vision and ability to help them create the right type of synagogue for themselves and their children. They also knew that he was interested in participating in their endeavor. As early as 1912 he had already urged "Joseph H. Cohen to induce his friends to establish an institution that would not only provide a place to worship for elders and a school for the children, but also an opportunity to all affiliated with it to develop their social life Jewishly." The "Jewish Center" that he visualized "would bring Jews together . . . who had recently moved to the West Side . . . for social, cultural and recreational purposes in addition to worship."[12] Kaplan likewise possessed, to their minds, the wealth of experience and expertise in synagogue and youth work necessary to make practical sense of their, and his, dreams and desires.

Erstwhile Kehilath Jeshurun members, they had witnessed firsthand his courageous efforts to Americanize procedures there. They knew that after Kaplan left Kehilath Jeshurun he participated in every one of New York's modern Orthodox initiatives. They were well acquainted with Kaplan's work as an innovative educator both at the seminary and in the Kehillah, two organizations Fischman personally supported. And, as former active members of the Yorkville Jewish community, they were aware of his work outside of the synagogue and school in attempting to reach those with minimal or declining connection to the faith.[13]

Kaplan began reaching out to local second-generation youngsters in 1912 when he conducted a series of Friday night services at the 92d Street Y.M.H.A. True to his Orthodox public posture, he accepted the appointment "only on the condition that the organ be removed." Although he confided to his diary that "personally [he] had no strong objections to an organ, [he] felt that [he] would shock his friends and folks if [he] would consent to officiate" if they had an organ. The Y acquiesced to his demand.[14]

Kaplan soon became disenchanted with the religious scene at the Y. There was little enthusiasm among its members for prayer, whether or not it was accompanied by an organ. On Friday night there were so many other, more attractive, diversions that better captured their attention and interest. Good Endeavorer that he had been, Kaplan tried to interest Yorkville youngsters in an innovative Saturday afternoon program where an open discussion session would immediately follow the Minchah (afternoon) service. The rabbi naively believed that local young people were religiously conflicted and would anxiously seize the opportunity to share their feelings with others in a nonjudgmental forum. But Kaplan found, to his dismay, greater interest "in most Jewish homes, even the most strictly observant [for] the young people to go to 'matinee.'" Essentially, Yorkville young people had reached their own comfortable solutions to discussion group questions like "what shall the young person do on Saturday afternoon" as "an outlet to uphold also the spirit of the law." The rabbi sadly explained that "to keep within the letter of the law" those youngsters who cared "provide themselves with theater tickets before hand and walk instead of riding" to the place of amusement. They did not feel a need for Kaplan's advice and guidance.[15]

Still, Kaplan perservered in his efforts to instill within Y members a more affirmative attitude toward the beauties of Judaism and, ultimately, to convince them to attend services. A year later, in 1913, the rabbi informed Felix M. Warburg, then president of the Y.M.H.A. Council, that he would attempt to identify "a group of those already interested in religion" and convince them to arrange "activities of a cultural sort" for their peers. "Then perhaps services would come as a natural development later."[16]

During these same years Kaplan also played a conspicuous role in the founding of the Central Jewish Institute (CJI), which reached out more effectively than did the Y to Yorkville youngsters. Established in 1915, the CJI was a Jewish social, cultural, and educational center that grew out of the Yorkville Talmud Torah and was adjacent to, but independent of, Kehilath Jeshurun. Kaplan spoke at the groundbreaking for this organization, which pledged to "not merely be [an ordinary Hebrew School], but also a Jewish Social Centre, wherein there are provided a gymnasium, room for club work, kindergarten classes, and a kosher kitchen; in short a centre where the ideas of traditional Judaism will be fostered and encouraged in the minds of American youth." Kaplan, who described himself as an inactive or "stationary director" of the CJI, was also consulted as a courtesy on the choice of a director. It is, however, unlikely that he was thrilled with the choice of Herbert S. Goldstein, his nemesis, for that post.[17]

But, for all of Kaplan's credentials, weren't Orthodox leaders Cohen and

Fischman deeply troubled about entrusting their new project to a man who they knew did not agree with many of the Torah's fundamental teachings? After all, unlike most of their contemporaries, Fischman and Cohen were fully aware of the dimensions of the rabbi's theological dissent. Kaplan himself already had had "occasion throughout the many years of my acquaintance with [Cohen] to explain to him my conception of the Torah."[18] It is reasonable to assume that Cohen shared what he had learned from and about Kaplan with Fischman. Of course, if either of them needed any additional information regarding Kaplan's views, they could easily have turned to the young people from Kehilath Jeshurun who frequented his Saturday afternoon study groups. There Kaplan was consistently far more open, and radical, in his articulations than he was in the Jewish press or from public rostrums. Yet, it is clear that when talk began about hiring Kaplan at the Jewish Center, these men were fully prepared to work with this dissenter so long as he did not actively promote his heterodox views among congregants and as long as he did not challenge the establishment and maintenance of Orthodox practices in the service. Optimally, they wanted him to behave like the rabbi they had known at Kehilath Jeshurun and would tolerate him as long as he did not embarrass them before other American Orthodox Jews. However, at no point during the few years before the Jewish Center was actually built did anyone explicate these essential requirements to Kaplan. We will presently see that the rabbi had a far different understanding of what he could do in his office and of how committed his lay leaders were to perpetuating Orthodox traditions and rites.

If appearances, cooperation, and propriety were paramount to Cohen and Fischman, Kaplan's behavior at the very dinner party where they and another Jewish Center founder, businessman Abraham Rothstein, informed the rabbi that "they had organized and were determined to carry out the plans . . . for having the kind of institution that [Kaplan] had been dreaming of" gave them no cause for concern. As Kaplan described and satirized the scene in his diary, he and his friends "were all duly 'capped.' We all washed our hands and stood silent until the waiter came around with the 'matzohs' in a silver tray and all of us made the 'motzi' [blessing over bread] in due form. We were as elegantly orthodox as we could be."

Kaplan personally felt a "heroic thrill" when he "dared to remove the cap after we got through with the meal." But since he "certainly would not have thought of doing so while we ate," what he really thought about those traditional cermonials did not become an issue.[19] And, Orthodox

communal mores among Upper West Side Jews at that time did not pre-
scribe that men had to keep their heads covered at all times. A month later
Kaplan again behaved as if he were part of the Orthodox community.
After a meeting where he and this committee of three sat down to talk
through some weighty religious questions, their gathering broke up just in
time for them all to go to afternoon services.[20]

More important, Kaplan did not cause any problems when questions
were first raised over whether the sexes would be separated by a mechitzah,
as would befit an Orthodox synagogue. He told the committee that he
"would leave the question of form of service to the members themselves.
If they insist upon having the sexes seated separately, I shall certainly not
object. And if they insist upon having them seated promiscuously, I shall
not oppose them either." Cohen wanted Kaplan "to come out strongly for
traditional customs" but contented himself with Kaplan's pledge that he
would be "tactful and circumspect" on sensitive issues of this sort.[21]

Cohen was more concerned about his rabbi on those occasions when
Kaplan personally "laid before Cohen [his] heterodox views." For example, soon after the session on synagogue seating, Kaplan met again with
Cohen and read him some of his "notes on Genesis." This was one of the
moments when Kaplan wanted Cohen to "know fully how far my radical-
ism went" on issues like evolution and the authorship of the Bible.[22]
Cohen quickly inquired "as to the *practical* form which these views would
take on" (emphasis added). Asked so directly, Kaplan "confined [himself]
to the statement that I should be exempted from holding any positive
views about the seating of the sexes and about the organ." With this position Cohen and his committee were satisfied that Orthodoxy would be
followed in their synagogue and that their rabbi would, at least publicly,
"advocate the strict observance of the traditional forms of worship."[23]

Actually, in the years before the Jewish Center opened in 1918, Kaplan
was not certain how important family pews were in his own plans for that
new synagogue. While he preferred mixed seating and was annoyed at
himself for not having "the courage," when Cohen questioned him, "to go
the full length of what my attitude logically should have led me to state,"
he also knew deep down that, for himself, "there are weightier problems
Judaism must deal with than ritual observance."[24]

Moreover, Kaplan, who clearly enjoyed interacting with Orthodox Jews
of the class and stature of Cohen and Fischman, had many reasons to believe
that these Jews were not unalterably opposed to the changes he wanted to

make and could ultimately be led to accept his ideas and positions. At that point the rabbi was not fully attuned to how important these issues were to the lay committeemen and, thus, was optimistic that this Jewish Center experience would not replicate his frustrating years in Yorkville, where he found the religious atmosphere at Kehilath Jeshurun so stultifying.

Kaplan was encouraged when, for example, in October 1915, Joseph Cohen asked him "to take steps about offering a prize of $500 for the best ritual poems to be composed for the coming High Holidays." Someone who felt that the traditional prayers alone were not touching the heart and soul of modern congregants and that some additional prayers were necessary was certainly a person with whom Kaplan could work. Had not the rabbi himself hoped some years earlier that "somebody would make a suggestion that a man like Bialik or Tchernochowsky write some Piutim in place of the ones we have now?"[25]

And then there was Cohen's suggestive remark, two years later, that "the Center should not confine itself to holding the services prescribed by our ritual." As Kaplan recorded their conversation, Cohen asked "why not have the people come together once or twice a week to take part in devotional readings in the vernacular? Why not," he continued, "satisfy our inner spiritual longings that cannot find expression in a language which no one understands?" Once again, Cohen appeared open to rethinking the viability of traditional synagogue practices along the lines being advocated by his younger friend.[26]

Cohen was, moreover, in Kaplan's view, "the most stimulating person in my circle of acquaintances." The rabbi was particularly intrigued when Cohen asked him about Christian Science. Cohen said that "he was very much interested in it, because it seemed to have a remarkably large following for a young movement, and to appeal to men and women of intellectual bent of mind." And, in the spirit of experimentation that Kaplan valued so much, Cohen wanted him "to find out what good there was to Christian Science that might be grafted upon the stem of Jewish life."[27] Cohen's request "somewhat surprised" Kaplan, "though pleasantly." He confided in his diary that "it made me feel that there were great possibilities for spiritual growth in Cohen and in the Center." Kaplan was elated further when he heard that Cohen discussed both of his "radical ideas" with Fischman—that of adopting the good in Christian Science and of having devotional gatherings—and "the latter readily accepted."[28]

Finally, Kaplan could not help but notice that Cohen had made some accommodations of his own with the technical strictures of traditional Jewish law in his personal quest to live comfortably as a well-to-do American Jew. Kaplan observed that when this Orthodox lay leader invited the rabbi to a lunch meeting at the Waldorf Astoria, "the waiters try to meet [Cohen's] wishes in every way so that neither he nor his guests should feel in the least embarrassed in washing, making the *Motzi* and saying grace after meals." In this regard, they were staunch and proud adherents of Orthodox regulations. However, the meal they ate was clearly not scrupulously kosher. While the fish that was undoubtedly served as the main course was surely kosher as prescribed in the Torah, the preparation of the meal—dishes, pots, etc.—as ordained by Jewish law was not properly performed. Such a man who was not unyielding in his own practices possessed, to Kaplan's mind, great potential for religious "growth" (i.e., change) and would not, over the long haul, he thought, stand in his way. However, Kaplan would ultimately be proven wrong. No matter what Cohen did at the Waldorf or ruminated to his rabbi in private, when it came to the Jewish Center he was determined that Orthodoxy be neither abridged nor compromised. The synagogue leader distinguished between the non-Orthodox behavior he would sanction for himself and what he would insist upon in the public precincts of the Orthodox synagogue.[29]

Nevertheless, at this early juncture, Kaplan did not focus on the consistency or depth of Cohen's belief and practice. Rather, in 1916–1917, he faced the real possibility that his Jewish Center might actually come to practical fruition. Kaplan lore has it that, as the building was going up, he would visit the site often, jumping from girder to girder with great anticipation and excitement.[30] He was enormously invested in a project that he had been thinking, hearing, and talking about for almost a decade. Whether or not Kaplan was the progenitor of the "synagogue center" idea of the 1910s,[31] he was influential within those intellectual circles that spoke openly about the needs a "Jewish center" would fill.

Kaplan had been a member, for example, of the Achavah Club, which, in October 1910, heard Judah Magnes call for the establishment of a new institution that would include a "house of worship" (*bet tefillah*), "a house of study" (*bet midrash*), and a "social centre" (*bet knesset*). Magnes further suggested that "a school for children, popular lectures on Jewish history and literature, charity work of a more individual character, social work and recreation ought to be the center of such an organization." In his talk, entitled "Some Suggestions for a Religious Organization in New York

City," Magnes, using terms he may have borrowed from Kaplan, asserted that "the organization should embrace the functions of the Jewish people as a whole. For it is only through the Jewish people that the Jewish religion can prosper."[32]

About two years later, in November 1912, Magnes came back to the idea in a letter lauding David Blaustein, a noted communal leader who was actively involved both in New York's Kehillah and in the Zionist movement. He wrote that "the idea common to both of them is that of the Jewish Centre. The *Kehillah* is endeavoring to establish itself as the Jewish Centre of the million Jews of New York City. The Zionist movement is endeavoring to establish the Jewish Centre for the Jewish people in the Jewish land." He went on to note the fact that, in the past, "the Synagogue was the only Jewish Centre which the Jews had" and continued, "It is significant of the trend of the times that the old idea of having a single Jewish Centre, in which should be gathered all kinds of Jewish activities, is again becoming fashionable."[33]

The synagogue center remained a very important component of Kaplan's thinking during this period. At a speech delivered in December 1913 before the seminary's Morais-Blumenthal Society, a student group that he had once headed, Kaplan stated: "Judaism must have a group of people who have some social interests in common. Hence the duty of the Jewish minister is no less that of building up the social and communal life of his people than to give the religious teachings and conceptions of Judaism. . . . Furthermore, he must strive to make the synagogue a social center."[34]

In addition, Kaplan was interested in how incipient "synagogue-center" activities were evolving away from New York as well. In 1914, for example, he wrote to a rabbi in Detroit for information about how his synagogue was run. His respondent, Rabbi Abraham M. Hershman, could only say "that the New Shaarey Zedek Synagogue . . . is designed to serve as a center of religious, social and educational activity."[35]

Then there was the work of Herbert S. Goldstein, both in Yorkville and then, beginning in 1917, in Harlem. We have already noted how Kaplan influenced the outreach activities that Goldstein ran at the Central Jewish Institute. Two years later, Goldstein left Kehilath Jeshurun and the Yorkville Institute and, with the financial help of his father-in-law, Harry Fischel, founded the Institutional Synagogue. This initiative was the first attempt to coherently integrate the synagogue with the Jewish school, the traditional bet midrash with the social hall or gymnasium. In articulating, in 1916, his own outreach program for the entire Jewish family, a proposal that was carried on the front pages of various Jewish newspapers throughout the country, Goldstein argued that his

> Institutional Synagogue must, first of all, be as Orthodox a house of worship as is prescribed in Jewish codes. It should then be a place of study for the elders in the evening and for the children in the afternoons. . . . It should be a place where men and women may come after plying their daily cares and spend a social hour in an Orthodox environment. . . . This institution would be a revival of the historic synagogue. The synagogue of old was the center for prayer, study, and the social life of the community, all in one.

He wrote further about the new synagogue giving young people the "opportunity to express their social instincts in good American style, under the auspices of the synagogue" by having the opportunity to "run a dance, attend a gymnasium, do social work, or study in a thoroughly Jewish atmosphere."[36]

Goldstein's activities may have spurred Kaplan on to rapidly make his own institutional mark with the help of the Jews of the new Upper West Side. He did not like Goldstein and he certainly did not want to leave the field of synagogue center work and the credit for pioneering in outreach work to a man whom he characterized as "the embodiment of all that I hate in narrowminded and bigoted Orthodoxy."[37] All told, Kaplan's pride, ambition, and confidence that he had the uncommon capacity to lead Jews within and without the Jewish Center toward his understanding of the essential elements that would ensure Jewish survival in the twentieth century convinced him that Cohen and his friends' Orthodoxy would not seriously stymie his efforts.

However, given Kaplan's and the Jewish Center committee's mutual misunderstanding of how each wanted the other to behave, it was inevitable that they would be drawn before long into irreconcilable conflicts. Indeed, struggles between Kaplan and his lay leaders began as soon as the Jewish Center started holding its first services, in January 1918, despite the fact that their building on West 86th Street between Amsterdam and Columbus Avenues had not yet been completed. According to Kaplan, "the reason they inaugurated the services . . . was that Max Weinstein, one of the members, celebrated the Bar Mitzvah of his son." And, some of the members figured that Weinstein, "one of the most successful cloak manufacturers in the city," who "is not affiliated with any congregation, . . . would show his appreciation by contributing liberally toward the building fund if his son's Bar Mitzvah were made the occasion for inaugurating services at the Center."[38] When Cohen actually went about creating the mechitzah to prepare the sanctuary for prayer, the rabbi, who earlier had raised no theoretical objections, now found himself deeply troubled and unwilling to acquiesce on this ritual matter. Quick to express his displeasure, Kaplan complained to Cohen that "he was gradually getting me to compromise with myself until there was nothing left to the ideals I value most."[39]

Kaplan's personal annoyance with Cohen was intensified by his belief that, deep down, his synagogue president was not really personally committed to the strictures of Jewish law and was only "ruining my soul" to satisfy some unnamed traditional Jews in the congregation. In his diary he opined that Cohen "consulted [Rabbis] Hyamson and Margolis about the gallery not for the purpose of knowing the actual law, but how to be sufficiently within the letter of the law and yet please the members." He now feared that Cohen might turn out to be "a Pharisee in the worst sense of the word."[40] Tensions between these two began to be palpable.

Three days after Kaplan and Cohen exchanged words, the highly exercised rabbi determined that he had to remind Cohen in no uncertain terms he was "not Orthodox" and to assert specifically that the *Shulchan Aruch* was not "the last court of appeal in matters religious." When Cohen heard this unequivocal "expression to my liberal thoughts," according to Kaplan, "he froze up as I had never seen him do before. That settles it, is what his whole bearing implied." And, at a subsequent meeting held just a day later, Cohen "stood his groundly firmly and would not concede to anyone's right to depart from the law as laid down in the Schulchan Aruch."[41]

After these confrontations, Kaplan's relationship with the Jewish Center was "settled," at least for a while. He severed his ties with the Upper West Side Orthodox and recommended his old seminary classmate, Charles Kauvar, for the position of rabbi. Cohen and the others accepted Kaplan's decision and recommendation, and Kauvar was invited to speak at the center in March 1918. But when the Denver rabbi did nothing to impress the synagogue's leadership, they asked Kaplan to reconsider. In April 1918 a committee of trustees consisting of Judge Otto Rosalsky, one of Manhattan's most distinguished Orthodox Jews, and Abraham Rothstein visited Kaplan to formally offer him the post of Jewish Center rabbi.[42]

While there is no explicit evidence available indicating why Jewish Center people were still willing to overlook Kaplan's antagonistic attitudes, it is entirely conceivable that, with the mechitzah in place, the synagogue's lay leaders hoped that Kaplan would calm down, accept the reality of the situation, and bring his unquestioned abilities to bear in building and promoting their institution. After all, notwithstanding his bluster when he fought with Cohen, he had not made the mechitzah nor his underlying views regarding it causes for public congregational debate. Besides which, having been disappointed with Kauvar's performance, they may have realized, even more than before, that in Kaplan they had a uniquely talented rabbi.

When the Jewish Center committee appeared with their offer, Kaplan confided to his diary that "it looks as though I have to make up my mind once and for all. I can by no means say that I am sorry that the state of uncertainty in which I have been living the last year or two will now finally and definitely come to an end."[43] However, it was not clear what this weighty decision would be. For, two months earlier, he had concluded that he could not work with those who would force him to abide by the strictures of the *Shulchan Aruch*. But, at the same time, he had second thoughts about walking away from the project of his dreams. He now wanted to stay on, if at all possible, and thus had to determine in his own mind whether his defeat over the mechitzah was but an isolated, temporary setback or indicative of Cohen's desire and ability to force him to conform to Orthodox strictures. Once Kaplan concluded that his own abilities would ultimately carry the day, despite or against Cohen, he was prepared to acccept Rosalsky's and Rothstein's offer. However, since a diametrically opposite set of reasons had convinced Kaplan and most Jewish Center leaders that their troubles were behind them, tensions were bound to reappear—which they did.

For example, when Kaplan gave his Bible lectures at the Jewish Center, he did not "suppress any of [his] convictions" about the origins of the ancient narratives. Interpreting his pledge of the year earlier to be "tactful and circumspect" very broadly, Kaplan, in his own view, "express[ed] quite frankly though not rudely [his] belief as to the pre-Israelite origin of the creation story, the Paradise story etc." These opinions did not sit well with some elements within the congregation. Indeed, "heresy" hunters "now and then would come to the class," and Kaplan pridefully reported that they "would not have to wait long before [they] got what [they] had come for." When these more traditional Jews complained about what the rabbi was espousing, Kaplan almost became a public issue. Interestingly enough, while Fischman and certainly Cohen may well have personally agreed with those who carped against Kaplan, they did not choose to confront the rabbi. Rather, in keeping with their commitment to maintain appearances and propriety in their synagogue, they elected "to find some way of drawing [the] fangs" of those offended.[44]

In the meantime, Kaplan was having his own difficulties, on a very different plane, with another segment of the Jewish Center's membership. At the close of the First World War, concomitant with the start of this new synagogue, Kaplan, a true child of his times, became infatuated with the promises of social justice and economic equality that Marxism held out to the world. This modern belief in an egalitarian social order accorded well with Kaplan's own faith in the ancient Jewish commitment to improving the world at large. He decided that, as rabbi of the Jewish Center, he had the obligation—and the ability—to convince the well-to-do Upper West Side Jews whom he had successfully attracted to his center to help him end the world's ills.[45] When he overheard some of his members saying that they did not like to hire Jews because they are too union-conscious, he knew he faced a difficult task. Committed as he was to labor's cause, he proceeded to "fulminate about this in public." He spoke out in favor of unions, workers' rights, and a five-day work week. Kaplan's pointed words of admonition, however, were, understandably, not well received in a congregation with many wealthy cloak and garment manufacturers who ran factories employing large numbers of people. They certainly did not like it when Kaplan would publicly point a finger at those whom he regarded as lacking business ethics.[46]

In a striking passage in his diary describing his social justice sermons and the tensions they evoked within the congregation, Kaplan wrote:

> From time to time I touched upon some of the vital political and economic questions, and gave expression to views which I deemed both Jewish and just. Whenever I spoke in that vein I was accused of being a Bolshevik. Not that I am ashamed of being classed with the Bolsheviki. I would rather be classed with them than with the bourgeois profiteers. But what I object to in their charging me with Bolshevism is that such charge was to them a sufficient reason for not taking my views seriously, or analyzing them to see whether there was any truth to them. I had this experience with the series of

sermons on Freedom that I delivered during the Passover season. A typical case was that of a wife of one of the members, a young woman in the thirties whose husband is just now growing rich on his investments in oil stock in Oklahoma. She . . . made up her mind to discontinue her attendance at the Synagogue because of the type of sermon that I was delivering. The sermons so upset her nerves that she could not sleep nights on account of them . . .[47]

Kaplan, who saw himself as the consummate preacher, teacher, and leader, was deeply frustrated by his inability to get through to those of the "self-satisfied bourgeois class." He complained to his diary: "The triviality and shallowness of the social life among that class of Jews is so wearying that I feel as though all the spirit has oozed out of me on account of the time I have been wasting in their company."[48] And, some time later, he continued in the same vein, "with nothing left to preach or teach and nothing that he can or dare change, what is there for the rabbi to do?"[49]

Kaplan did not include Cohen and Fischman among the "smug self-complacen[t] . . . Jewish bourgeois" who, he feared, lacked "a larger vision and a deeper insight into the problems both of general and of Jewish life."[50] However, there was little they could do to ease Kaplan's frustration when he had to deal unproductively with individuals whom he characterized in moments of anger as "out and out materialists," "social climbers," and even as vulgar, uncouth slobs. In fact, once, in describing a prominent member he actually wrote, "as far as I can see, his vulgarity measures up to his reputed wealth."[51]

Moreover, as a man of boundless pride and considerable self-esteem, Kaplan was severely wounded when congregants, whether they agreed with his philosophies or not, failed to accord him the proper respect. A dinner held on April 18, 1920, "to celebrate the finishing of the building" was one such occasion where Kaplan felt dishonored and considered "throwing up the sponge." That gathering, Kaplan reported to his diary,

> was noisy and long drawn out. The desert was hardly served when the young folks, they upon whom we stake all our hopes, rose as one man and walked downstairs to dance. This was too much for me. The lack of manners, the crassness that makes it possible for a banquet in the interest of a religious cause to be unattended by a word of prayer or blessing aroused my resentment to such a degree

that I too walked out. No speeches were delivered that evening. Not that anyone took it to heart.[52]

Yet, despite tensions, misunderstandings, and bad feelings, Kaplan's association with the center continued unabated through the second half of 1920. No one moved against Kaplan on religious grounds because, although he was "anxious to introduce changes in the ritual," he did not push the point with Joseph Cohen, who "suspects every move I make."[53] Moreover, as late as January 1920, Kaplan was still tactful and circumspect—or maybe just disingenuous, as we have already seen in other contexts—in keeping his theological opinions largely to himself. It was then that H. P. Mendes, his former colleague, wrote to Kaplan. At a recent meeting of the Union of Orthodox Congregations he objected to the fact that they did not recognize the Jewish Theological Seminary as an institution "that stand[s] for the Torah and traditional Judaism." The rabbi of Congregation Shearith Israel continued:

> It has been alleged that the Seminary does not stand for Orthodox Judaism. It was stated to me that you teach that Revelation is not as the Orthodox believe, "Min Hashamayim," direct from God to man, even by voice; and further that you teach that there is no evidence of Divine Providence in human affairs.
>
> Will you put me in a position to use your name denying these statements? Or kindly let me know your actual views. . . . I want [the] Seminary to stand where Dr. Morais and I and others placed it.[54]

Joseph Cohen and his friends could not have been displeased with Kaplan's answer, which carefully avoided addressing the issue placed before him. He clearly kept his true beliefs off the public record when he responded:

> In reply to your favor of January 5th, I beg to say that I do not see my way clear to discuss, by mail, theological questions of an important a character as those you mention in your letter. I am inclined to think that the opposition to the Seminary is not altogether due to theological zeal, but is inspired by sulks and ill-will which people naturally develop toward anything which they are unsuccessful in getting under their control.[55]

Kaplan himself was not pleased with the Jewish Center's unresponsive rank and file nor with the lay leader who doggedly watched his every move. Still, he was not prepared to leave an active, maturing institution. The synagogue building grew from a three-story structure, completed in March 1918, to ten stories ready for occupancy in July 1920. Membership likewise saw an increase from sixty-one families in April 1918 to over a hundred by June 1921. In the course of those few years the synagogue was able to boast of a full range of activities: daily services, two separate schools—an afternoon school as well as a day school, special holiday celebrations, study and sewing circles, social programs utilizing the center's athletic and restaurant facilities, a children's club, a choral group, and a complete range of congregational committees. In addition, the center sponsored a number of communitywide events on behalf of the New York Kehillah, the United Synagogue of America, Hadassah, and more. In his more optimistic moments Kaplan had to have thought that, with time and given his own efforts and abilities, he could attract an even larger number of Jews to the center and ultimately influence both old and new about what, to his mind, it really meant to be a Jew in America at the beginning of the third decade of the twentieth century.[56]

However, the question of Kaplan's patience with the congregation became moot in the latter months of 1920 when the rabbi violated, in bold unequivocal terms, Cohen's implicit injunction to "refrain from giving expression to his liberal thoughts." The lay leader could not countenance Kaplan's series of frontal attacks against Orthodoxy, which began appearing in the August 1920 edition of the *Menorah Journal*. From that moment onward Kaplan's relationship with the Jewish Center would become increasingly untenable as his now very public heresies emerged as a major cause célèbre within and without the congregation.

CHAPTER 6 • *The Struggle for Control of the Jewish Center*

On December 24, 1920, the *Hebrew Standard* printed an editorial entitled "Heresy in Our Rank?" This weekly, reporting on and advocating American Orthodox programs and initiatives, had until then always given the Jewish Center and its rabbi excellent exposure and publicity. Joseph Cohen and his colleagues in the leadership of the center could always be proud to know that American Orthodox rabbis like Drachman, Mendes, and Goldstein and lay people like Fischel and Dukas, whose approbation and opinions they valued, were, through the *Hebrew Standard*, kept abreast of Upper West Side efforts to reach the community's youth and adults. But now the weekly cited statements the center's rabbi had recently made in the *Maccabaean* and in the *Menorah Journal*, declaring that "the above quotations express even to the uninitiated mind plain unmistakable heresies." They warned that "our youth is in danger when such views are being thrust upon them" and asserted that "Orthodoxy cannot remain silent." Whether Cohen's rabbi had intended to or not, Mordecai Kaplan had deeply embarrassed the Jewish Center leader.[1]

Cohen was further upset one month later, in January 1921, when the *Jewish Forum*, a monthly with sympathies and a readership very close to the *Hebrew Standard*, took note of his institution and wondered out loud how Kaplan could continue as its rabbi. In an essay entitled "Reconstructing Judaism?" Bernard Drachman, managing editor of that weekly, took off after his former student:

> The utterances of Kaplan . . . on some of the fundamental
> doctrines of religion and his proposals for the Reconstruction of

Judaism (?) . . . have come as a great shock to all Jews who believe in
the traditional faith of Israel and desire its perpetuation. . . . True
Jews, that is to say, believers in a Supreme Being and a genuine
Divine Law interpreted by authoritative tradition, cannot look upon
such theories and proposals otherwise than with feelings of horror.

Seeing Kaplan's statements as a problem both for the Jewish Center and
the seminary, Drachman continued by averring that

these views would have been bad enough coming from the lips of an
avowed representative of Radical Reform but emanating as they do
from one who holds a high position on the faculty of a Theological
Seminary which declares that it stands on the platform of Orthodox
Judaism and who also is the spiritual guide of an Orthodox congregation, they are amazing and disconcerting in the highest degree.

Drachman then suggested that "considering the nature of Professor
Kaplan's views and proposals, it is somewhat surprising that the learned
professor does not see their inconsistency with the official positions which
he holds." And, Drachman was quick to suggest, "if he cannot bring himself to endorse or uphold these tenets, the honorable and manly thing is
to withdraw and not remain in official connection with a cause to which
he is inwardly utterly antagonistic."[2]

William Fischman also experienced some bad moments over Kaplan's
remarks. In December 1920 Edwin Kaufman, chairman of the Religious
Observance Committee of the United Synagogue of New York, expressed
his astonishment to Cyrus Adler over "how in the world [the Jewish Cen-
ter] can tolerate a Rabbi in its pulpit who does not profess to be an Orthodox rabbi." Fischman, who was a member of Kaufman's committee, surely
heard from his chairman on the now controversial issue.[3]

Cohen and Fischman, likewise, could not have been pleased with what the
Agudath ha-Rabbanim had to say about Kaplan. While these uptown American Orthodox Jews really had little to do with the East European rabbinate,
as men who were keenly sensitive to bad publicity they were concerned that,
at its semiannual convention held on January 11, 1921, these rabbis attacked
Kaplan for leading Jewish youth to Reform. Referring to him as "half-Ortho-
dox," they appointed a committee to stop the spread of what they considered a danger to Judaism. They gave Kaplan one week's time to stop his activities, threatening, if he did not, to engage in an all-out attack against him.[4]

What had Kaplan done to provoke such ire within a community that previously had not really reacted to even his most antagonistic published statements? What had he written in the 1920 *Maccabaean* and *Menorah Journal* that made those who usually did not examine those journals turn quickly to his pieces and tell others about them? The Jewish Center rabbi had now finally taken two large steps across an invisible religious line that would separate him from Orthodoxy. First, he had dared to identify and specify the real and practical implications of his heresies: the traditional Sabbath, the festivals, the *Shulchan Aruch*, the dietary laws, and the liturgy were all formally and publicly denigrated. Second, Kaplan presented himself as a leader of a new movement—a new expression of Judaism—far more radical than the United Synagogue, which would compete, not only ideologically, but institutionally and organizationally, with Orthodoxy.

For example, in the *Maccabaean* essay of November 1920 the rabbi clarified those core teachings and observances he considered to be outmoded or untenable and suggested his role in a new society that would take up these issues "with due regard to the principle of continuity, yet also with an eye for the social value of that which is to be declared authoritative and binding." Here Kaplan enumerated "those very practices [which] are, to a large extent, responsible for the problem of Jewish adjustment." He unequivocally stated that

> the observance of the Sabbath in complete conformity with the letter and spirit of the Schulchan Aruch is entirely out of the question. The celebration of the two-day holiday imposes a great burden upon those engaged in commerce and industry. To demand a scrupulous observance of the Dietary Laws is to place a handicap upon pioneer effort on the part of the Jew who wants to remain loyal to his faith. The repetitious character of the ritual, and the limited scope of the content of the prayers, are responsible for Jewish worship failing to be recreative and comforting to those of the newer generation. The position of woman in traditional Jewish Law is still no higher than that which she was accorded in the ancient laws of the Romans, a position that puts her in the same class with minors and slaves.[5]

The society to which he alluded was the Society of the Jewish Renascence, consisting of a group of seminary alumni who themselves chafed at the conservative tendencies of the still-young United Synagogue.

Led by Kaplan friends Rabbi Jacob Kohn of New York's Temple Ansche Chesed and Rabbi Herman R. Rubenovitz of Temple Mishkan Tefila, Roxbury, Massachusetts, they attempted "to establish an organ outside of the regular channels of the movement [the United Synagogue] to achieve their purpose" of bringing "Jewish belief and practice into vital relationship with the actual life of the Jew." It was before this audience, people with whom Kaplan felt very much at home, that he, in June 1919, spoke about "Judaism and Reconstruction." This presentation contained the core of the thoughts that found their way into his controversial article, "A Program for the Reconstruction of Judaism," which appeared in the August 1920 issue of the *Menorah Journal*.[6]

In other words, Kaplan was no longer coming across in the same manner as previously, that is, as a United Synagogue leader who greatly respected the traditions of the past and wanted to make the most minimal of changes in America's synagogues. Rather, he was emerging as the most forceful spokesman for a real third movement in Judaism that called for a "Program of Progressive Judaism" with its own newly formulated "modern code of Jewish practice" as opposed to the "religious anarchy of the Reform Movement" and "the spiritual despotism of Orthodoxy."[7] He was specifying that "in the case of the liturgy, not only are its contents and length entirely out of keeping with the requirements of present-day life, but there are parts in it which have been made entirely obsolete by changes in social conditions and in the intellectual point of view." Kaplan was advocating that "any movement which aims at reconstructing Jewish life must revitalize the entire system of ceremonial observances by adjusting them to the spiritual needs of our day."[8]

The movement Kaplan appeared to be spearheading was particularly galling to those American Orthodox leaders who, as late as 1920, still viewed the seminary as an institution that served their community well. It will be recalled that for over thirty years (circa 1887–1920), people like Drachman, Mendes, Goldstein, Fischel, Dukas, and others, each in his own way, had worked with and supported JTS activities. Although Drachman, for example, was not happy with Schechter's ideas, he did not, in 1904, back the Agudath ha-Rabbanim's reviling of Schechter's seminary. If anything, for another generation he freely associated with JTS people in a myriad of communal institutions even as he pined for the days before 1902 when the old seminary was solidly within the Orthodox camp. Goldstein himself had graduated from the new seminary and was proud of his training—as was his father-in-law, Harry Fischel. The founding of the United Synagogue of America in 1913 did not sit well with men who were closely linked with the Orthodox Union. They did not like institutional competition and feared that Schechter's views on Catholic Israel would significantly alter the nature of American congregational life. But in the first years of the USA's existence its constituent congregations were slow in changing synagogue services. Now, however, these traditionalists saw in Kaplan's ideas and moves the personification and realization of their worst dreams. Much to their chagrin, an element more radical than Schechter was trying to capture the Conservative movement and move the seminary irretrievably away from Orthodoxy.

The January 21, 1921 edition of the *Hebrew Standard* expressed these American Orthodox leaders' anger and fears very well. In an editorial entitled "Official and Personal Heresy" it referred to the criticism of Kaplan expressed there a month earlier and called upon the seminary community to align itself with Orthodoxy and oppose the dissenter. The *Hebrew Standard* was especially exercised by the fact that Kaplan was still respected enough to be scheduled for a major presentation on "The Function and Organization of the Synagogue" at the forthcoming convention of the United Synagogue. It referred to Kaplan's "treason to the cause he affects to serve" and called his ideas nothing less than "official heresy." Kaplan continued to be attacked, in similar terms, in a subsequent issue of the weekly as well. Meanwhile, Rabbi Henry Morais, another loyal Orthodox supporter of the seminary, expressed all of his friends' feelings best when he excoriated Kaplan from the pulpit of Congregation Shearith Israel, calling him "a wolf in sheep's clothing."[9]

Edwin Kaufman was also apprehensive over the possibility that Kaplan and his group would come to dominate the seminary and the USA. Focused on the potential harm Kaplan might inflict upon the faith commitments of students at the seminary, this USA lay leader called for the rabbi's outright dismissal from the school that, for him, "stands for adherence to strict traditional Judaism." He wrote:

> Dr. Kaplan has a perfect right to preach his kind of religion if he
> so desires, as an independent minister to those who believe as he
> does . . . but as a Professor of the Seminary, I believe he should not
> be permitted to continue his present teaching, for . . . if his present
> beliefs are inculcated into the young men studying for the Rab-

binate . . . and those studying for teachers at the Teachers College, Judaism in America will suffer greatly.[10]

Seminary leader Cyrus Adler tried to soft-pedal and sidestep his harboring of a renegade from Orthodoxy. His dilemma was that if he defended Kaplan too strongly, American Orthodox supporters of his institution would reconsider their association with a school they might see as having gone astray forever. On the other hand, as a believer in academic freedom, befitting the head of an American theological seminary, he could not in good conscience summarily remove Kaplan from his post. So he wrote to Kaufman that he had "casually" read both of Kaplan's controversial articles and had "heard something" about the Society for the Jewish Renascence. But, he continued, "I did not take the matter very seriously because I thought that it was part of the unrest in the world which follows the war, when everybody felt that they must talk about reconstruction." Although he distanced himself from Kaplan's pronouncements ("I am not certain what they are and think they are expressed rather clumsily") and stated that he considered the society's platform "not so much dangerous as childish," he felt that no action against Kaplan was appropriate. He preferred to say that "if an issue is now made with Dr. Kaplan, he will become a martyr. . . . The men of his synagogue who like him may support him." He concluded with the assertion that Jewish tradition does not consider deviant opinions to be heresy, only deviant behavior. "As long as a man *observes* the Jewish law, which Dr. Kaplan says he does, and I am convinced he does, he may speculate about philosophical matters." After all, even Maimonides' *Guide for the Perplexed* was burned by his opponents while his *Mishneh Torah* was universally respected, he added.[11]

None of these issues were lost on Cohen and Fischman. As supporters of seminary organizations, they too shared their American Orthodox friends' concerns with the state of that school's soul. They were also, certainly, "worried" about being tarred for keeping on the dissenter as their spiritual leader. But, beyond their fears "for maintaining their own reputations as being Orthodox," they developed great anxiety over whether Kaplan could still be "tactful and circumspect" and respectful of Orthodox tradition within the Jewish Center.[12] Given what he had said publicly about "revitalizing the entire system of ceremonial observance," would Kaplan not move to alter synagogue life, starting with new seating patterns? And now that he was emerging as a spokesman for a new movement in Judaism, would he not want his Jewish Center to be its flagship synagogue? Having lost total faith in a man who was not living up to any of the essential requirements for employment as their rabbi, Fischman and Cohen, especially the latter, wanted to be rid of Kaplan.

However, they would soon learn that Kaplan would not resign quietly and that it would be very difficult to force him to leave. Despite all his frustrations and all the criticisms that were being leveled against him, Kaplan "was determined to stick" for two basic reasons. First, the Jewish Center was still the institution of his dreams. He believed that he could withstand the current "trouble in the Center" and, if forced into a showdown, prevail through the force of his rhetoric or the power of rank-and-file votes. In the end he still hoped that the Upper West Side synagogue would become his society's lead congregation. Second, Kaplan fought to hold his line at the Jewish Center because he feared that the American Orthodox rabbinic and lay leadership being arrayed against him would continue to pressure the seminary to fire him. He struggled to at least maintain his congregational affiliation, no matter what might take place at the school. In a conversation with Rubenovitz when the battle within the center was just beginning, Kaplan intimated that "he would not mind withdrawing from the Center provided he felt his Seminary position were secure and that he could go on with his work." Kaplan suspected that his "moneyed interests" synagogue opponents "will withhold their support from the Seminary on the ground that his presence there constitutes a taint and that, in such an event, the authorities of the Seminary may feel inclined at least to muzzle him."[13]

Committed to staying, Kaplan dismissed Rubenovitz's view that his

> own highest interests, as well as of the Renaissance Movement . . . demand that you free yourself from the trammels, which association with intolerant and bigoted men must, of necessity, impose upon you. . . . You should be free to throw all your ability and strength in the direction which will count most, and not be obliged to fritter it away in the Sisyphian labor of trying to convert the magnates of the Eighty-(Fifth) [Sixth] Street Synagogue.[14]

While Kaplan was prepared, if necessary, to engage his critics, he initially tried to safeguard his position with a few well-placed words, even if they did not really represent his true position. We have already seen how Kaplan, by temperament, often preferred verbal obfuscation to direct confrontation with his adversaries. That proclivity may explain the purpose of his January 16, 1921 Hebrew letter printed in *Der Morgen Zhurnal* where he denied his intention to break away from Orthodoxy. Instead, he claimed that the sole purpose of his new society was

> to bring closer to Judaism those who, as a result of their secular education which they received in secular schools, distanced them- selves from religion. . . . These young people who were ensnared by alien cultures and were influenced by the (views) expounded within them—the heart of these and only these do we strive to attract to the Jewish religion.[15]

This time, however, Kaplan's critics were quick to ridicule his apologia. Bernard Drachman spoke for many Orthodox Jews when he stated that "mere vague disclaimers and professions of loyalty cannot counteract the most radical negations of the fundamental doctrines of Judaism." The editors of the *Hebrew Standard* articulated comparable views when they scoffed, "When the professor declares, however, that he never attacked Orthodox Jewish principles, we suspect that he was incorrectly quoted. In our columns we recently gave chapter and verse of each of Professor Kaplan's attacks on Orthodoxy. If those were not attacks, we do not know what attacks are."[16]

Undeterred, Kaplan continued to try to carry the day without a fight by calling for a private meeting with his congregants where they could have a "heart to heart talk, in order that the atmosphere might be cleared of all false rumors and misunderstandings." At that gathering, which was closed to "outsiders" (the Jewish media?), Kaplan treaded warily and cautiously on sacred turf, as had been his wont already on a number of different occa- sions, chose his words carefully and offered an interpretation of his *Mac- cabaean* and *Menorah Journal* articles that did not really reflect what he believed and had said about Orthodoxy. Here Kaplan made every effort to neither discourage those who liked his ideas nor inflame those who were troubled by them. He began his presentation by declaring that "historical traditional Judaism is what I stand for and what I work for." He then ten- dered a hazy statement, which did not fully explain his *Maccabaean* remarks that "the observance of the Sabbath in complete conformity with the let- ter and spirit of the Schulchan Aruch is entirely out of the question" or that "the celebration of the two day holiday" is a burden on most Jews. The rabbi said that "his position was that the second day was not really necessary, but as long as the law was in effect, it must be obeyed. People had the right to express their dissatisfaction." And, after telling his audience, that "if you must violate some of the Sabbath laws don't feel you have to overthrow the entire institution," he closed his remarks with the cry "We all stand for a Hebrew Judaism, for a Torah Judaism, and for a Zionist Judaism. . . . We stand on tradition and history."[17]

A series of carping pulpit comments was the closest Kaplan came, at this point, to publicly confronting his critics or even to chastising those within the congregation who had consistently stymied his efforts. When he spoke on "Confidence in People" on Saturday morning, January 1, 1921, he adeptly implied that, like Moses who lost confidence "in the people whom he was to lead out of slavery," so was he losing faith in his own stiff-necked "people" who did not appreciate his efforts to free them from servitude to the religious past. The next Saturday he delivered a talk entitled "Gratitude," subtly suggesting that while "inherent to human nature is the trait of gratitude . . . based on a sense of indebtedness for that which one could not obtain by his own efforts, and is thus a recognition of one's limitations . . . on the recognition of the duty of making some return for sacrifice or effort made in one's behalf," that trait was lacking among some of the people to whom he spoke. And then, some two weeks after the private congregational meeting described earlier, on Saturday, February 26, he expatiated on "The Readjustment of Ideals," concluding, "If men would learn to carry out this principle of the readjustment of ideals in the manner suggested, they will not become cynical, skeptical, or despondent as soon as they will find reality in conflict with their ideas, but they will broaden and deepen those ideals." This was as far as he would presently go in telling his opponents to be less rigid in their thinking and behavior.[18]

Kaplan's nuanced public apologia and his pulpit implications did not impress Joseph Cohen at all. Certain of what Kaplan believed in, embarrassed by what he had written, and fearful of what the renegade would do next, Cohen remained determined to have the rabbi out of the Jewish Center. Yet, he and the other stalwarts "best qualified to be considered the representatives of Orthodox Judaism" in the center were not ready to move precipitously against their rabbi. Years later Bernard Drachman would suggest that they "felt unable to oppose" Kaplan because his "reputation for learning was so great, and his articles were so full of apparently profound erudition."[19]

But a more likely explanation of why they were "afraid to ask [Kaplan] to resign"[20] was their worry that if the rabbi called for a final congregational showdown he might have the votes to sustain his post. Then they would lose control of the Jewish Center and he would be free to do as he pleased with the institution. Or, the congregation would become hopelessly split and a substantial number of disgruntled members would leave an institution in turmoil. For the unavoidable reality was that, whether it was by dint of Kaplan's charisma or the panoply of social and religious activities the center offered, the institution had been successful in attracting a sizable group of Jewish Upper West Siders to its upscale West 86th Street home. And Cohen and his friends understood that many of these Jewish Center members did not share their dogged concerns about the content of Kaplan's messages or, for that matter, their commitments to Orthodox teachings.

Cohen knew of people like I. L. Philips, vice president of the center's Building Committee, who openly told his fellow board members at a meeting held on a Saturday afternoon that, earlier that day, "he was called to the telephone" when he returned home from the synagogue and "rushed downtown to the Hotel Biltmore for a meeting." Cohen, likewise, was aware of center men "who never come to the Saturday morning services because they work in their offices" but who attended Saturday afternoon fund-raising gatherings and carried money in their pockets. Indeed, he once had sharp words with one irreligious member who, moved by a solicitation, "was about to hand a thousand dollar bill to the committee." Quick to react, Cohen spoke up and told this offender that "we don't take money on the Sabbath." Then there was another nonobservant center family that arrived late for their son's bar mitzvah and "had to be telephoned for twice before they came." These Jewish Center members, whose own religious observances were far from punctilious, did not care what Kaplan really thought about Orthodoxy. They, and maybe even the majority of the synagogue's rank and file, were content simply to be in the company of an accepting tolerant rabbi who preached that they had a place within an Orthodox institution. All they desired was to avail themselves of this upscale congregation's facilities, to listen to a refined and highly skilled preacher, and to pray, when the spirit moved them, in the traditional manner that reminded them of the best of their Jewish heritage.[21]

Cohen's own concern about how his raising a hue and cry over Kaplan would be heard in his congregation may explain his reaction to Bernard

Drachman, who pressed him to endorse his polemic against the dissenter. In February 1921 Cohen received a prepublication copy of Drachman's excoriation of Kaplan, "An Examination of Prof. Mordecai M. Kaplan's Views on Judaism," which was slated for appearance in the next issue of the *Jewish Forum*. Worried that Drachman's arguments might galvanize Kaplan's friends and splinter the congregation, Cohen gave the following careful response:

> I read the article very carefully and I am bound to say that, while you treat the subject in a most temperate manner, laying emphasis on the point that your opposition is "to the book, not the author," your arguments are nevertheless most thorough and logical and will, I am sure, appeal not only to the believing and observing Jew, but to the skeptic as well. Would that we had more such able, valiant and ready advocates of Jewish principles and ideals in the defense of which, to quote from your article, "countless numbers of men and women have made the supreme sacrifice and died as martyrs."

Cohen's letter to Drachman essentially made three points: thank you for sending me your article; your arguments are good but, remember, they are not against Kaplan personally; if only the Jewish people could have more advocates like you. His reply possessed none of the vitriol that infused Dr. Joseph Bieber's reaction to a reading of the same as yet unpublished article. A leading member of Drachman's own congregation who did not have to worry about splitting Ohab Zedek over Kaplan, Bieber had no problem writing passionately to his own rabbi about the heretic's "malicious views" and "agnostic and sophistic opinions" and their "terrible effect" upon the community.[22]

A month later Cohen had more than intuition and experience to convince him that Kaplan truly had significant support within the Jewish Center. On March 17, even as attacks against Kaplan grew outside the synagogue, the board of directors tendered its rabbi a vote of confidence as it offered him a salary of $10,000 and asked him to depart from his standard procedure of rejecting any remuneration for his services.[23]

Constrained from moving directly against Kaplan, Cohen attempted a last-ditch effort to show him—even at this late date—the error of his ways. However, their encounter in April 1921 did nothing but antagonize both Cohen and Kaplan and remind them of how problematic their relationship had become. At a meeting that Fischman and Rothstein also attended, Cohen attempted to engage Kaplan in "a theological discussion on the question as to whether the Jews exist for the Torah or the Torah for the Jews." When Kaplan bristled and asserted that he would not debate this issue with those he deemed "unqualified," Cohen proposed that "the matter [be] referred to a committee of rabbis who are authorities on Jewish law." Presumably, these higher rabbinical authorities would be Orthodox. Kaplan would have none of this. He replied: "There are very few rabbis to whom I would submit my case. They would have to possess a modern education and to think as moderns in addition to being authorities on Jewish law."[24]

However, despite their growing antipathy toward one another, because both Cohen and Kaplan were unsure of their ultimate strength within the congregation, neither was quite ready for a showdown. Thus, when William Fischman moved that, since the rabbi had previously requested a leave of absence, he should again apply "with the understanding that it was to be for one year, and that if by the end of that time either Cohen or [Kaplan] changed . . . attitudes," Kaplan would then return to the pulpit rabbinate, both "accepted the suggestion heartily."[25]

Kaplan's public stance when he followed Fischman's suggestion and reapplied for the sabbatical did not at all reflect the conflict then underway. He wrote, "I am planning to give up my rabbinical duties for the present, in order to catch up with my literary work and my studies to which I have done very scant justice during the last three years that I have been giving my services to the Center. . . . By the end of the year I shall, with God's help, be in a position to resume my duties as Rabbi . . . with greater zest and vigor than ever before."[26] We may surmise that the rabbi also planned to spend some time gauging and shoring up his support within the congregation.

Cohen agreed to this temporary truce because he had seen, just a month earlier, that only a minority of the center's leaders shared his degree of outrage. His greatest hope of the moment was that, with time off, Kaplan would find other affiliations more fulfilling and ultimately volunteer not to return to the Jewish Center.[27]

This truce was never effectuated. On May 2, 1921, the board of trustees met to discuss Kaplan's request for a leave. Despite Cohen's advocacy, seven of the nine trustees present were opposed, and a committee was appointed to further discuss the matter with Kaplan. Those who voted against the leave included the rabbi's supporters, who saw no reason why their leader should not continue his important work at the center.[28] Feeling that he now had the upper hand, a more confident Kaplan immediately stopped talking about a sabbatical. At a general membership meeting only two days after the board gathering, the rabbi, for the first time, defiantly indicated that he not only planned on staying at the Jewish Center but that he had every intention of teaching his conception and practice of Judaism within its confines. He "pleaded" with the rank and file to take "their Judaism seriously" and help him determine once and for all whether "the educational work in the Center . . . be dominated by the orthodox point of view, or the point of view upon which [he] had been laboring all these years." As always, Kaplan was sure to temper his remarks by asserting that his own views regarding faith were "irrelevant to the larger purposes for which the Center stood . . . so long as [he] did nothing in [his] own life or in the Center that could be objected to by the Orthodox wing." Still, his conclusion that he "should be allowed to work out these plans which [he] considered essential to the work of Judaism" confirmed Cohen's worst fears.[29]

Three days later the rabbi took an additional provocative step when he attempted to rally his forces within the board for a victory over Cohen. Kaplan believed that "unless something happens whereby Cohen's spell on some of the leading trustees will be broken, it is useless for me to work in the Center." When a committee came to Kaplan to reinitiate the deliberations over his leave of absence, he lobbied hard "to convince them that Cohen had been pestering my life ever since we began to discuss the Center. . . . [Kaplan's] advice to them was that they should ignore Cohen and promise me the cooperation which I needed to make the Center a success."[30]

But even as Kaplan felt increasingly sure that, should his disagreements with Cohen "be aired" at their forthcoming annual meeting, he "would have no difficulty getting a large majority of members to support [him]," the rabbi still had some nagging reservations about whether this triumph might turn out to be "a Pyrrhic victory." Not unlike Cohen, as much as he wanted to control the synagogue he too was concerned about splintering his Upper West Side constituency. Kaplan fully recognized that if Cohen and Orthodoxy were totally disenfranchised, the most traditional of his lay leaders would leave the congregation. The bottom line was that neither he nor the center could afford to lose their substantial financial commitments. Given these realities, Kaplan "made it [his business]" at an informal dinner meeting with the center's leadership at the Astor Hotel (excepting Cohen who was ill and left) "to make peace overtures right there and then."[31]

Kaplan soon found out that if he wanted peace he would have to compromise on his bold assertion of just a few days earlier that he intended to actively promote his views within the congregation. It became clear that, minimally, he would have to agree not to teach his controversial ideas to "the children and the young people at the Center." Fischman, for one, told Kaplan outright "that if he had a daughter going to the Center he would take her away if she was taught that the Torah was not given by God at Sinai."[32] Indeed, for Fischman, the problem already existed. Heresy, he alleged, was secretly being introduced into the center's school curriculum. Apparently, Fischman had recently "got into an argument . . . [with] one of the pupils in [Max] Kadushin's class . . . and in the course of that argument," she revealed, "that she had been taught not to disclose to people at home the views on the Bible that she was being given in the classroom." An implacable Fischman was determined that the center had "to have a Committee on Education that would safeguard the orthodoxy of the instruction."[33]

Seizing the "opportunity to bring about peace in the Center," Kaplan agreed "to the appointment of that committee," even at the expense of "compromising with myself" and "with the principle of intellectual honesty." As long as his opponents could not and would not move against him, Kaplan was again willing to bide his time. He held out hope that, "before long," everyone in the synagogue would recognize the wisdom of his teachings.[34]

However, Cohen remained unconvinced that Orthodoxy and heterodoxy could really coexist within the Jewish Center. Just two days later, at a May 10, 1921 board of trustees meeting called to discuss Kaplan's proposed leave of absence, Cohen demanded that the group discuss the rabbi's views and relationship with the center "in our shirt sleeves," without "beating around the bush," without "veils [obscuring] the issues." Kaplan, he contended, "wants to give us a new Judaism. We, however, cannot permit ourselves to be experimented with. We are bound by the constitution to be orthodox." Moreover, "in accepting the rabbinate of the Center," Kaplan "was pledged to make it 100% Jewish according to the 'Din Shulhan Aruch.' " The Jewish Center rabbi had no choice, argued Cohen, but to conform to these strictures.[35]

Stung by Cohen's uncompromising attack, and yet anxious still to reach a compromise that both he and all center people could live with, Kaplan retreated. He suggested rhetorically that "it was not a new Judaism that I was trying to formulate but on the contrary, that I was doing all in my power to enable traditional Judaism to live." More important, he promised that he would not attempt to change the center's traditional rite. He said that "as far as my relations to the center are concerned I am prepared to uphold the Shulhan Aruch as the code to be followed in our practice inasmuch as we have no other authoritative code to go by." However, Kaplan reserved the right to preach what he believed from the center's pulpit, since he claimed that "there is nothing in the Constitution which says that the Center must be Orthodox." Turning to the critical question of what would be taught to impressionable youngsters, Kaplan conceded that, "if the principal directors of the Center object to having such unorthodox ideas as I hold taught to the young people, they have a perfect right to appoint an Education Committee to supervise the teaching and see to it that it be conducted in the orthodox spirit."

Eager to sustain his point, Kaplan offered a graphic illustration of how he could, in fact, compromise on the teaching of his heresies to children, as long as he had the freedom to preach in his pulpit:

> If the teacher in the school would be asked by a young person whether the Red Sea was actually divided as described or not, the teacher would be obliged to say that we must accept the story as narrated in the Torah. On the other hand, when I shall have occasion to speak of that incident, I will say that it could not have taken place as described in the Torah, because such an occurrence is contrary to the laws of nature.

Under this scenario, Kaplan continued, Orthodoxy and heterodoxy could coexist at the Jewish Center. Indeed, he told the board frankly that with all

> the logical inconsistency it is better for the Center to harbor this inconsistency than to be sacrificed to logical consistency. For if either side insists upon having its point of view prevail to its full extent, the Center is bound to be wrecked. Holding the unity and integrity of the Center higher than the views of either group, I believe that it [is] advisable to adopt the compromise suggested.

However, Cohen and his followers would not hear of this sort of arrangement. Kaplan's articulation of how praying, preaching, and teaching would take place within the Jewish Center caused one perplexed board member to wonder out loud: "Does this arrangement mean that we are going to have two religions in the Center, one for the children and another for the parents?" And, as Kaplan remembered the meeting, for the next two hours, six other board members joined Cohen in "a violent fire of questions and sneers." The attacks continued until midnight.

Cooler heads were not destined to prevail that night. For, after midnight, one of Kaplan's supporters counterattacked on the rabbi's behalf. Stating that "my principle is that when a man meets you more than half way you must not repel him," Abraham Rothstein spoke sternly to Cohen and his supporters: "Dr. Kaplan has done his utmost to accede to your wishes. He has consented to the appointment of a committee that should guard the orthodoxy of the teaching. He wants peace. Then why refuse to accept his proposal."

When, moments later, Kaplan's supporters, obviously the board's majority, moved that their leader be reelected rabbi, the moment of truth that Kaplan originally wanted to avoid, and Cohen, at first, felt less than powerful enough to pursue, was at hand. Outnumbered, Cohen and Fischman attempted several parliamentary maneuvers to block the motion, but to no avail. Ultimately, Kaplan was reelected rabbi, with Cohen casting an opposing vote. A half-hour later, after much cajoling from those within the board, Cohen changed his vote to permit them to announce at the general membership meeting to be held the next night that Mordecai M. Kaplan had been unanimously reelected as rabbi of the Jewish Center. According to Kaplan, "the members seemed satisfied with the outcome of the controversy."[36]

Although Kaplan was pleased to have retained his post and gratified that his staying on had not splintered his congregation, he remained less than sanguine about the future. While he was quick to publicly assert, at the general membership meeting held less than twenty-four hours after the tumultuous board gathering, that "in re-electing me as Rabbi [you] initiat[ed] a new conception of the rabbi [namely] that he has a right to his own point of view, and must not be expected to be simply the mouthpiece of the ideas of his congregation," in his heart he knew that there was no way he could really articulate what he believed without interference.[37] Indeed, just a week after the membership meeting, he confided to his diary that "the arrangement" he had struck at the center was not really "workable." He believed that Cohen and Fischman were not interested in his compromises and were, indeed, intent on forcing his resignation. At the same time, Kaplan was resolute in his determination not to allow his enemies to push him from his pulpit. If necessary, he would pick the time and moment of his eventual departure and "do so with as little a jolt and shock as possible to all concerned."[38]

Proof that Kaplan's opponents were prepared to renew their campaign against him came immediately to hand. To Kaplan's profound dismay, five days later, on May 22, 1921, he was informed that some of the Cohen-led leaders had drawn up a new set of resolutions regarding Orthodoxy at the Jewish Center, to be presented to the entire board the next evening. When Kaplan read the following declarations, he knew that the struggle had been rejoined:

> Whereas it is of vital importance to place a record in written form [of] the religious principles which underlie all the activities of our institution
>
> and Whereas recent events have shown how easily misunderstandings arise when such clear expression of principles is lacking,
>
> Be it resolved that it is the sense of this Board that it go on record as reaffirming that the underlying religious principles of The Jewish Center were conceived in the spirit of orthodox Judaism, and
>
> Be it further resolved that in letter as well as in spirit, every activity of The Jewish Center shall be carried on in accordance with the principles of Orthodox Judaism.

Initially, Kaplan had not planned on attending the meeting to again press his case. His friend, Rothstein, had promised to prevent the resolution from reaching the floor. However, in the middle of the evening, at 9:30 P.M., Kaplan was called to the meeting because the resolution was, in fact, being considered and the board was, again, in the midst of an angry debate. Given the floor, Kaplan expressed shock that his opponents, "after having elected me as Rabbi the week before, knowing full well that I am not orthodox . . . could pass a resolution that every activity should be carried on in the letter as well as in the spirit of Orthodoxy."

The Cohen group's response—a concession on their part—was that the phrase "every activity" did not include placing restrictions upon Kaplan's preaching. Unmoved by this explanation, Kaplan demanded that the following amendment be written into the resolution: "The Rabbi shall have the right to teach and preach in accordance with the dictates of his conscience." However, recognizing that this statement virtually "counteracted the force of the resolution," the Cohen group pressed further for their position that the rabbi be "bound by Jewish law." Quick to respond, Kaplan offered a reworded amendment that "readily incorporated the words, 'shall have the right within Jewish Law.'" But Cohen was not taken in because Kaplan's reformulation "did not imply that he must teach and preach Orthodoxy." The battle continued for hours, with Kaplan's opponents heaping calumnies upon him and the angry rabbi, setting aside his customary caution, threatening that "if they opposed my amendment they automatically voted for accepting my resignation."

Caught between the proposed amendment and the threatened resignation, Kaplan's supporters and opponents deadlocked. As the clock approached 1:30 A.M., the most moderate people in the room appealed to Kaplan to "trust them on their honor that they would not harass [him] in [his] work." Kaplan was unmoved. Ultimately, it was a very divided board that "adjourned on condition that the vote be taken [the next evening] without further discussion."

The showdown was averted in the course of the next eighteen hours because Kaplan backed off from his threat. Sensing that the Cohen forces might now carry a vote that would cost him his job, Kaplan decided that he could stay at the Jewish Center despite his deep mistrust of those who had promulgated what he considered to be that most offensive resolution. As he told the story to his diary: "Tuesday . . . afternoon a number of people urged me not to resign." Judah Magnes was among those who "came to see me especially for that purpose." Kaplan met later on in the day with Rothstein, Fischman, and Rosalsky, each possibly representing different factions in the board, "and told them of [his] decision to withdraw [his] conditional resignation, allowing them to pass the resolutions in the original form except that [Kaplan] would [be] on record as opposed to them." The three board members were apparently pleased with Kaplan's decision and advised him that, to ensure no further flare-ups with the board in its entirety, he should stay away from that evening's gathering. Kaplan complied.

The board as a whole was also more than satisfied with Kaplan's accommodation. Through his concession, the congregation had been drawn back from the brink of a disastrous split. And, as if to emphasize that most board members still wanted Kaplan to remain in his position, after "they passed the resolution . . . they decided to vote [Kaplan] an annual salary of $12,000."

Kaplan greatly appreciated the gesture but he liked the salary increase even more. He noted in his diary that "should I consent to remain in the Center it will probably be the attractive salary that will justifiably appear to have been the main deciding factor." He further reconciled himself to the new limits imposed upon him by privately holding out hope of eventually bringing all Jewish Center people to his side. "There is another factor," he wrote, "that will also play something of a part, and that is the desire to work with this group which despite its limited Jewish vitality, holds out so far as I know, more promise of enabling Judaism to strike root in this country."[39]

At this moment, in May 1921, a concordat was reached between this Orthodox synagogue and its singular rabbi. "Two Judaisms," as one board member had previously characterized it, would be living side by side at the Jewish Center. If board leaders were to be true to their word, Kaplan would be free to preach without interference. Those in the pews who liked his opinions could be appropriately inspired while those troubled could listen with civility and then conveniently forget what he said. Most of the rest of the congregants would continue to care less—that is, if they attended services at all. In the meantime, the Orthodox liturgy and practices at the Jewish Center would not be abridged or changed and restraints on Kaplan propagating his questionable beliefs among the congregation's youth would be effected. An education committee was in formation to ensure that Kaplan kept to his word in his dealings with impressionable youngsters. This arrangement did not fully please the rabbi, and Joseph Cohen and his friends were also not totally satisfied with it; after all, Kaplan was still around and could continue to embarrass them. They might have to endure the censure or the raised eyebrows of people like Drachman or the leaders of the Agudath ha-Rabbanim for consenting to this pact. Still, against all odds and despite residual mistrust on both sides, a way had been found for the congregation to remain together; an objective that both sides wanted, each for its own purposes.

The agreement held during the summer of 1921. Kaplan spent three months (June 7–September 8) in Long Branch, New Jersey, during which time he met with a group of young people with whom he discussed the "Development of the God Idea in Judaism." Interestingly enough, while on vacation, Aaron Garfunkel, Kaplan's old admirer, once again invited him to occupy that summer community's Orthodox pulpit. Kaplan refused because he did not want to occupy the same rostrum with "students and graduates of the . . . downtown yeshiva [the Yeshiva Rabbi Isaac Elchanan]." He explained in his diary that he "could not bring [himself] to pass in review together with a lot of ignorant, young boys who, as a rule made it their business to attack all liberalism in thought and action." Kaplan did agree to "interpret the *perek* [chapter of the *Ethics of the Fathers*] on two successive Sabbaths." Despite what was being said about him back in the city, there is no indication that this Orthodox community on the shore, led by Garfunkel who, during the winter was vice president of Drachman's home synagogue, Congregation Ohab Zedek, had any difficulties with him or his views. Once again, Kaplan felt comfortable among Orthodox synagogue-goers who admired his talents and were not concerned with his dissenting ideas.[40]

The treaty of May unraveled immediately upon Kaplan's return to New York. He claimed that Cohen was the first to violate the concordat and dispel the spirit of cooperation when he started "dealing high handedly in dismissing teachers and appointing others in their stead." But there is also evidence suggesting that Kaplan too had second thoughts about coexistence. By his own admission, when Kaplan appealed to his supporters within the board to again "take up cudgels on [his] behalf . . . if [they] sincerely believed [he] was right in [his attitude] towards Orthodoxy," their goal was to ensure Kaplan's "stay" through "victory," not compromise, at the center. As these backers began "deliberating what action to take," battle lines were again drawn within the center's leadership.[41]

The struggle reached a new level of intensity when Kaplan and his friends subsequently challenged the veracity and reliability of the text of a resolution that had supposedly been "presented, discussed and unanimously carried" the previous May. Kaplan claimed that he never agreed to a resolution that stated:

> Resolved that the educational system of the Jewish Center be placed under the direction and control of a committee to be known as the School Board to be appointed by the Board of Trustees and to be responsible to the Board of Trustees. At regular intervals, reports of the progress of the work in the educational system of the Center are to be submitted to the membership body.

The entire basis for any level of continued cooperation came completely undone when the rabbi asserted that "it never entered [his] mind to confine [his] activity in the Center to preaching" and that all he had agreed to was for a committee "merely to look after the Orthodoxy of the instruction." Cohen countered that in May Kaplan had "abdicated all control of the educational work." It is impossible to determine whether Kaplan or Cohen was disingenuous in their recording and recollection of the May debate. What is certain is that over the summer of 1921 the level of their personal distaste had intensified. Kaplan would now write in his diary that Cohen "was a self-deluded hypocrite and not [just] an honest fanatic." And, reportedly, Cohen "mumbled to himself," while Kaplan was arguing his point at a hotly contested board meeting of September 19, "'The cancer must be cut out,' alluding to [Kaplan] as the cancer of the Center."[42]

The next day, Tuesday, September 20, 1921, Kaplan wrote to Fischman requesting the year's leave of absence they had earlier discussed, effective immediately.[43] If Kaplan's move was designed to energize his supporters, it surely had the desired effect. With their rabbi's future at the center once again in question, a group of "over 100 members" met during the following week, to constitute "a committee of fifteen to represent [Kaplan's] side of a question that has been agitating the entire membership of the Center." Their position was that "peace" within the Jewish Center was essential "at any price but one—Dr. Kaplan and what Dr. Kaplan stood for was not to be the price." They were soon to find that the "other side" had also calcified: "A few members of the Board of Trustees had made up their minds that they would only consider peace at the sacrifice of Dr. Kaplan." Or, as this same pro-Kaplan adherent put it, the institution was now "divided by two distinct elements—one element refusing to function with Dr. Kaplan—and the other element refusing to function without him." No longer was anyone talking of factions staying together for the sake of a unified congregation.

As "conferences and negotiations" proceeded, it became apparent that further compromises would be impossible. At long last the power of events was forcing the congregation to unequivocally articulate its identity, to decide once and for all whether it wanted to be unquestionably Orthodox and be rid of Kaplan or to chart another religious course with this decidedly iconoclastic rabbi at the helm. Presently, pro-Kaplan forces boldly claimed that it had never been their leader's intention to build an Orthodox synagogue and that the theological differences between Kaplan and Cohen and his counterparts "existed before this institution was built, and they knew it." Moreover, they asserted that Kaplan had "pointed out" his non-Orthodox views "time and again" and that "he insisted that" the men who now opposed him so vehemently "knew the difference between them before he would assume the leadership and they acknowledged it publicly." As proof of their contention, pro-Kaplan people pointed out that the constitution and bylaws of the synagogue did not contain the word *Orthodoxy*. They further asserted that it was Joseph H. Cohen who had asked that this restrictive word "be expunged." The words *Shulkhan Aruck* were substituted as the "protection the by-laws contained for traditional Judaism." From where they stood, "Dr. Kaplan was ready at all times to live up to it."[44]

It is unknown what Cohen's specific responses were to these new allegations. But we may presume that Cohen told anyone who would listen that these latest statements were incontrovertible evidence of the dangers that this heretic rabbi continued to pose to their congregation. And, now, influenced by the single-minded Cohen, a majority of Jewish Center people agreed with the position that Kaplan had to go. While the historical record is silent on how exactly Kaplan was forced out of office or why he chose to leave, we do know that, by the end of 1921, many of those "members who joined with Dr. Kaplan because of his religious and educational leadership," and most of those who, upon joining the Center, "found Dr. Kaplan functioning in it to their satisfaction," had lost their struggle and began the process of "parting in peace" from Cohen and his backers.[45]

At the end of December 1921 Judah Magnes volunteered his services as a mediator for this hopelessly split congregation. His agenda was to find an equitable way of dividing the synagogue's wealth between those who were leaving and the majority who were staying behind. After all, every member of the center had made a substantial commitment to it upon joining the congregation. Membership dues were $200–$250 per member and $1,000 for trustees. In addition, members bought their seats for anything between $800–$3,000 per seat, depending on its location within either the men's or women's sections. When a member "retired," the constitution stipulated that the money paid to purchase a seat be returned. It also appears that the membership made substantial loans to the center to help it meet various building expenses. Financial considerations were, as expected, a major residual issue. After a month of delicate negotiations, Magnes reached a settlement with the warring factions.[46]

Some of Kaplan's supporters immediately moved, with their rabbi's encouragement, "to take the next step toward establishing an institution founded on the ideals [Kaplan] laid down years ago." Indeed, they seemed to have coordinated Kaplan's formal resignation from the Jewish Center to coincide with the opening of the Society for the Advancement of Judaism (SAJ). Kaplan tendered his letter to Fischman on January 16, 1922, and SAJ was officially founded the very next day. Five days later, on Friday night, January 22, 1922, services were held under its auspices for the first time at 41 West 86th Street, just one block east of the Jewish Center. Reflecting upon what had just transpired, Kaplan told his friends that "to me it has been heartrending. To see one's ideals shattered by idle worshippers because one cannot stand for deception, is indeed heartrending. They have made my life Hell because I came out with the Ideals which they knew I stood for, but did not want me to express."[47]

Their perspicacity vindicated with the defeat of Kaplan, Joseph Cohen's faction within the Jewish Center's leadership moved rapidly to restore and enhance their reputation within the larger Orthodox community. They earned themselves the approbation of Rabbis Drachman and Goldstein as well as that of their Orthodox lay colleagues throughout the city when they chose Rabbi Leo Jung as the dissenter's successor. Possessed of impressive religious and secular educational credentials, Rabbi Jung came to this post in 1922 with the clear potential to be an outstanding advocate of Orthodoxy's continued viability within the modern world. He had received talmudic schooling from his early youth in Hungarian yeshivas and was later trained as a modern Orthodox rabbi in Rabbi Ezriel Hildesheimer's Berlin rabbinical seminary. He was the holder of a Ph.D. from the University of Giessen (in Hesse) and also studied at the Universities of Berlin, Vienna, Marburg, Cambridge, and London. He would earn a second doctorate from the University of London in 1922. Jung also pleased and impressed the American Orthodox spokesmen as a young firebrand for the faith who would help them extend their battle against Kaplan beyond the precincts of their Upper West Side synagogue. While still serving a Cleveland congregation—his first American post—he had spoken out against Kaplan three months after the latter moved on to the Society for the Advancement of Judaism. In an article in the *Jewish Forum*, Jung made it abundantly clear that "Kaplanism . . . was downright 'Epikorsuth' . . . [for] this is unmitigated kefiroh [heresy]. It sweeps away the foundation of Jewish tradition with its walls and roof, the authority of the

Torah, the observance of Shabbos and Kashruth." Indeed, he continued, it is worse than even the "genuine reform of the past. It is its most insidious, most dangerous form."[48]

In the summer of 1923 Jung more than lived up to his reputation as a fighter for Orthodoxy when he joined a renewed American Orthodox effort to unseat Kaplan from his seminary job. At this point he helped Cantor Josef Rosenblatt of Drachman's congregation, Rabbi Herbert S. Goldstein, and layman S. I. Israel edit a Yiddish language weekly, the *Light of Israel*, a periodical whose apparent primary mission was exposing "Kaplanism" and those who tolerated the heretic. Writing about the dissenter in very harsh terms, they called "upon the parents of the East Side to withdraw their support from the Teachers' Institute" so long as Kaplan was its principal.[49]

Jung was also very likely a force within a group that sent protest letters directly to Cyrus Adler asserting that we "who had read [Kaplan's] articles ... feel that an institution of your kind, if it really stands for what we presume it should, should not tolerate the teachings of a man who disrobes Judaism of all its ceremonies, precepts and vital laws."[50] These activists pointedly told Adler and the seminary's board that they would be "held accountable" by "the community and public in general, for the welfare of the institution, by reason of the responsibility that is vested with you now."[51] Israel, the point man for the group, minced no words when he threatened "that the prolonging of your inactivity in this matter would cause a 'Negah Tzorahas' [plague of leprosy] to spread and take root further and much deeper than you might imagine."[52] Indeed, at one point, he was even ready to darkly predict that Kaplan will "be disposed of, if not by your action and the Board, [then] by the members of the community at large."[53]

Jung's forces nearly achieved their objective. Mordecai Kaplan's long-standing fear that he would be expelled both from his pulpit and his professorship was almost realized, for Cyrus Adler and his advisers still desired the support of American Orthodox Jews. The seminary needed the financial support of people like S. I. Israel, a real estate and mortgage broker. Equally important, the Teachers Institute maintained friendly relations with many Orthodox schools—their graduates taught in Orthodox talmud torahs—and the Teachers Institute, in turn, drew many of its own pulpils from these institutions. Thus, there was significant pressure on Adler to avoid having his school tarred as a hotbed of heresy.[54] One answer would have been to let Kaplan go,[55] but, ultimately, Adler drew back from that solution and tried to mollify his critics by downplaying Kaplan's actual influence and impact within the seminary community and student body. For example, Adler wrote to Israel that "Professor Kaplan's position in the Seminary is that of Professor of Homiletics. His work is to teach the art of constructing a sermon, not the knowledge of Judaism which goes into the construction of the sermon."[56]

When Adler's remark became public, thanks to the *Light of Israel*, which was unimpressed with this apologia, Mordecai Kaplan was deeply offended. He wrote to the seminary head outlining in some detail, and for the record, his history of involvement with JTS and the range of substantive courses he had taught in Adler's school.[57]

Adler's response reassured Kaplan only slightly. The distressed faculty member was told that "we are all modern men, we do not engage in inquisitions or excommunications or heresy hunting." At the same time, Adler did suggest that the question of how far academic freedom "applies in a theological seminary . . . in which faith, tradition, even inherited prejudice . . . must have a part" had to be a subject for future faculty consideration. Most important, Adler alerted Kaplan to the realities with which the JTS seminary president had to deal. Kaplan's "articles were giving [him] a great deal of trouble both because of interviews which people sought with [him] as well as correspondence from various parts of the country."[58]

But even as Jung fought the spread of "Kaplanism" throughout New York, he was soon to find, to his utter horror, that interest in and support for his opponent persisted still at the Jewish Center. Indeed, twice in the late 1920s to early 1930s some of his Upper West Side Jews actually seemed ready to turn the clock back to 1917. Despite everything that everyone now knew about Kaplan, these leaders made overtures to Kaplan to head their Orthodox institution once again. When discussions took place about having Kaplan back at the Jewish Center, Jung must have deeply questioned the Orthodox commitments of some of his leading congregants. He also had to have wondered whether he was about to lose his job, for a part of each draft agreement included the provision that he be removed from his pulpit. Thus, ironically, in the 1920s both Kaplan and Jung had reason to fear each other's influence in the institutions where they earned their livelihood.

The first brief overture took place in 1928 when, according to Kaplan, "some of the most influential members of The Jewish Center," approached

SAJ board member H. L. Simmons about the feasibility of the "amalga-mation" of the two synagogues. Simmons had negotiated the separation agreement between his friends and the Jewish Center some six years earlier and remained friends with Reuben Sadowsky, who had sat across the table from him during those tension-filled days of 1921–1922. It was Sadowsky who pressed for "a merger of the organizations," along with Samuel C. Lamport who "belonged to both institutions." Protective of Kaplan's interests, Simmons told the Jewish Center people that for a consolidation to be considered, Rabbi Jung would have to be "eliminated . . . from the rabbinate," a new rabbi, of Kaplan's choosing, would have to run the day-to-day operations of the center, and the Orthodox members would have "to back . . . the SAJ in its wider scope." It was the envisioned game plan of this Reconstructionist lay leader "to emancipate [Kaplan] from having to do with the congregational aspects of the movement and to enable [him] so to represent the SAJ movement that its true character as a means of strengthening the organic . . . character of Jewish life as a whole should not be missed." Kaplan gave Simmons "carte-blanche in carrying on nego-tiations" for acceptance of what was, in essence, a blueprint for the capit-ulation of Upper West Side Orthodoxy to SAJ. Merger discussions did not proceed, however, because Sadowsky and his friends probably balked at this patently one-way deal.[59]

Four years later, under a somewhat different set of circumstances, more serious, more evenhanded, and more extensive negotiations took place. The severe financial straits in which the center found itself at that time, during the height of the Depression, was the stimulus for reconsideration of the matter. In 1931 the center owed $38,000 to the Bank of the United States with which they had been negotiating "to compromise the claim of The Jewish Center to the sum of $18,000.00." Members were asked to sign promissory notes of $1,000 each to bolster the synagogue. Indeed, at this critical juncture, Otto Rosalsky actually raised the possibility of foreclo-sure in a special trustees meeting. One of the great fears that had kept the Jewish Center together during the extended debate over Kaplan's status in 1921–1922 was now becoming a reality. Simply put, there were not enough families affiliated with the center to keep it fiscally viable. Faced with grim financial exigencies and desirous of increasing its dues base, Jewish Cen-ter officials put past history and long-debated ideological differences aside. They looked for a way of recapturing SAJ families back to their syn-agogue of origin, even if that meant having the heretic Kaplan back in their Orthodox pulpit. Implicit also in this contemplated move was the sense that Rabbi Jung had not attracted enough strictly Orthodox families to the synagogue and that he would not minister effectively to a variegated constituency. Joseph Cohen and William Fischman may not have agreed with this analysis of the center's staffing needs, but, as we will see, their influence had waned within the synagogue's leadership.[60]

For Kaplan, it must have seemed like old times when Rabbi Ira Eisenstein, assistant SAJ leader, conveyed to him the results of a meeting that had taken place on May 21, 1932, "between representatives of the Jewish Center Board and of the Board of Trustees of the S.A.J." Kaplan had gotten early wind of the new possibility of merger some months earlier when his assistant rabbi Eisenstein told him that "the Center People are making overtures to the S.A.J." and that a major stumbling block to consolidation might be out of the way since the Orthodox contingent "expect that Jung, whose salary has been reduced from $12,000 to 6,000, would return to England," a courteous way of saying that he would be politely dismissed. Now Eisenstein informed Kaplan that an agreement was falling into place whereby "Jung would be given two years' salary and resign and . . . Eisenstein and [Kaplan] would take charge of the Center." However, in return for "control" of the institution, the Reconstructionist rabbis would accede to giving up "the innovations worked out in the S.A.J. service" and the Jewish Center service would keep its Orthodox ritual. Yet, given the chance to return victoriously to the seat of his great defeat and there have the opportunity to recapture his dream of leading much of Upper West Side Jewry, Kaplan conceded this point for "the present." What he did demand was a written "stipulation that [he] would be given full charge of the educational work and unqualified freedom to teach and preach." Kaplan told the SAJ board members who were conferring with the Jewish Center people that, in any future discussions, "they must insist upon the removal of the clause in the Center Constitution which was adopted a few years ago," after the very painful Kaplan-Cohen battle, "to the effect that the Center must be governed in its religious activities by the Shulhan Arukh." Kaplan wanted to be certain that even if the Orthodox could have their style of service for a while, he would be unquestionably free to say his piece in support of Reconstructionism without any interference whatsoever.[61]

As talks continued apace, Jewish Center spokesmen showed a basic willingness to accept Kaplan as their leader. And it must be noted that those within the center's family who sought out this cooperation did not consist merely of a few marginal disgruntled members. While Fischman and Cohen were not part of this "unofficial committee," the six-man delegation did include esteemed leaders of that institution. Morris Asinof was the center's treasurer and Gustavus A. Rogers had served as its they president from 1926–1928. Samuel Bayer, if he is the "Bayer" indicated in the documents, served as president from 1928–1930. Their names, as well as those of Nathan and Reuben Sadowsky, Julius Schwartz, and Abraham Landau, all appeared in the special act of the New York State Legislature, dated a little more than a year earlier, on April 6, 1931, that reincorporated the center, stating that it was to be governed according to the strictures of the *Shulchan Aruch*. Almost all of these men would also be listed by Leo Jung, in his own memoirs, as being among the men who "opposed Dr. Kaplan and voted for his dismissal" back in the early 1920s. And yet, when they left a meeting on May 9, 1932, they tacitly agreed that if "men and women be seated separately at the service," they "definitely would follow Dr. Kaplan." As far as Rabbi Jung's status was concerned, one of the center people again suggested that it would not be a problem since "Jung wants to go abroad anyway." The rewriting of the center's constitution to Kaplan's satisfaction remained to be done. That would be accomplished once the respective congregations formally certified their committees "and authorized [them] to continue negotiations."[62]

This critical, final step, however, never took place. The SAJ trustees certified their negotiators but "the Center Committee [was] not made official." And, although Sadowsky's group publicly "claimed that it was merely a matter of form, and that they could be made official if necessary," from the tone and substance of their stance when the groups next met, it was clear that something, or someone, had challenged the probity of a merger. For they now "suggested that in view of legal and technical difficulties, a complete merger would be very difficult, if not impossible." Their new idea was that "the S.A.J. take over the Center building; that as many of the Center people as would desire to join the S.A.J. in their new quarters might do so; and that the men who are now on the bond of the mortgage would remain on that bond."[63]

SAJ leaders immediately recognized that as "a far different proposition from the one originally made, and far less attractive, because it deviates from the purpose of the original proposal." One of Kaplan's followers further explained their position:

> We were interested in the invitation extended to us by the Center
> to negotiate because we felt that for the sake of unity in our neigh-
> borhood, every effort should be made, but here apparently the pro-
> posal is to take over the institution. If, as it is very likely, a large
> number of Center members will not be eager to join the S.A.J.,
> they would perhaps like to rent the S.A.J. building and continue
> their activities. Thus we would be confronted again with the situa-
> tion of two synagog[ue]s on the same street.[64]

More likely than not it was Rabbi Jung who caused the negotiation ultimately to flounder. Obviously, he was not on the way back to England.
Committed to staying the fight on the Upper West Side, he rallied his
forces within the center to stop Kaplan. He called "a special meeting of a
number of the leading members of the Center" in which "an attempt
[was] made by the Center people to have their first mortgage extended five
years." Jung understood that if the center's financial ills could be
addressed, the fiduciary forces that were moving the Jewish Center and SAJ
together—and precipitating unacceptable religious compromises—would
be arrested. In any event, Rabbi Jung's intervention was decisive, no further meetings were ever held, and the remarkable project was dropped. Still
in all, it heightened Jung's resolve to stop the spread of Kaplan's influence
both for the sake of Orthodoxy and to ensure his own position.[65]

When the Jewish Center-SAJ merger talks broke down for good,
Mordecai Kaplan's half-century of association with Orthodox institutions
finally came to an end. Yet, during the next half-century of his long life,
some segments of the Orthodox community continued to relate to him.
Although they could not countenance his heretical theology and considered it to be totally unacceptable, they acknowledged that this dissenter
had talents and ideas from which they could benefit as they sought to lead
their American Jewish communities through the twentieth century.

CHAPTER 7 · *Learning from a Heretic?*

When Mordecai Kaplan formally separated from the Jewish Center in 1922, the forty-one year old rabbi was only at the beginning of his long career. Ten years later, when his divorce from the West Side synagogue was finalized, Kaplan was just entering the most productive and influential years of his life. For the next fifty years or more, his name would be associated with almost every plan and program proposed by non-Orthodox Jews to fight assimilation, strengthen Jewish identity, and improve education among their second, third, and fourth generation coreligionists in America.

From his perch on Morningside Heights this head of the seminary's Teachers Institute would have a direct impact on the training of generations of American Jewish educators. One Kaplan scholar has written that "as a primary force in Jewish education in America . . . all the principal leaders of Jewish education who themselves were educated between 1910 and 1940 were students, if not disciples, of Kaplan."[1] Another has suggested that the rabbi created "a hothouse for the nurturing of ideas that captured the imaginations of a larger public of Jewish educators between 1920 and 1950."[2] Kaplan would retire as dean of the Teachers Institute in the mid-1940s but would continue to teach his version of Judaism at the seminary's rabbinical school until past his eightieth birthday.

During his tenure Kaplan articulated many of the basic truths that would permeate formal and informal American Jewish education through to the end of the twentieth century. Israel Chipkin, one of those disciples who was nurtured at the Teachers Institute's "hothouse," took out time, on the occasion of his mentor's seventieth birthday, to set down what were, for him, the essential messages of Kaplan's pedagogic creed. Jewish youngsters had to be "given insight into the meaning of spiritual values" and taught how these values could be applied to their lives. Pupils had to "develop an attitude of respect towards human personality," had to "gain an appreciation of individual and group creativity," and had to "seek peace and ideals of justice and kindness in our economic relationships" even as they were taught to "seek a creative Jewish life in Israel as well as in America." In terms of specific Jewish skills and functions, youngsters had to be helped to feel comfortable in the synagogue or Jewish center, educated and inspired to "celebrate the Sabbath and Jewish festivals, [and] observe the Jewish customs and ceremonies." They had to be shown how to acquire a taste for Jewish art, music, theater, and literature. The knowledgeable, committed young Jew had also to acquire a knowledge of Hebrew and an awareness of the storehouse of traditional Jewish sources that were part of his or her cultural heritage.[3]

Kaplan's friends and associates would also credit him as "an all-pervading influence through the written and spoken word, and through direct counsel and teaching, that helped shape the basic philosophy of the Jewish Community Center." While willing to admit that "it is difficult to identify many direct references to the purpose of the Jewish [Community] Center in the writings and addresses of Dr. Kaplan," Louis Kraft of the National Jewish Welfare Board saw the rabbi, from the 1920s on, as particularly influential among the lay and professional leadership who "had been motivated by the feeling that the Jewish purposes" of the largely recreational and secular "Jewish Center constituted its chief rationale."[4]

Similarly, Kaplan is closely connected with the evolution of the field of Jewish social service from an area of interest that, before the 1920s, was concerned only with promoting the economic well-being and rapid assimilation of its clients to its becoming, by mid-century, acutely interested in Jewish group survival. One Jewish social worker, who was on the scene prior to Kaplan's impact, remembered the belief expressed by many of his colleagues that "Jewish life has no content, that Jewish culture has no significance, that Jewish social work has nothing to do with either of these, and therefore has nothing to contribute to American or any other civilization." Kaplan fought that notion in his classes at Manhattan's Training School for Jewish Social Work, where from 1925–1940 he taught courses on "Social and Religious Institutions of the Jew" and "Problems of Jewish Adjustment to American Life." There he emphasized not only the enduring content of Jewish life but also the necessity for social service agencies to address specific Jewish group needs and objectives. When the school closed at the start of World War II, Kaplan continued to interact with and influence Jewish social work professionals through his appearances and addresses at the annual meetings of the National Conference of Jewish Communal Service.[5]

All of these activities fit into and grew out of Kaplan's overall scheme for Jewish survival, which was fully articulated in his magnum opus, *Judaism as a Civilization*, published in 1934. It is a major work of both Jewish theology and sociology that offers an exhaustive compendium of specific remedies for meeting the spiritual ills of those Jews with whom he had always worked, the American-born generation that attempted to live in two cultures and who had difficulty reconciling Jewish and American values.

Central to this work is Kaplan's understanding that Judaism is, and has always been, a human-directed civilization with sets of significant symbols, ceremonies, mores, and traditions that have changed over time as Jews responded to different cultures and political realities. The problem facing modern Jewry, as he saw it, was that it had yet to respond adequately to the new worlds of freedom, rationalism, and science. Here, in this forum, all his thoughts about God, the Bible, and Jewish observances harbored since the beginning of the twentieth century came together. Now he firmly asserted that the Jewish civilization of the past to which the Orthodox still clung and which Reformers were unable to effectively change, was both senseless and caused problems for most modern Jews. He personally had not believed, for, by then, at least thirty years, that God had spoken to Moses on Mount Sinai. And he suggested that his contemporary community was, likewise, far too skeptical, educated, and sophisticated to follow a system of rigid laws based on what he considered, essentially, to be a myth. Moreover, the concept of the chosenness of Israel explicit in God's supposed revelation was a monumental barrier to Jewish integation into general society. How could Jews, he wondered, hope to be accepted by their fellow Americans in a democratic society when they were linked to a doctrine that defined them as superior to all others.

It was this assertion in particular—the rejection of the notion of chosenness or election—that highlighted the extent to which Kaplan's ideology radically deviated from traditional beliefs. For this idea was absolutely central throughout the history of Jewish thought, deeply rooted in biblical concepts and further developed in the talmudic, philosophical, and kabbalistic literature of ancient, medieval, and modern Judaism. The explicitly stated biblical formulation of Israel's role in the world as God's chosen "kingdom of priests and holy nation" (Exodus 19:6) as well as its reference to Jews as God's "special treasure" (Exodus 19:5) indicate the absolute centrality of the concept of election in the earliest Jewish sources. Although aware of a universalist element in Jewish tradition, later rabbinic thought stressed this principle of chosenness or election as the central feature of Jewish faith and behavior. As a contemporary scholar has written, chosenness was "affirmed and retained at the center of the set of ideas which locate Israel's place in the world: God, revelation, covenant, messiah, exile."[6] Any attempt to repudiate it struck at the very heart of Jewish tradition.

For Kaplan, however, the key to contemporary Jewish survival was the reconstruction of Jewish civilization to bring it in consonance with what Jews as modern thinkers could believe in and with what they could subscribe to as American citizens. He envisioned a two-step process. First, the usable Jewish past of ideas, concepts, and practices had to be plumbed and examined for what it still contained of value to the contemporary Jew. Those ceremonies or observances that still warmed the Jewish soul or brought this ethnic group together had to be maintained and invigorated. As Kaplan saw it, whether or not a supernatural God created the Sabbath or sanctified the holidays or gave a special value to the Hebrew language or instilled in Jews a unique sense of national identity, these ideas still had relevance for twentieth-century Jews. That is, of course, if they could be projected as being in accord with American doctrines and social patterns. Zionism, for example, could certainly captivate Jewish attention and peak the popular interest, but it had to be formulated in such a way as not to threaten the minority group with charges of dual loyalty. Out of this philosophical and social analysis came the rabbi's practical call for reeducating Jews about some of the beauties of their people's past even as he attempted to infuse Jewish values with forms of American culture to which Jews were already strongly committed.[7]

Seven months after *Judaism as a Civilization* first appeared, Kaplan began his own process of ongoing, public exegesis of Reconstructionism's basic text with the *Reconstructionist* journal. Over the next forty years Kaplan would publish several hundred short and long comments and reflections on his thoughts in that organ. And, a year after the *Reconstructionist* first appeared, Kaplan, in 1936, felt a need to express "in non-technical language, the essence of his message to the popular reader." *Judaism in Transition* "elaborated certain aspects of his philosophy and program, clarifying some mis-understandings that had arisen concerning the first book and attacking directly some of the immediate burning issues of the day."[8] And, over the ensuing twenty years, the period of his greatest literary productivity, Kaplan wrote and revised five books that essentially reiterated his Recon-structionist creed and responded to the changing American and Jewish scene he saw as challenging the future of the Jewish people in this country.[9]

Through all this time, Kaplan's synagogue home, the Society for the Advancement of Judaism, remained his experimental laboratory for inno-vations in prayer and ritual. At the very beginning of his tenure the soci-ety was the site of the first bat mitzvah when his daughter Judith was con-firmed there in March 1922. In subsequent decades SAJ was where Kaplan's *New Haggadah* was generated as well as his Reconstructionist *Sabbath Prayer Book*, which, we will presently see, caused a particular uproar among some segments of the Orthodox community. Kaplan, who saw himself as the consummate teacher of all Jews and his society as a "school of thought" more than a movement, was very pleased when elements of his teachings and his evaluation of Jewish rituals resonated within the Conservative and Reform movements.[10] Indeed, on more than one occasion he seriously considered leaving the seminary for Rabbi Stephen S. Wise's Reform Jew-ish Institute of Religion. Had that change eventuated, he would have had direct, immediate influence on generations of Reform rabbis.[11] He would also have liked Orthodox Jews to appreciate his work and honor him as this century's master teacher of Jewish survival, but such accolades were, understandably, not forthcoming.

To be sure, given Kaplan's radical theological stances, there was no way he would ever have been allowed to teach what he thought about God and Jewish tradition at any Orthodox educational institution. In fact, the very idea that this heretic could somehow end up teaching Orthodox rabbini-cal students effectively scuttled whatever chance there had been for a merger, in the mid-1920s, of the seminary and the Yeshiva Rabbi Isaac Elchanan, America's two schools for the training of traditional rabbis. At that juncture some lay leaders felt that, since both institutions served the same constituency of second-generation Jews and produced rabbis who respected traditional Jewish ways while projecting Jewish identification in an American style, it was sensible to pool the resources of these two finan-cially weak schools to more effectively serve communal needs. (It will be recalled that a decade earlier, Solomon Travis, brother-in-law of Yeshiva's head, Bernard Revel, had mulled over a comparable plan with Kaplan.) But as discussions progressed in 1926, it became clear that even the most "liberal" members of the Yeshiva delegation, which included Joseph H. Cohen, would not countenance amalgamation if Kaplan were considered for a spot on a consolidated faculty. Such was the observation of Rabbi Max Drob, who negotiated on behalf of the seminary with Yeshiva's lay leaders. Drob reported to Cyrus Adler that

> the Yeshiva group considers the Teachers Institute the citadel of atheism because it is headed by Professor Kaplan. Under no conditions will they countenance a union with the Seminary as long as he is retained on the faculty. I have spoken to the most liberal minded of the group and they tell me that this is the crux of the entire problem.[12]

But if Orthodox Jews were unanimously opposed to Kaplan the theologian, they were not all convinced that everything he had to say about the social condition of American Jewry and the practical pedagogic advice he had to offer could not serve their own purposes. Indeed, the question of whether and how to use Kaplan and his works to strengthen their own community was frequently discussed and debated within Orthodox circles during the last half of the dissenter's life. The answers that were given both by nationally recognized leaders and by that denomination's rank and file in different parts of this country reflected the multiplicity of American Orthodox attitudes and life experiences existing in the middle of the twentieth century.

The Agudath ha-Rabbanim, Mordecai Kaplan's Orthodox enemies of longest standing, took the most extreme position on interaction with the dissenter. If they would have had their druthers, no Jew would ever have anything to do with the heretic, at any time or on any level. Joining with their colleagues at the Rabbinical Council (Vaad ha-Rabbanim) of Greater New York, lay leaders, and many yeshiva students, they punctuated their consistent animosity toward Kaplan in 1945 when, in a solemn ceremony at the McAlpin Hotel in midtown Manhattan, these rabbis unanimously agreed to excommunicate the Reconstructionist, to "separate him from the congregation of Israel" until such time as he desisted from his heretical activity and "repents completely in full accordance with the Law." The punishment they pronounced, as derived from the Code of Jewish Law that governed their lives, was meant to ensure that no Jew sit within four *amot* (fig. feet) of the sinner, nor speak with him from a closer distance, nor break bread with him, nor count him toward a *zimmun* (quorum for reciting grace after meals), nor toward a minyan for prayers.[13] At the close of the gathering—in keeping with the traditional teaching that (even) a Torah scroll written by a heretic must be burned—Kaplan's prayerbook was publicly set on fire.[14] The act of book burning, which means setting afire the name of God, was traditionally reserved for only the most extreme circumstances—so great was these Jews' contempt for Kaplan and his work.

The activity that caused these rabbis to attack Kaplan so vehemently was his coediting of a new *Sabbath Prayer Book* that the Reconstructionist Foundation published for the "many Jews who do not find that the prayer books now in use fully answer their spiritual needs." There he had put into concrete liturgical form his "modification of traditional doctrine" to reflect his creed that "Jews are not a divinely chosen race; that the Torah is a human document and not one supernaturally inspired and that modern Jews no longer look forward to the advent of a personal Messiah."[15]

Of course, Mordecai Kaplan's prayerbook was far from the first modern liturgy that deeply offended Orthodox sensibilities. Reform Judaism itself had a long history of prayerbooks that ran totally counter to traditional Jewish practice and belief. And yet of all modern dissenters and of all offensive texts, it was Mordecai Kaplan and his siddur that were singled out for such extreme and dramatic condemnation. The rabbis publicly addressed the roots of their very focused and personalized anger during the meeting at which Kaplan was excommunicated and his prayerbook burned. "They [Kaplan and his ilk] are much worse for us than the Reformers," declared Rabbi Israel Rosenberg, one of Agudath ha-Rabbanim's most important leaders. Reform Judaism was so far removed from traditional Judaism and so alien to its letter and spirit, he said, that it no longer posed a threat to Orthodoxy. No Orthodox Jew could possibly ever be tempted to consider this brand of Judaism as genuine or authentic. Not so Kaplan and his colleagues, however, he continued, who masquerade under the guise of tradition and who were thus in a position to mislead well-meaning traditional Jews into thinking that they too represented authentic Judaism. Kaplan's prayerbook was "not heresy for heretics but heresy meant for religious Jews . . . presenting it in the name of Jewish faith and Jewish tradition." In an interview with the *New York Times*, Rosenberg stated that "there was danger that the book might be confused with the traditional volume of prayer," something that would be impossible with the Reform *Union Prayer Book*, with its predominance of English and its opening—as an English book would—from right to left. That prayerbook was "clearly not Jewish—not in form or in spirit," but Kaplan's prayerbook was dangerous, cloaked as it was in the mantle of tradition.[16]

Compounding Kaplan's offense and energizing the Agudath ha-Rabbanim toward definitive action was the fact that, to their minds, the siddur was the dissenter's second grievous offense against the basics of traditional liturgy. In 1941 Kaplan and his Jewish Reconstructionist Foundation colleagues had published his own version of the Passover haggadah. In that work Kaplan took one crucial step that elevated the level of his heresy to new and unprecedented heights. Although the classic *Union Prayer Book* of the Reform movement reflected Reform's teachings that the Torah was of human origin and that neither a corporeal Messiah nor the reinstitution of sacrifices were to be anticipated by contemporary Jews—beliefs that ran totally counter to traditional Judaism—it still did liturgically proclaim—in keeping with its traditional counterparts—that the Jews were a chosen people, chosen for a specific purpose by a supernatural God. Kaplan's haggadah, however, boldly rejected chosenness and excised all references to it from the Passover seder liturgy. Furthermore, it also eliminated the passage beseeching God to "pour out [His] wrath upon the nations." True, when *The New Haggadah* first appeared in 1941, it elicited a fierce attack from traditional circles for its "sacrilege" and "blatant desecration of the name of God." The Orthodox *Morgen Zhurnal* opined that Kaplan was much worse than the Reformers who had never lowered themselves to such a level of heresy. Nevertheless, no excommunication or book burning was yet forthcoming. It was Kaplan's second offense, and one which would adversely affect Jews every week rather than just once a year, that elicited excommunication.

Indeed, in his speech condemning Kaplan's siddur, Rabbi Rosenberg reminded his listeners of how far the heretic had gone previously with his haggadah. By "expressing atheism, heresy and disbelief in the basic tenets of Judaism," as Rosenberg put it, even to a greater extent than did the Reformers, the Kaplan of the haggadah and the siddur had taken modern Jewish religious deviance to an even higher level and his dissent therefore necessitated this most extreme of responses.[17]

Bernard Drachman, Leo Jung, and many of their American Orthodox colleagues who published both in the harshly presented *Light of Israel* and in the genteel *Jewish Forum* felt basically the same way about Kaplan. While these spokesmen did not sign on to the Agudath ha-Rabbanim's extreme representation, they were, for the two decades leading up to the *cherem* (excommunication), outspoken in their denigration of all Kaplan's ideas and consistently emphasized the threat he posed to impressionable young minds. In 1925, for example, the *Light of Israel* excoriated the Agudath ha-Morim (Hebrew Teachers Union), an organization composed of the "so-called European type of teacher," instructors "who came to this country from Eastern Europe as adults" and possessed (only) of "pedagogic experience in the countries of Eastern Europe,"[18] for inviting Kaplan to address its annual convention on the seemingly innocuous topic of "character development." S. I. Israel, Jung, and their fellow traditionalists were extremely upset that the men, and sometimes the women, who made up the faculties of the city's early congregational and communal talmud torahs and who, through the 1920s, worked in and ran New York's Orthodox and Conservative-sponsored afternoon schools, would offer a public forum to a "mesiach u-maydeach" (a false prophet who would lead Jews astray).[19]

Similarly, when *Judaism as a Civilization* appeared, Orthodox rabbi Aaron Rosmarin, a frequent contributor to the *Jewish Forum*, wrote fearfully that Kaplan's ideas were percolating down among his seminary students to influence the masses of American Jews. Sensing a threat in everything Kaplan taught, and renewing his group's refrain that the heretic had to be purged from the seminary, Rosmarin reminded his readers that while students may, or may not, be interested in Talmud and Kabbalah, "the sermon, however, is of immediate use to them. It is the basis for their bread and butter." Indeed, Rosmarin continued, "even after graduation, they attend Kaplan's class though never entering any of the other classes. They need themes, topics for sermons, and ideas—and Rabbi Kaplan supplies them."[20]

Leo Jung, Kaplan's neighborhood nemesis, also doggedly focussed on the threat the dissenter posed long before the Agudath ha-Rabbanim's cherem. In 1936 Jung asserted that

> the time has come for our people to be told what Reconstructionism is! Reconstructionism is the destruction of the Jewish faith, a definite abrogation of the Jewish tradition, the abolition of the authority of the Torah—the creating of a new "religion" with terms and phrases borrowed from sources hostile and foreign to historical Judaism.

Explicitly referring to Kaplan, Jung continued that Reconstructionism's "leader ... arrogates the right to change or cancel laws of the Torah, forms of ritual, texts of the prayer book." And Jung warned that "there is nothing to stop Reconstructionism from carrying on its destructive activity," except seemingly "to open the eyes of the general public to what Reconstructionism really means."[21]

However, notwithstanding his personal animosity toward Kaplan—a feeling that seemed to have been mutual[22]—and despite his abhorrence for all the Reconstructionist stood for, Leo Jung could not always avoid interacting with him. Unlike the members of the Agudath ha-Rabbanim who, on principal, resisted public discussions with denominational leaders of all other stripes—they defined such meetings as tantamount to a religious recognition of their theological foes—Jung was a nationally recognized leader of the type of American Orthodoxy maintaining that cooperation with other Jews on communitywide issues not strictly religious was acceptable and warranted in an effort to help and serve the entire Jewish community. (A major public rift on this issue would separate the European and American Orthodox rabbis in 1956 when the Council of Sages of the Agudath ha-Rabbanim condemned Orthodox rabbinical participation in the interdenominational Synagogue Council of America.[23]) Thus, Jung met up with Kaplan, for example, in 1941 when the Reform Central Conference of American Rabbis sponsored a Fellowship Day "to discuss how to augment the authority of the rabbi, attitudes towards interfaith work and towards Jewish defense work." As Kaplan described the encounter, he found Jung and his other Orthodox colleagues "intransigent and separatist despite their mingling with Conservative and Reform Jews." At the same time, Kaplan thought Jung to be "quite affable"; they shook hands, chatted, and promised to continue their dialogue at some future time.[24]

However, the promised private meeting did not take place, and it would be another ten years before the two would meet again in a public forum. In 1952 Jung was the spokesman for Orthodoxy at an interdenominational symposium in Boston attended by Kaplan on "Our Religious Faith and Future." Ever the gentleman in demeanor, Jung opened his remarks with the statement that "we shall agree to disagree agreeably" before articulating his Orthodox position and surrendering no ideological ground.[25]

There were, however, other leaders and segments of American Orthodoxy who saw real value in much of what Kaplan had to teach in all areas other than Jewish theology. To begin with, there were the Orthodox leaders of the Agudath ha-Morim. People like Kalman Whiteman, whom Kaplan's friend, Alexander Dushkin, eulogized as "a deeply religious, orthodox Jew [who] scorned the pretensions of the 'ultra' orthodox . . . a traditionalist [whose] reactions to educational problems and situations were ever fresh . . . and unexpected," firmly believed that this master teacher had something to offer all who might listen in upgrading the methodologies of Jewish education. In 1925 he and his "nationalist" and "Hebraist" colleagues refused to withdraw their invitation to the Teachers Institute's head to address their meeting, referred to above. In his own private way Isaac Allen, the son of the rabbi who had been one of Kaplan's downtown teachers when the professor was a youth, made an even more positive judgment of Kaplan as a teacher of teachers. Not only did Allen, also an Orthodox member of the Agudath ha-Morim, attend Kaplan's talk, but he actually approached the rabbi afterward "about having his [own] daughter admitted to the [Teachers] Institute." Allen's young daughter would be part of that generation of Orthodox young women who studied education within Kaplan's school.[26]

The Orthodox Jews in Borough Park in the 1920s also debated whether it was right and safe for teachers and students to study with Kaplan. What set that community buzzing was the Teachers Institute's effort to create extension school courses, which later bore the name "Israel Friedlaender Classes," in their community. Ultimately, such courses were established in three Brooklyn neighborhoods, the Bronx, and Newark, New Jersey. The aforementioned Israel Chipkin organized the seminary effort. But the foot soldiers, "the leading spirits" in this activity—at least in Borough Park—were, according to Kaplan, "two brothers by the name of Green, sons of an Orthodox rabbi . . . graduates of the Institute and attendants of the Institute." They were "part of the most orthodox part of the community . . . identified with a congregation known as the Shomre Emunah." And it was the "elder one of the brothers" who audaciously rose during Sabbath morning services the weekend before Kaplan was to launch the program to announce that their seminary professor was scheduled to speak at a neighboring Conservative Temple. Green wanted his fellow young people of the community to take advantage of the modern pedagogic training he was so proud to be receiving. However, the very "mention of [Kaplan's] name called forth violent protestations both from a Mr. Roth who is a president of a yeshiba [sic] or parochial school in Borough Park" and from, of all people, Kaplan's old acquaintance, the Rev. Meyer Peikes. Kaplan's predecessor from his earliest Kehilath Jeshurun days may have mixed feelings of revenge with zealotry for the faith in underscoring the dangers Kaplan posed. He led the chorus of denunciations of the "notorious epikorus" from Manhattan. Peikes's remonstrations did not, however, deter "a dozen people at least"—presumably the young people from Shomre Emunah—from coming to hear Kaplan at Temple Emanuel of Borough Park "and among them contributed to the fund."[27]

Back in Manhattan, nothing Drachman and Jung had written and none of the *Light of Israel's* exposés convinced Orthodox rabbi H. P. Mendes that Kaplan had to be opposed on all counts. Indeed, as late as 1927 this erstwhile colleague of Kaplan still turned to him for advice and assistance on how to maintain and upgrade *Orthodox* standards of observance in communities "out west." So great was Mendes's respect for Kaplan's understanding of the contemporary Jewish scene that he could ask him for help in uniting the "Unions (the Seminary, the Orthodox, the this and the that)" to "keep up the fight" for Sabbath observance and for the maintenance of kashruth standards. Mendes also believed that his controversial colleague had both the power and the interest to see all traditional Jews brought together.[28]

With the publication of *Judaism as a Civilization*, an open, intense debate took place among the Upper West Side's Orthodox over Kaplan's abilities and liabilities. In 1932 Dr. David de Sola Pool, Mendes's successor at Congregation Shearith Israel, defended Kaplan's work against Aaron Rosmarin's angry attack in the *Jewish Forum*. While de Sola Pool was sure to assert that he was among those "who differ" from Kaplan's work, which "invites dissent at so many points," he also upbraided Rosmarin for "descend[ing] to criticisms which seem strangely indistinguishable from a complete perversion of [Kaplan's] teachings." He was particularly exercised that Rosmarin falsely alleged that Kaplan approved of intermarriage. For de Sola Pool, notwithstanding its heretical elements, *Judaism as a Civilization* was a "remarkable volume" and a "monumental work."[29]

These positive characterizations of Kaplan's work simply caused Rosmarin to wonder out loud about the depth of de Sola Pool's commitment to Orthodox Judaism. "Is it not paradoxical," Rosmarin chided, "that when the Jewish Religion is done away with, the orthodox Rabbi Pool, though he 'can say much in honest criticism' of the book, says nothing." Moreover, he continued, is it not the irony of the fate of the Jewish religion that when a book appears which denies the very religious principles and views to which Rabbi Pool adheres and which he preaches (am I perverting the truth?), the orthodox Rabbi, instead of saying "much in honest criticism" rather finds such laudations for it as "remarkable volume" and "monumental work."[30]

A friendly letter from Mendes to Kaplan in May 1935 offers a credible explanation of both his and de Sola Pool's attitudes toward a man whose new theologies they opposed fully. In this letter Mendes, one of American Orthodoxy's most experienced rabbis, asked his controversial colleague for strategies and techniques useful for interesting teenage and young adult girls in Judaism's messages. For Mendes, Kaplan was "from days of old of the experimental nature," a widely acknowledged innovator of methodologies for reaching the second-generation Jew. Kaplan surely had shown that skill in his career as an American Orthodox rabbi. And if, in evaluating Kaplan, one could divorce oneself from his heresies—as Mendes apparently did—there were many social truths and pedagogical verities to be imbibed from this teacher, especially in a "remarkable" and "monumental" work like his 1934 magnum opus.[31]

When *Judaism as a Civilization* appeared, Rabbi Joseph H. Lookstein was among those within that same variegated American Orthodox rabbinate who clearly denounced the Reconstructionist denigration of halakhah. In this regard, Lookstein was no different from Leo Jung or the rabbis of the Lower East Side who were very angry with Kaplan when he, for example, treated kashruth merely as a popular folkway and not "as a legal ordinance." What especially irked Lookstein was the assertion that "since the main purpose of these practices is to add Jewish atmosphere to the home, there is no reason for suffering the inconvenience and self-deprivation which result from a rigid adherence outside the home." Yet, Lookstein, who was a successor to Kaplan at Kehilath Jeshurun—he was also Ramaz's grandson-in-law—appreciated other aspects of the controversial book. He certainly felt that its articulation of the problems faced by second-generation Jews was worthy of consideration by his students at Yeshiva College, many of whom were studying to be Orthodox rabbis. Indeed, from the 1930s through the 1950s, Professor Lookstein candidly discussed Reconstructionism in his "Sociology of the Jews" class and recommended that his students read *Judaism as a Civilization* as part of its syllabus. Lookstein's tacit advocacy of this degree of freedom of inquiry fit well with his growing reputation as American Orthodoxy's most accommodating and widely cultured rabbi.[32]

However, his openness and willingness to have his students become aware of these nettlesome Jewish thoughts and issues did have, in at least one case—even to Lookstein's own mind—disastrous results. In or before 1943 a Yeshiva College student, the son of a rabbi "of the Old European type" who was planning to follow his father's footsteps into the Orthodox rabbinate, selected Kaplan's opus for his term essay in Lookstein's class. Joseph Tabachnik did more than a credible job on the book and earned a superior grade. Returning the paper to his student, Lookstein asked to see Tabachnik after class. Lookstein must have picked up a certain degree of sympathy for Reconstructionism in this paper. In all events, Tabachnik frankly admitted to "having fallen under the spell of the book, and as a result, his having decided not to apply for the Orthodox rabbinate." Taken aback, Lookstein told him that the place for him to study was not Yeshiva but the Jewish Theological Seminary. More generally, however, students of Lookstein read the work without incident or damage.[33]

In the 1950s Rabbi Emanuel Rackman, a younger colleague of Lookstein, and Rabbi Herschel Schacter, a devoted disciple of the Kehilath Jeshurun rabbi, emerged as two of the leading spokesmen for American Orthodoxy. True to its creed, they were willing participants in communitywide activities and interdenominational symposia and ignored the Agudath ha-Rabbanim's proclamations against Orthodox rabbis publicly interacting with Conservatives and Reformers. Rackman was a leading member of New York's Board of Rabbis. Schacter later became the first Orthodox rabbi to chair the Conference of Presidents of Major American Jewish Organizations. When it came to the question of working with Kaplan or publicly acknowledging his abilities, Rackman and Schacter followed Lookstein's teaching. They gave Kaplan due credit for his unique ability to formulate the questions and identify the problems that affected American Jewry while respectfully declining to share his Reconstructionist solutions. In this regard, they were far more collegial toward Kaplan than was Leo Jung, another one of their friends and mentors.

For example, in 1956 Schacter took part, along with Kaplan, in a program on "The Dynamic Aspects of Judaism and the Educational Process" sponsored by the National Council for Jewish Education, an organization that linked educators of varying Jewish orientations, in some ways a successor to the Agudath ha-Morim. And in 1964 he was the key respondent to a paper on "Intermarriage from a Religio-Ethnic Perspective" that Kaplan gave before the Commission on Synagogue Relations of the New York Federation of Jewish Philanthropies.[34]

On each of these occasions Schacter respectfully agreed with Kaplan the sociologist and forcefully disagreed with Kaplan the theologian in analyzing the problems and solutions for these most significant of communal concerns. Thus, when Kaplan argued in front of the Jewish educators that "all accounts of miracles or of events in which the natural order is said to have been superseded must be taken as ahistorical," Schacter immediately defended traditional Judaism. Indeed, when the Orthodox rabbi defined what is "dynamic" in Judaism, his answer was that "its dynamic character consists in [the] inherent elasticity" of the divinely given Halakhah. And, in taking the offensive against Reconstructionism, he averred, "The notion that Judaism should adjust itself to the climate of ideas is contrary to [everything] Judaism stands for."[35]

Similarly, in responding to Kaplan's position paper on intermarriage, Schacter not only addressed that "most distinguished and revered speaker" in the most dignified and gentlemanly like terms but also allowed that he "substantially agree[d]" with the professor's understanding of "the immediate and ultimate causes" of this problem. Of course, as an advocate of Orthodoxy, he went on to strongly challenge Kaplan's theological doctrines and their implications for solving this vexing issue.[36]

On a somewhat different communal front Rackman acknowledged Kaplan's special expertise in articulating what American Zionism's needs were in the period following the founding of the Jewish state. He accepted those ideas of Kaplan for reversing declining American Jewish interest in the national movement that would do no damage to Orthodoxy. At the same time, the politically sagacious Rackman was very careful not to be co-opted into supporting positions that implied assent to Reconstructionist views.

The American Zionist Council's Committee on Zionist Ideology was the forum for this interaction and interchange. This group brought together representatives of all Zionist persuasions—from Labor Zionists to Religious Zionists, from Hadassah to the Progressive Zionist League, and from the Revisionists to the mainstream Zionist Organization of America. In 1959 it set out to ascertain the continuing role Zionism might play in the lives of diaspora Jews in a world where, happily, the State of Israel was an accepted reality. Mordecai Kaplan was a central participant in these deliberations because, a year earlier, he had chaired a comparable committee on Zionist ideology of the zoa that had deliberated on the centrality of Israel in the spiritual and cultural life of all Jews, the role Zionism had to play in unifying world Jewry, and the essential partnership shared by diaspora Jews and Israelis both in supporting the state and in projecting "the Jewish people throughout the world . . . as an indispensable factor in the civilization of mankind." This "so-called Kaplan platform" was the starting point for the azc discussions even as it was clear that other proposals could be heard and that, ultimately, an ideological consensus would have to be reached with which all of American Zionism's special interests could be comfortable.[37]

As the Religious Zionist (Mizrachi-Hapoel Hamizrachi) representative on this committee, Rackman had no real difficulty with Kaplan's ideas, which formed the backbone of the council's draft position, when he spoke of concepts or issues like Israel as the Jews' spiritual home, the need for aliyah, or even the Law of Return "as sacred and inviolate . . . to the Jewish people." They did part company, however, when it came to Kaplan's assertion that "notwithstanding *diversity of religious beliefs and practices*, Jews throughout the world constitute one People united by a common past and a common destiny (emphasis added)." Ever sensitive to the affirmation of doctrinal heterogeneity, a cause so dear to Kaplan, Rackman told the committee that "from the point of view of many orthodox Jews it was incorrect to speak of diversity of religious beliefs and practices." The Orthodox rabbi then proposed a revision that spoke of unity but made no reference to religious values. After several meetings and a number of rewrites, a compromise plank was approved that undoubtedly pleased Rackman more than Kaplan. The council formally recognized the diversity in beliefs and practices that indeed existed among Jews worldwide but made no positive statement about heterogeneity in "religious beliefs and practices."[38]

Outside of New York and away from Orthodoxy's elite circles, in the denomination's hinterlands of the Midwest, South, and Far West, where Orthodox cooperation and interaction with the wider group was an acknowledged fact of traditional Jewish life, Kaplan's broad experiences and suggestions were almost universally recognized and often utilized. Between the 1920s and the early 1960s Kaplan frequently toured outlying Jewish communities either on behalf of the seminary, as a lecturer sponsored by the Jewish Welfare Board, or to promote his Reconstructionist creed and cause. While on the road he was often approached by local community leadership—which very often included Orthodox representatives—either to speak to some general group concern or to help solve some outstanding Jewish issue. Conservative and most Reform leaders were usually thrilled to have the benefit of Kaplan's expertise. Orthodox lay spokesmen or rabbis kept their theological reservations about their visitor largely to themselves and went along because they were convinced that Kaplan's advice would be of great value to their town's needs and would not undermine traditional faith. Or they cooperated because they did not want to be seen as undermining communal unity, particularly when reassured that the Reconstructionist would stick to noncontroversial themes.

Kaplan hastened to accept these invitations because he had a particular affinity for those Jews whom he called the "Enlightened Orthodox." He saw them, along with "the Conservatives," as "the only Jewish groups that evince a tendency to deal with Jewish life as a problem in social and spiritual adjustment." He strongly believed that they "held out promise of evolving as complete a Jewish life as we can hope for in this country." In other words, they reminded him of the Orthodox Jews with whom he once had been so comfortable back in New York City. They were like the ones who had started their lives in old-line Orthodox synagogues and who subsequently found that "a shul where they can 'daven' on Sabbaths and holidays and where they can occasionally listen to a maggid or an itinerant Rov" was unsatisfying.[39] They were also akin to the people with whom he had hoped to build a national movement at the Jewish Center, only to find that its synagogue leaders did not share his formulae for meeting their mutual aspirations. Now, on the frontiers of American Orthodoxy, he had a second chance to recruit, with due subtlety and circumspection, a different mass of foot soldiers for his Reconstructionist creed. And, although Kaplan may have felt somewhat constrained to soft-pedal the controversial aspects of his religious thought so as not to antagonize the Orthodox leaders who invited or welcomed him, he still felt very much at home among these traditional Jews who had little connection with his enemies back in the metropolis.

In April 1929, for example, while on tour through Canton, Ohio, a community of some 3,500 Jews, the executive director of the local Jewish Federation approached Kaplan "to straighten out the talmud torah tangle in this town." He was requested "to induce some of the leading representatives of both Reform and Orthodox to start a campaign for a community talmud torah." Kaplan readily agreed and met with the president of the small incipient Conservative temple and "two men representing the

Orthodox," all of whom were enthusiatic about Kaplan serving as a consultant on this pressing local communal concern. At meeting's end Kaplan determined that ultimately "it would be impossible to get the Orthodox to come as a group to work with the Reform on behalf of a community hebrew school." Still, he advised those anxious for communal unity to inaugurate their campaign. Kaplan "assured them that many of the present Orthodox group would come into the work as individuals." Whatever difficulties Canton's Orthodox experienced in working with their Reform neighbors on an ongoing basis, they did not carry over to opposition to Kaplan, the visiting dissenter, who served as mediator.[40]

In March 1950 Fort Worth, Texas Jews of all denominational stripes turned together to Kaplan for his views and guidance in directing their community when they invited the Reconstructionist to speak over a weekend in a number of congregations, including the Orthodox one. En route to Texas, Kaplan could not help but intuit that he was in for a most pleasant experience when he happened to meet the Orthodox, Conservative, and Reform rabbis who together had tendered the invitation. Significantly, the three colleagues were on the way home from an interdenominational rabbinical retreat in Beaumont, Texas. The Orthodox rabbi, a graduate of Chicago's Hebrew Theological Seminary, took great pains to emphasize to Kaplan how well they cooperated despite their clear theological differences. And they all seemed to agree that the Orthodox and Reform rabbis' experiences as chaplains in the American armed forces during the Second World War predisposed them to "get along in the community."

For the Orthodox rabbi there was no problem having Kaplan speak to his congregants about issues that concerned all the Jews in town. It is also entirely possible that that rabbi's involvement with his colleagues in sketching out the questions Kaplan would address ensured his equanimity about hosting this guest. Kaplan helped the situation too, for he agreed to examine such concerns as "the problem of intermarriage, the proper Jewish educational foundation for our children, what is the sustaining force in Jewish life today and the future of Jews in Russia," topics that could relate only tangentially to his Reconstructionist opinions. A more typical Kaplan presentation, like the one he would give several days later before a purely Conservative congregation, included such issues as "is the American Jewish community dying, what is your conception of God, why ritual in modern Judaism and what is left of the 'chosen people' concept?"[41]

Two years later, in 1952, a group of Orthodox rabbis in Minneapolis was somewhat less favorable to his appearance under local auspices in which they were included. But after some pressure and admonitions from their more religiously liberal colleagues, they fell into line and greeted Kaplan respectfully. When the Rabbinical Council of the Twin Cities tendered its original invitation to Kaplan to address their group, the Orthodox members expressed no reservations. However, when a local Anglo-Jewish newspaper suggested that Kaplan would use his speech "as an occasion to present the case for Reconstructionism," they had serious second thoughts. Indeed, the night before Kaplan was to come to town, "the Orthodox rabbis met among themselves and decided not to attend." It took some very harsh words from their Conservative counterparts emphasizing the need for communal unity to bring them back to the meeting. Fortunately for all concerned, Kaplan did not talk much about his radical theological views. Rather, as he recapped the speech, "I argued for organized community . . . answered their objections and left everyone in the group in ironic spirit."[42]

A few years later, in February 1960, an Orthodox rabbi in Tulsa, Oklahoma, who was convinced that Kaplan had much to contribute to all the Jews of his city, held fast to his invitation to the guest from New York, even when subjected to outside pressures. Rabbi Arthur Kahn, a graduate of Yeshiva University's Rabbi Isaac Elchanan Theological Seminary, invited Kaplan to deliver a series of lectures to the entire local community at his Orthodox synagogue. However, this engagement did not sit well, neither with a certain member of his congregation nor with Orthodox Jews outside of town. To "immunize the Tulsa Jews against Kaplan" this antagonist proceeded to send reprints of "an onslaught against Reconstructionist theology by renowned Orthodox theologian Eliezer Berkovitz" that had recently appeared in *Tradition*, a "journal of Orthodox Jewish thought" sponsored by the Rabbinical Council of America. This very explicit critique of his choice of guest lecturer failed, however, to faze Rabbi Kahn. He firmly believed that opening Orthodox synagogue doors did not constitute assent to Reconstructionst theology and he continued to appreciate Kaplan's insights on contemporary Jewish social and political problems. Rabbi Kahn personally introduced his guest the first night of the series and then permitted his Reform rabbinic colleague to do the honors the following evening.[43]

It remained for the Orthodox members of the Board of Rabbis of Southern California in 1966 to take American Orthodox appreciation of Kaplan as a teacher to the highest possible level, leaving themselves perilously close to endorsing Kaplan the Reconstructionist—or at least to saying that Reconstructionist ideas had something to teach Orthodoxy. On the occasion of Kaplan's eighty-fifth birthday these rabbis joined their Conservative and Reform colleagues to publicly "acknowledge the indebtedness of all wings of Judaism for your tremendous contribution to the field of *Jewish theology and Jewish thought in general* (emphasis added)." Here Orthodox rabbis participated in lauding Kaplan not only for his work as a pedagogue and social scientist but also as a religious thinker. They signed on to a statement that concluded with the following: "The impact of your mind and the amazing influence of your spirit has wrought great things in Israel. It may take generations to assess the range of your achievements, but we rabbis, Orthodox, Conservative and Reform, have felt the immediacy of your presence in the course of many decades."

This tribute truly moved Kaplan. He would exult to his diary that it was "the most thrilling testimonial I have ever received." He was heartened "that not all Orthodox rabbis are of one mind with regard to the insistence on uniformity in Jewish life." And he prayed that the tolerant Orthodox rabbis of Los Angeles and environs would "serve as examples to their Orthodox colleagues in the rest of the world." Even at this late date in his life he still desired masses of Orthodox Jews to look upon him as one of their foremost teachers.[44]

As his long life drew to a close, Mordecai Kaplan slowly exited the American Jewish scene. The last significant achievement of his career was the establishment, in 1968, of the Reconstructionist Rabbinical College in Philadelphia. Although the octogenarian rejoiced that finally there was an American Jewish seminary to espouse his teachings on Jewish life, he regarded the creation of his own separate denominational institution with less than total satisfaction. He had always wanted to be a teacher of all Jews and have all Jews see him as their teacher. Now he had defined himself as a leader of only one segment of the community.[45]

In 1973, at the age of ninety-two, Kaplan retired to Israel and, concomitant with that move, ended his close to seventy years of diary and journal keeping. From that point on he was an infrequent contributor to his own *Reconstructionist* publication even as portions of his most important books were republished and scholars and disciples continued to evaluate his contributions. On the occasion of his one-hundredth birthday, in 1981, a new edition of *Judaism as a Civilization* was reissued by the Jewish Publication Society. Kaplan returned to the United States during these final years of his life and died in Riverdale, New York on November 8, 1983.

By the time of his passing, Mordecai Kaplan's works and activities had long ceased to stir the emotions of Orthodox Jews. In fact, in the days after Kaplan's death—he was buried close to the grave of Ramaz on the cemetery grounds of his old synagogue, Kehilath Jeshurun—that institution, continuing the tradition of civility toward opponents that its late rabbi, Joseph H. Lookstein, had established, joined the many mourners who described him in favorable terms. Unlike the Jewish Center, which submitted no obituary to the *New York Times*, Kehillath Jeshurun did, and it stated: "Congregation Kehilath Jeshurun mourns the passing of a great religious leader of American Jewry who, shortly after the turn of the century, served as Assistant Rabbi in our synagogue. His words and thoughts have enriched Jewish civilization in our time."[46]

Yet, there is impressionistic evidence to suggest that Orthodox Jews have continued to be of several minds over whether it was permissible to learn from the writings of the heretic. For example, in 1976, in a Yeshiva University ambience that had changed somewhat from the one familiar to Joseph Lookstein, a young professor of American Jewish history encountered a qualitatively different stance toward reading Kaplan's works on the part of one of his rabbinical students. On his first day of teaching Professor Jeffrey S. Gurock handed out a syllabus that included *Judaism as a Civilization* to his class in Yeshiva's Bernard Revel Graduate School of Judaic studies. Kaplan's work was to be read, Gurock calmly explained, neither to promote his views, nor to refute them. Rather, the book was, to this professor's mind, an important source for understanding the religious life of American Jewry during the interwar period, a major focus of the course. This scholarly appraisal sat well with all but one of the some half-dozen students in the class who characterized the work as *minus* (heresy). And, in an after-class discussion of a type very different from the Lookstein-Tabachnik chat some three-and-a-half decades earlier, the student informed his teacher that the only conceivable way he could read this book would be "to know how to answer" the Reconstructionist. In other words, he had put Kaplan's book in the category of heretical works that might only be studied to refute their views. This fundamentalist student did not remain long in the course, and the other students read Kaplan without complaint.

That student's fears about the dissemination of Kaplan's ideas within his yeshiva would have been heightened had he known that, almost a decade later, a passage from *Judaism as a Civilization* would be used in *Hamevaser: A Student Publication of Traditional Thought and Ideas* at Yeshiva University "to appreciate more fully the insight of one of the Chasidic rabbis regarding the *mitzvah* of *sukkah*." That fundamentalist's only consolation would be that Kaplan's words were not identified by name, but rather as the statement of "one modern Jewish thinker." For the author himself, at that later date—almost two years after Kaplan's demise—there was a concern about the resonance of Kaplan's name, even as he tacitly asserted the dissenter's ability to teach.[47]

Rabbi Shlomo Riskin showed no concern about what others might say as he went even further in publicly crediting Kaplan as possessed of a unique message that all Jews would do well to emulate. In April 1993 this Orthodox rabbi who, from his Lincoln Square Synagogue pulpit, had reached out to fourth-generation Jews on the Upper West Side—as the young Kaplan had done fifty years earlier to second-generation Jews—was outspoken in asserting that if this country's Jewish leaders want to halt "rampant disaffection" they "must emblazon in gold letters atop every Jewish institutional building Mordecai Kaplan's definition: Judaism is a civilization." Borrowing directly from the Reconstructionist's work while making sure not to endorse his theological position, Riskin continued: "A civilization has its own language, its own land, its own history, its own literature, its own days of celebration and mourning and its own lifestyle." Mordecai Kaplan would have been pleased to join with Riskin in "an indefatigable effort to 'convert' the masses of American Jews to become conversant with, and hopefully passionately involved in, their Jewish civilization." He had called for such a campaign over the course of his entire life. He also would have seen in Riskin's proposed "Operation Exodus from Assimilation, which would secure the opportunity for every Jewish high school graduate to spend one year in Israel in a special program of exposure to [their] unique heritage," an affirmation of the central role that he had always asserted the culture of Zionism had to play in ensuring Jewish survival.[48] Of course, Riskin and Kaplan would have differed on the role traditional religious belief and practice would play in the Jewish civilization both promoted. But Kaplan probably would have been prepared to defer consideration of these weighty matters for some later date, hopeful that everyone would ultimately see the correctness of all his positions. Shlomo Riskin and his generation of American Orthodox rabbis, on the other hand, would not have entered into any sort of alliance with Kaplan the theological dissenter. Such was the limit of Orthodox respect for Kaplan's views and ideas by the last decade of the twentieth century.

CONCLUSION • *Walking with Mordecai Kaplan
and Understanding Orthodoxy
and American Judaism*

Our tracking of Mordecai Kaplan's
footsteps as he strode among American Orthodox Jews for almost a century has revealed much about this modern dissenter's disengagement from
his traditional faith but even more about the community that he once
called home. As a biography of Kaplan, it presents a thoughtful and troubled heretic who, while still a young man, was tortured by Orthodoxy's
teachings and strictures and anxious to be unencumbered by all it represented. And yet, for a combination of personal, strategic, and careerist reasons, Kaplan was not eager to separate himself from those who still subscribed to what he perceived of as an antiquated faith.

Indeed, for close to twenty years, unwilling, unable, or simply not ready
to alienate his traditional friends, Kaplan kept the full import of his
unconventional understandings and solutions for dealing with the modern
Jewish condition largely to himself. From his time at Kehilath Jeshurun
through his early encounters with the Jewish Center community, Kaplan
had innumerable opportunities to articulate much of what he did not have
in common with Orthodox Jews. But he consistently shied away from sep-
arating himself from most elements of that community. He obfuscated
issues when interrogated and went out of his way to hide the full extent
of his disagreements. If anything, to the uncritical observer—and most
Orthodox Jews fell into that category—Kaplan's constant presence and
personal kinship with them bespoke an allegiance they assumed he still
shared for what they believed. Nothing could have been further from the
truth. But, meanwhile, their positive perceptions of this peripatetic
rabbi—and maybe their own desire to believe that this extremely bright

young man who grew up in their midst shared their views—does much to explain why Kaplan was not really challenged until 1920.

In the early 1920s the force of issues, events, and personalities brought his views fully to the surface. As a result, Kaplan's relationship with Orthodox institutions became untenable. And, yet, another decade would elapse before the final irrevocable divorce. That twice during the late 1920s-early 1930s this controversial rabbi was almost called back to the Jewish Center pulpit suggests that even then a segment of West Side Orthodoxy cared far less about what Kaplan advocated than his ability—which they still acknowledged—to attract Jews to the synagogue. For them it was solely what he would insist upon in synagogue ritual that could determine whether or not their former rabbi would still be considered Orthodox.

What Kaplan's own involvement in these last-gasp efforts says about this dissenter is no less significant. For all his abhorrence of traditional teachings, he was still, even at these late dates, willing to compromise with the aim of eventually capturing the masses who belonged to Orthodox synagogues. If anything, that patient approach would continue to characterize his activities throughout his long life. He never stopped believing in his ability to bring all American Jews to his side. Kaplan was deeply hopeful that Orthodox synagogue-goers, the men and women who shared his East European background and heritage, would turn to Reconstructionism when they realized, as he had, that the traditional faith could no longer sustain them in modern America. He prayed that these Jews, whom he sometimes called the "Enlightened Orthodox," would help him create a new twentieth-century Judaism.

Our recognition, through Kaplan, that the American Orthodox community of his times had such "enlightened" types, including those who did not punctiliously observe the religious commandments, is just one of the ways in which this dissenter's life defines this community in the nineteenth and twentieth centuries. No less important is what our walk with Kaplan tells us about Rabbi Jacob Joseph and his supporters and the Agudath ha-Rabbanim's own resistance to Americanization and objection to other Jewish movements.

To be sure, the chief rabbi and the downtown Orthodox we have met were intent on transplanting a beloved and revered religious civilization to the United States. The Etz Chaim Yeshiva that grudgingly imparted the barest of secular knowledge to its boys was their ideal institution. It was the correct alternative to the public schools. Elements of the association that hired the chief rabbi were also antagonistic to the early JTS's own efforts to reach out to the youth of the immigrant ghettos.[1] However, much of the Kaplans' family life and the saga of young Mordecai's education point to an alternative understanding of Rabbi Joseph's "court." The members of this group were not unqualifiably resolute in their rejection of the new world they encountered.

Some association people—including the Kaplans themselves—remembered a Jewish Eastern Europe that was itself experiencing change under the impact of modernization. They already understood, from their own old world experiences, that some social and religious adjustments were going to be necessary as Jews lived in new environments. Moreover, while downtown rabbis extolled Etz Chaim's efforts, many also demonstrated ambivalence toward that yeshiva's mission when they chose to send their own sons to public schools. And, as far as the seminary was concerned, the outspoken association leader, Judah David Eisenstein, was only one of the people within the circle of Rabbi Joseph and the Kaplans who saw real value in the seminary's mission even if he—and they—harbored reservations about how that mission was carried out. There were downtown lay people who experienced no conflict in backing both the chief rabbinate experiment and the JTS initiative. They had no problems with the modern school and were proud of the boys from their neighborhoods who trained there to serve their acculturating community. In other words, as we enter the Kaplans' world we find that, for those who gathered around the chief rabbi, old European ways were essentially ideals toward which they would always strive. But accommodations to America and modernity itself were often the order of the day.[2]

Our encounter through Kaplan with the Agudath ha-Rabbanim reveals that even this rejectionist front was not consistent in its opposition to other Jewish expressions. Once again, like the chief rabbi before them, they certainly harbored staunch allegiances to traditional Jewish belief and practice, opposed Americanization, and were outspoken in their condemnation of modern religious alternatives. In 1904 the Agudath ha-Rabbanim excoriated JTS as a home of apostasy. As part of their tirade against Schechter's school they pilloried old seminary graduates who, within the Orthodox Union, were trying to influence downtown youngsters. The Agudath ha-Rabbanim demurred that even the Orthodox Union could not be a valued and trusted ally in the fight to perpetuate Judaism. And, as the story of Kaplan's first year at Kehilath Jeshurun reminds us, the

Agudath ha-Rabbanim concretized their contempt for the seminary and their disdain for the Orthodox Union by supporting their elder statesman, Rabbi Judah David Willowski, in his humiliation of the Yorkville congregation's young minister. This would be the first of several nasty encounters between Kaplan and those whom he would castigate for promoting "mental narrowness and confusion that reigns supreme in the Jewish ghetto, reinforced by fanaticism."[3]

Nevertheless, the trail of Kaplan's life experiences also leads us to occasions where distinguished members of the Agudath ha-Rabbanim recognized and worked with those supposedly tarred forever by their seminary associations. For example, a second look at the Ridbaz story reveals that while Willowski did demand that as long as he was associated with Kehilath Jeshurun all sermons there had to be delivered in Yiddish, he did not object to sharing the pulpit with a JTS minister. The Ridbaz's colleague, Ramaz, a longtime member of the Agudath ha-Rabbanim's presidium, did far more than just tacitly recognize the rabbinic authenticity of an old seminary and Orthodox Union man. Ramaz worked harmoniously with Kaplan at Kehilath Jeshurun and approved of his modern Orthodox efforts to transform the ambience, social message, and even certain elements of the service of their synagogue.

In 1914 Kaplan tells us that Rabbis Avraham Udelewitz and Joseph Konvitz, two other leaders in good standing of the Agudath ha-Rabbanim, went much further in actively recognizing their opponents. When they spoke at Roxbury's Blue Hill Avenue Synagogue—albeit in Yiddish and in that synagogue's Orthodox minyan—they favorably recognized Schechter seminary graduate and United Synagogue founder Phineas Israeli, a rising leader in the nascent Conservative movement. In other words, despite their excoriation decrees, important Agudath ha-Rabbanim leaders, including Konvitz, the son-in-law of Willowski, sometimes acknowledged not only American Orthodoxy's best young men but Conservatism's early stars as well.

Our journeys with Kaplan, likewise, make it clear that the seminary was also part of the Orthodox Union's own community consciousness, particularly when it confronted a dissenter within its midst. The fears and anger expressed by Drachman, by the *Hebrew Standard* editorialists, and by the *Light of Israel* campaign against what Kaplan was doing to *their* seminary strongly suggests that, to these modern Orthodox minds, JTS was still one of their institutions. Some twenty years after Solomon Schechter set JTS on the road to becoming the Conservative movement's flagship educational institution, that school still had a following among Americanized Orthodox leaders. Cyrus Adler's weak defense of Kaplan reflects both his recognition of significant Orthodox ties to his seminary and his interest in having his school supported by these upwardly mobile Jews. All told, Kaplan's travels emphasize well how long and how strongly the seminary was linked to an inclusive American Orthodox community during the first decades of this century.

This part of Kaplan's story does much to explain why Jewish lay leaders from Samuel Travis in the 1910s to a group that included Joseph H. Cohen in the late 1920s could consider merging JTS with RIETS. For them, both schools largely stood for the same mission of promoting Americanized Orthodoxy through the training of modern rabbis and teachers to a new generation of young people. It took Mordecai Kaplan's continued presence on the seminary faculty, as much if not more than any other factor, to derail this endeavor. The seminary's tolerance for the dissenter within its midst is what ultimately set that school apart from its Orthodox counterpart. In no way could RIETS or Yeshiva College possibly countenance his teachings.

Indeed, it was here, while we began to chart the final bends in Kaplan's road which took him forever away from Orthodoxy, that we saw how reactions to the dissenter exposed American Orthodoxy's multiple faces as the twentieth century unfolded. In answering the questions of if, when, and how to turn to Kaplan, Orthodox Jews once again revealed themselves to be a complex community. Their group was home to resisters of varying sorts—including now an unyielding Agudath ha-Rabbanim—to accommodationists of differing stripes, and, of course, to Kaplan's favorites, the marginal or "Enlightened Orthodox" who could be found both on New York's Upper West Side and in communities throughout America's hinterland. While some Orthodox Jews excommunicated him and burned his prayerbook, others respectfully joined him on various communal platforms. All told, Mordecai Kaplan, professional pedagogue that he was, would have been pleased to see his heretical life used as a point of departure for understanding how a far-flung and multifaceted traditional community defined itself in this country and during this century.

NOTES •

Introduction

1. Jeffrey S. Gurock interview with Sam Hartstein, January 30, 1994, and recollections of the interviewer. See also "The Oldest Alumnus of Yeshiva University Dies," press release, November 1, 1993, Yeshiva University Public Relations Department.

2. William Berkowitz, ed., *Dialogues in Judaism: Jewish Dilemmas Defined, Debated, and Explored* (Northvale, N.J.: Jason Aronson, 1991), p. 32.

1. An Orthodox Rabbi's Son on the Lower East Side

1. "Constitution of the Association of the American Hebrew Orthodox Congregations"; Broadside of the Association of the American Orthodox Hebrew Congregations, appendix 3 in Abraham J. Karp, "New York Chooses a Chief Rabbi," *Publication of the American Jewish Historical Society* (hereafter *PAJHS*) 44, no. 3 (March 1955):191–93.

2. Broadside, p. 191. For a comprehensive description of the many religious abuses that the association hoped to address, see Moses Weinberger, *The Jews and Judaism in New York* [Hebrew] (New York, 1887). Weinberger's important work of criticism has been translated into English by Jonathan D. Sarna as *People Walk on Their Heads: Moses Weinberger's "Jews and Judaism in New York"* (New York: Holmes and Meier, 1982).

3. Broadside, p. 191.

4. On the relationship between the founders of Etz Chaim and the leadership of the association, see Jeffrey S. Gurock, *The Men and Women of Yeshiva: Higher Education, Orthodoxy, and American Judaism* (New York: Columbia University Press, 1988), pp. 12–13. For information about Etz Chaim, the forerunner of today's Yeshiva

University, see Gilbert Klaperman, *The Story of Yeshiva University* (London: Macmillan, 1969); Aaron Rothkoff, *Bernard Revel: Builder of American Jewish Orthodoxy* (Philadelphia: Jewish Publication Society of America, 1972); and Jacob J. Schacter, "Torah u-Madda Revisited: The Editor's Introduction," *Torah u-Madda Journal* 1 (1989):3–4.

5. Weinberger, *People Walk on Their Heads*, pp. 55–56.

6. Kaplan's description of "old time Rovs" from Eastern Europe appears in volume 4, p. 217 (January 17, 1929) of his unpublished journals. The twenty-seven volumes of the journals (hereafter "Journals"), which Kaplan kept from 1914–1972, were examined at the library of the Jewish Theological Seminary of America.

In many instances the journals are the major source on Kaplan's life and activities extant. At times, particularly with reference to his family background discussed in this chapter, the journal entries and his several autobiographical sketches written many decades after the fact are the only sources on Kaplan's activities. Thus, for all their unquestionable value, the journals and, especially, his few published autobiographical articles, all of which were composed after he personally broke with Orthodoxy, have to be approached judiciously. The scholar has to consider the prejudices that might have informed all these accounts. Even as we carefully utilize Kaplan's recollections in our presentation, we will note problematic entries.

7. See Mordecai Kaplan, "Journals," 1:256 (January 30, 1917), 1:256–57 (February 1, 1917), and the few loose pages attached to 1:257; "Journals," 4:217 (January 17, 1929), 5:181 (October 4, 1929), and 19:264 (March 7, 1959). See William Berkowitz, *Let Us Reason Together* (New York: Crown, 1970), p. 71, where Kaplan refers to his father as a "student-colleague" of Rabbi Reines. See also Mordecai Kaplan, "Response," *Proceedings of the Rabbinical Assembly of America* 15 (1951):113.

The Mordecai Kaplan Archives, Reconstructionist Rabbinical College, Wyncote, Pennsylvania (henceforth MKA), also contain two letters written by Rabbi Reines to Israel in 1908 that reflect their friendship. See also Jacob J. Schacter, "Mordecai M. Kaplan's Orthodox Ordination," *American Jewish Archives* 46, no. 1 (Spring/Summer 1994):1–11, which discusses this relationship. The archive is divided into two parts. Most of Kaplan's correspondence can be found in a filing cabinet in the college library and has already been catalogued. See Richard Libowitz, "A Catalogue of the Correspondence in the Mordecai M. Kaplan Archives," *Jewish Civilization: Essays and Studies*, 3 vols. (Philadelphia: Reconstructionist Rabbinical College, 1981), 2:207–78. Other correspondence as well as Kaplan's pocket diaries, notebooks, and assorted papers, which fill some 150 folders, can be found in file boxes in one of the administrative offices of the college. They have not yet been catalogued, although the files are numbered. Wherever possible, we will refer to Kaplan's papers by their file number.

8. Mordecai Kaplan, "The Influences That Have Shaped My Life," *Reconstructionist* 8, no. 10 (June 26, 1942):28; Kaplan, "Journals," 1:257 (February 1, 1917).

9. See Ira Eisenstein, "Mordecai M. Kaplan," *Great Jewish Thinkers of the Twentieth Century* (Clinton: Colonial, 1963), p. 253. See also Simon Noveck, "Kaplan and Milton Steinberg: A Disciple's Agreements and Disagreements," in Emanuel S. Goldsmith, Mel Scult, and Robert M. Seltzer, eds., *The American Judaism of Mordecai Kaplan* (New York: New York University Press, 1990), p. 147. On Kaplan, Fuenn, and Kohut, see Kaplan, "Journals," 1:257, 258 (February 1, 1917). On the Haskalah circle in Volozhin, see Jacob J. Schacter, "Haskalah, Secular Studies, and the Close of the Yeshiva in Volozhin in 1892," *Torah u-Madda Journal* 2 (1990):91–96.

10. Kaplan, "Journals," 19:264 (March 7, 1959). In an interview in 1971 Kaplan said that he believed his sister was "the first girl in town, or for that matter in Russia, to have studied together with boys in the *heder*." See Richard Libowitz, *Mordecai M. Kaplan and the Development of Reconstructionism* (New York and Toronto: Mellen, 1983), p. 215, n. 2. For Israel Kaplan's relationship with Rabbi Reines, see note 7 above. Mordecai Kaplan probably overstated the possibility that his father might actually have been deemed a heretic. What was more likely is that Israel Kaplan had an interest in the Haskalah that was considered controversial in his circles.

11. See Kaplan, "Journals," 17:300 (December 10, 1955): "According to what my father once told me, I was born on Friday night June 10, 1881 a few minutes before midnight." See also Berkowitz's transcript of his interview with Kaplan in *Let Us Reason Together*, p. 71: "I was born on a Friday night. Since it was forbidden to record anything on the Sabbath, my father stopped the pendulum of the pendulum clock. It was then seven minutes before midnight." It is interesting, however, that Kaplan's passport gives his date of birth as June 11, 1881, MKA. See also the *Jewish Theological Seminary Students Annual* (New York, 1914), p. 39. Berkowitz's interview was reprinted in William Berkowitz, ed., *Dialogues in Judaism: Jewish Dilemmas Defined, Debated, and Explored* (Northvale, N.J.: Jason Aronson, 1991), pp. 29–46.

12. Mordecai Kaplan, "The Way I Have Come," in Ira Eisenstein and Eugene Kohn, eds., *Mordecai M. Kaplan: An Evaluation* (New York: Jewish Reconstructionist Foundation, 1952), p. 286. See also Berkowitz, *Let Us Reason Together*, p. 71; Kaplan, "Journals," 1:257–58 (February 1, 1917). For more information about Kaplan's early childhood in Russia, see Mordecai Kaplan, "How to Live Creatively as a Jew," in R. M. MacIver, ed., *Moments of Personal Discovery* (Port Washington: Kennikat, 1952), p. 94.

13. Kaplan, "The Way I Have Come," p. 287.

14. Kaplan, "Response," pp. 213–14.

15. Several years earlier Israel Kaplan had decided to go to America, only to change his mind in Hamburg when he "saw the kind of people that emigrated there." See Kaplan, "Journals," 1:257 (February 1, 1917).

16. Kaplan, "Influences," p. 29. See also Kaplan, "Journals," 1:257 (February 1, 1917).

17. Kaplan, "Journals," 16:185 (July 16, 1953), 18:231 (March 19, 1957), 19:265 (March 7, 1959), 25:121 (April 24, 1971).

18. Kaplan, "Response," p. 214. See also Kaplan, "Journals," 1:257 (February 1, 1917), 23:101–02 (July 17, 1965). In Kaplan, "Journals," 19:264 (March 7, 1959), he wrote that he left Swentzian "at the age of seven and about two months (August 1888)."

For Kaplan's meeting with Rabbi Yitzchak Elchanan, see Kaplan, "Journals," 15:159 (June 29, 1951): "In Kovno we met father who took me to R. Yizhak Elchanan to be blessed by him."

Rabbi Yitzchak Elchanan Spektor served as rabbi of Kovno from 1864 until his death in 1896. See Ephraim Shimoff, *Rabbi Isaac Elchanan Spektor: Life and Letters* (New York: Yeshiva University Press, 1959), p. 41 f. On Rabbi Spektor's less than antagonistic attitude toward religious Jews migrating to the tref (unkosher) land of America, see Aryeh Gartner, *The Jews in the United States from the Earliest Days to the Present* [Hebrew] (Hakibutz Hameuchad, 1980), p. 82. Kaplan suggested that this encounter made an "everlasting impression" on him. Sixty-three years later, and generations after he had fully broken with Orthodoxy, Kaplan would reflect that "no books, no theories, no ideas, can mean what that [Spektor's blessing] has meant in my life." See "Response," p. 214. It is, however, impossible to determine what precisely that impression was. While clearly evincing great respect for Rabbi Spektor, our view is that this statement is more a rhetorical flourish than an accurate portrayal of fact.

19. Kaplan, "Journals," 4:217 (January 17, 1929).

20. Kaplan, "Journals," 1:110–12 (October 28, 1914), 1:256–58 (February 1, 1917), 7:256 (November 29, 1934), 15:171 (July 16, 1951), 16:185 (July 16, 1953), 18:141 (September 23, 1956), 21:153 (July 16, 1962), 22:13 (July 16, 1963), 23:101 (July 17, 1965), 24:200 (July 18, 1968); Berkowitz, *Let Us Reason Together*, p. 72.

21. On the curriculum of Etz Chaim in its earliest days, see Gurock, *The Men and Women of Yeshiva*, pp. 11–12, 15.

22. For a discussion of the unavailability of either all-day or supplementary Jewish schooling for immigrant girls of East European heritage on the Lower East Side until 1894, see Gurock, *The Men and Women of Yeshiva*, pp. 186–88. The few girls' schools run by American Orthodox congregations in uptown neighborhoods would not have been an option for unacculturated girls like Sophie Kaplan. For information on the basic training Sophie had before coming to America, see Kaplan, "Journals," 19:265 (March 7, 1959).

23. M. Kaplan, "Response," p. 214.

24. In these schools Kaplan had some difficulties dealing with his observance of Jewish holidays and the demands of the French school schedule. See Kaplan,

"The Influences," p. 29; see also Kaplan, "Response," p. 214; and "The Way I Have Come," p. 287.

25. M. Kaplan, "Response," p. 214.

26. There is a lack of clarity in Kaplan's memoir sketches, both about his educational experiences before arriving at Etz Chaim and how long he remained there before returning to public school. For varying recollections, see Kaplan, "Response," pp. 214–25; Kaplan, "The Influences," p. 29; Kaplan, "The Way I Have Come," p. 287; Berkowitz, *Let Us Reason Together*, p. 72.

As for how long Kaplan stayed in Etz Chaim, there are, again, conflicting accounts. See Berkowitz, *Let Us Reason Together*; p. 72; Kaplan, "The Influences," p. 28; Kaplan, "Response," pp. 214–15; and Kaplan, "Journals," 18:188 (December 22, 1956). In all events, by age twelve, as we will see, he was off to the Jewish Theological Seminary.

27. Klaperman, *The Story of Yeshiva University*, p. 27.

28. The word *cherpah* was written by Kaplan in his journal in Hebrew letters. See Kaplan, "Response," p. 215. See also "The Way I Have Come," p. 287: "Speaking Yiddish meant to me being a Jew, so that when my schoolmates spoke English in the synagogue I resented it and told them so." This recollection also may not exactly reflect what Kaplan, who had been a student in public schools in France and America, may have felt about the sanctity of the Yiddish language. And, in describing himself as a zealot, Kaplan may have been trying to deepen the contrast between his early and later years. For other examples of Kaplan's youthful piety, see Libowitz, *Mordecai M. Kaplan*, p. 10. See also Kaplan, "The Influences," p. 29; Berkowitz, *Let Us Reason Together*, p. 72.

29. Ehrlich was the author of the three-volume Hebrew *Mikra Ki-Feshuto* (Berlin: M. Poppelauer, 1899–1901) and the seven-volume *Randglossen zur hebräischen Bibel* (Leipzig: J. C. Hinrichs, 1908–1914). On Ehrlich's return to and relationship with the Jewish community, see Richard J. H. Gottheil, *The Life of Gustav Gottheil* (Williamsport: Bayard, 1936), pp. 75–77; Richard M. Stern, "Arnold B. Ehrlich: A Personal Recollection," *American Jewish Archives* 23, no. 1 (April 1971):73–85; *Encyclopaedia Judaica*, 16 vols. (Jerusalem: Macmillan, 1971), 6:512; Louis I. Rabinowitz, ed., *Encyclopaedia Judaica Year Book 1973* (Jerusalem: Keter, 1973), p. 196; Libowitz, *Mordecai M. Kaplan*, pp. 10–11. See also Jacob Kabakoff, "New Light on Arnold Bogomil Ehrlich," *American Jewish Archives* 36, no. 2 (November 1984):202–24. On the Kaplans' relationship with Ehrlich, see Kaplan, "Journals," 14:239 (June 24, 1949), 19:104 (June 13, 1958), 19:254 (February 7, 1959); Berkowitz, *Let Us Reason Together*, p. 73; Eisenstein, "Mordecai M. Kaplan," p. 255; Mordecai Kaplan, "A Founding Father Recounts," *Alumni Association Bulletin*, Teachers Institute and Seminary College of Jewish Studies, Jewish Theological Seminary of America (1959), p. 6. See also Kaplan, "The Influences," p. 30; Kaplan, "The Way I Have Come," p. 289; and Kaplan, "How to Live Creatively," p. 96.

30. Kaplan, "Journals," 14:239 (June 24, 1949); Eisenstein, "Mordecai M. Kaplan."

31. Regarding Kaplan's mother's hopes that he become chief rabbi of England, see his interview with Gladys Rosen (November 18, 1971), cited by Libowitz, *Mordecai M. Kaplan*, p. 215, n. 1. See also Ira Eisenstein, "Kaplan the Human Being," *Reconstructionist* 49, no. 7 (June 1984):19; Berkowitz, *Let Us Reason Together*, p. 71. Kaplan later claims, ironically, that he turned down an opportunity a few years later to be elected chief rabbi of England. See Mordecai Kaplan, "Solomon Schechter and Ethical Nationhood: A Personal Memoir," *Proceedings of the Rabbinical Assembly of America* 37 (1975):351.

In general, Kaplan's father was more easygoing than his mother. See Kaplan, "The Way," pp. 287–88:

> When I began attending public school in my twelfth year, I tried to get my parents to speak English at home. They, on the other hand, still planned to make a rabbi of me. There were times when I preferred playing with the boys in the street to studying the dialectics of the law of damages. Mother would then haul me back into the house, and when my reluctance persisted, Father would say to her, "Why do you force him to study? The worst that can happen to him is that he will have to sell newspapers for a living. If that's what he wants, let him be." That had more effect on me than Mother's insistence.

See also Mordecai Kaplan, "A Heart of Wisdom," *Reconstructionist* 17, no. 6 (May 4, 1951):10, where Kaplan refers to his having been raised by "an indulgent father and a strict mother." Kaplan's mother was very traditional and the Kaplan Archives contains several letters she wrote to her son expressing her great upset at his religious nonconformity. See also Kaplan, "How to Live Creatively," p. 93; and Carole S. Kessner, "Kaplan and the Role of Women in Judaism," in Emanuel S. Goldsmith, Mel Scult, and Robert M. Seltzer, eds., *The American Judaism of Mordecai Kaplan* (New York: New York University Press, 1990), pp. 336–37.

32. See Ira Eisenstein, "Mordecai M. Kaplan and His Teachers," in Ira Eisenstein and Eugene Kohn, eds., *Mordecai M. Kaplan: An Evaluation* (New York: Jewish Reconstructionist Foundation, 1952), p. 17. For more on Enrlich's influence on Kaplan, see Kaplan, "How To Live Creatively," p. 96.

33. On Sossnitz, see Hutchins Hapgood, *The Spirit of the Ghetto: Studies of the Jewish Quarter of New York* (New York: Funk and Wagnalls, 1902), pp. 65–66. For Sossnitz at the Uptown Talmud Torah, see Jeffrey S. Gurock, *When Harlem Was Jewish, 1870–1930* (New York: Columbia University Press, 1979), p. 98.

34. Israel Kaplan's behavior apparently never fully alienated him from the most Orthodox of colleagues downtown. Although he was a member of the chief rabbi's court from only 1888–1891, his departure from the court was, reportedly, unrelated to issues of acculturation or schooling. As his son told it, Israel Kaplan

was rather dismayed over "the rabbinic politics which centered around the exploitation of the Kashruth business." Moroever, before Rabbi Jacob Joseph's death in 1901, and long after Mordecai's removal from Etz Chaim, Israel Kaplan was "reconciled" with his former colleagues. In addition, for all his idiosyncratic ideas, Israel Kaplan very much wanted to communicate with his fellow Russian-American rabbis and they seemingly accepted him. He was an early member of the Agudath ha-Rabbanim (Union of Orthodox Rabbis of the United States and Canada), even if he did not totally share that organization's point of view. See Kaplan, "Journals," 1:258 (February 1, 1917), 4:217 (January 17, 1929), 24:248 (June 15, 1967). See also *Jubilee Volume of the Orthodox Agudat ha-Rabbanim of the United States and Canada* [Hebrew] (New York: Oriom, 1928), pp. 145–46. For Kaplan's negative recollections about his father's position as dayyan, see his "A Heart of Wisdom," p. 12.

Not incidentally, the veracity of the suggestion that the Kaplans were not critiqued for their apparently less than fully traditional positions is heightened by the fact that Mordecai Kaplan, writing long after he broke with Orthodoxy, never noted—neither in his diary nor in his published memoirs—problems of an ideological nature involving his father and the chief rabbi or the Orthodox establishment.

35. For information on Rabbi Hurwitz, see Bernard Drachman, *The Unfailing Light* (New York: Rabbinical Council of America, 1948), p. 259. See also Isaac Rosengarten, "Intimate Touches of Dr. Hurwitz," *Jewish Forum* 3, no. 2 (February 20, 1920):71.

36. Needless to say, the inability to create a cadre of youngsters trained and committed to the transplanted East European lifestyle was but one of the many failures of the chief rabbi's administration. For a comprehensive study of all the difficulties confronted by this attempt, see Karp, "New York Chooses a Chief Rabbi," pp. 129–98; and Gurock, *The Men and Women of Yeshiva*, pp. 15–16.

2. Training at the Seminary for the American Orthodox Rabbinate

1. On the processes and goals of the yeshiva in Eastern Europe, see Gedalyahu Alon, "The Lithuanian Yeshiva," trans. Sid Z. Leiman, in Judah Goldin, ed., *The Jewish Experience* (New York: Bantam, 1970), pp. 450–52. For a discussion of the courses and curriculum offered at the seminary and an enumeration of the faculty during its early years, see Robert E. Fierstien, *A Different Spirit: The Jewish Theological Seminary, 1886–1902* (New York: Jewish Theological Seminary of America, 1990), pp. 81–86. For the early years of the seminary, see Cyrus Adler, ed., *The Jewish Theological Seminary of America Semi-Centennial Volume* (New York: Jewish Theological Seminary of America, 1939); Herbert Rosenblum, "The Founding of the United Synagogue of America," Ph.D. diss., Brandeis University, 1970, pp. 9–91.

2. For a delineation and discussion of the background of the heterogeneous

group of rabbis who joined together in founding the Jewish Theological Seminary, see Jeffrey S. Gurock, "Resisters and Accommodators: Varieties of Orthodox Rabbis in America, 1886–1983," *American Jewish Archives* 35, no. 2 (November 1983):160–62 and nn. 2–6.

3. *Ha-Ivri* (September 17, 1897), p. 1a; (October 15, 1897), p. 1e, cited in Gilbert Klaperman, *The Story of Yeshiva University* (London: Macmillan, 1969), p. 40.

4. *Yiddishe Welt* (July 3, 1902), p. 4, cited in Klaperman, *The Story of Yeshiva University*, p. 42.

Joffe (b. 1862) came to the seminary as instructor of Talmud and librarian in 1892–1893. See *American Jewish Year Book 5665* (Philadelphia: Jewish Publication Society of America, 1904), pp. 125–26; and Fierstien, *A Different Spirit*, pp. 84, 87, 94. Joffe retired from the seminary in April 1917. See Adler, *The Jewish Theological Seminary*, p. 82.

5. J. D. Eisenstein, "The Establishment of the New Seminary" [Hebrew], in *New Yorker Yiddishe Zeitung* (1886), republished in Eisenstein's *Memoirs* [Hebrew] (New York: J. D. Eisenstein, 1929), p. 210.

6. For a useful biographical sketch of Eisenstein's early years in America, see Lloyd P. Gartner, "From New York to Miedzyrecz: Immigrant Letters of Judah David Eisenstein, 1878–1886," *American Jewish Historical Quarterly* (hereafter *AJHQ*) 52, no. 3 (March 1963):234–43. For Eisenstein's own early history of that downtown congregation, see his "The History of the First Russian-American Jewish Congregation: The Beth Hamedrosh Hagodol," *PAJHS* 9 (1901):63–74.

7. Eisenstein, "The Establishment of the New Seminary," pp. 206–11.

8. It is unclear from Eisenstein's rhetoric what he meant precisely by this phrase. One possibility, in keeping with rest of the sentence that describes "conservative faith" as including "even the most minor mitzvah of the commandments of the Torah," suggests that the term *conservative* is used as an adjective referring to what we might more properly call traditional Orthodox practice. However, it is noteworthy that in an earlier part of the essay, when he describes the nature of Orthodoxy in America, Eisenstein never used the word *conservative* in his description. The other possibility, of course, is that Eisenstein is referring to the same "Conservative" Judaism that he pilloried earlier in the essay. If such be the case, it suggests a certain degree of ambivalence toward Conservatism on Eisenstein's part and certainly points to him being tolerant of the seminary producing what we might call traditionally oriented Conservative rabbis. All told, Eisenstein's entire approach breathes not a word of difficulty with Orthodox young men attending the seminary.

9. Eisenstein, "The Establishment of the New Seminary," pp. 206–11. Whatever its weaknesses, Eisenstein displayed no fear that the seminary would ruin good Orthodox students. After all, as he explained elsewhere in his essay, were not modern seminaries basically "trade schools" that provided candidates with the practical skills of their profession, leaving them the choice of determining

what sort of rabbi they wanted to be? The key, of course, was that students not be misled by the wrong types of teachers. We may readily assume that Eisenstein would have told Kaplan to approach Joffe with care, but he would not have required him to avoid the experience of studying with him.

10. Mordecai Kaplan interview with the *Intermountain Jewish News* 63, no. 21 (May 21, 1976):28.

11. In his recent biography of Mordecai Kaplan, Mel Scult suggested, paren-thetically, that Kaplan's father once entertained the notion of sending him back to Eastern Europe for rabbinical training. However, Scult offers no source for his suggestion. See Mel Scult, *Judaism Faces the Twentieth Century: A Biography of Mordecai M. Kaplan* (Detroit: Wayne State University Press, 1994), p. 41.

12. See note 4 above, especially Fierstien, *A Different Spirit*, p. 87.

13. *American Hebrew* (November 24, 1899), p. 86, quoted in Fierstien, *A Different Spirit*, p. 126.

14. The sources cited earlier, chapter 1, note 26, indicate that Mordecai Kaplan attended the Machzike Talmud Torah before entering Etz Chaim.

15. *Yiddishes Tageblatt* (March 6, 1888), p. 1, referred to in Fierstien, *A Different Spirit*, p. 123, n. 24.

16. *Yiddishes Tageblatt* (December 2, 1896), pp. 2a–b, quoted in Klaperman, *The Story of Yeshiva University*, p. 197.

17. *Yiddishes Tageblatt* (November 17, 1901), 4b, (July 3, 1902), 4a, and (May 5, 1904), English page, quoted in Klaperman, *The Story of Yeshiva University*, p. 58.

18. For a listing of the members of the original board of trustees of the Jew-ish Theological Seminary Association, see "Certificate of Incorporation of the Jewish Theological Seminary Association," in Moshe Davis, *The Emergence of Con-servative Judaism: The Historical School in Nineteenth-Century America* (Philadelphia: Jewish Publication Society of America, 1965), pp. 386–87. For a historical description of Kehal Adath Jeshurun that includes a biography and evaluation of Jarmulowsky's role in the congregation, see Jeffrey S. Gurock, "A Stage in the Emergence of the Americanized Synagogue Among East European Jews, 1890–1910," *Journal of Amer-ican Ethnic History* 9, no. 2 (Spring 1990):169–85.

19. Jarmulowsky served as treasurer of that organization beginning in 1887. See Abraham J. Karp, "New York Chooses a Chief Rabbi," *PAJHS* 44, no. 3 (March 1955):189–93, especially pp. 189–90.

20. Another connection between this East European congregation and the seminary was the appointment, in the late 1880s, of the congregation's cantor, the Rev. P. Minkowski, as one of the instructors in *hazzanut* and "the conduct of syn-agogue services." See *Proceedings of the Second Biennial Convention of the Jewish Theological Seminary Association* (New York: Philip Cowen, 1890), p. 11.

21. For information on Levin, see "Certificate of Incorporation of the Associ-ation of the American Orthodox Hebrew Congregations," in Karp, "New York

Chooses a Chief Rabbi," pp. 189–90, and *Proceedings, 1890*, title page. It should be noted that among the nineteen trustees listed as members of the original JTS board, there was another individual with a Lower East Side address and possibly an East European name. If Newman Cowen of 207 Canal Street indeed fits that profile, then three members of that board were of downtown community extraction. See *Proceedings, 1890*, title page.

22. For a laudatory biography of Fischel that notes his many communal associations, see Herbert S. Goldstein, *Forty Years of Struggle for a Principle: The Biography of Harry Fischel* (New York: Bloch, 1928). See below for discussions of the Kaplan-Fischel relationship.

23. Germansky and a "S. Bernstein" of 89 Division Street are listed as "Subscribers" to JTS throughout most of the 1890s. See *Proceedings, 1890*, p. 68, and *Proceedings of the Sixth Biennial Convention of the Jewish Theological Seminary Association of America*, March 20, 1898 (New York: Philip Cowen, 1898), p. 55. This Germansky and a Moses Bernstein, also of 89 Division Street—very possibly the same person as S. Bernstein—are also listed as founders of RIETS. See "Certificate of Incorporation, Rabbi Isaac Elchanan Theological Seminary Association," in Klaperman, *The Story of Yeshiva University*, p. 244.

It is also possible that Jarmulowsky was not the only leader of Kehal Adath Jeshurun to actively support JTS. *Proceedings, 1898*, p. 55, lists an A. Feinberg of 36 Essex Street. Could he, in fact, be the Avrohom Feinberg noted in the minute books of the congregation from the 1890s through the 1910s as either a trustee, president, or gabbai? See the unpublished minute books of the Eldridge Street Synagogue, 1890–1916, passim. As far as rank-and-file downtown supporters are concerned, an informal survey of the names and addresses of the "Subscribers" or "Patrons" of JTS from 1890–1900 reveals that approximately one in six were of downtown addresses with East European-sounding names.

24. For the early history of RIETS, see Jeffrey S. Gurock, *The Men and Women of Yeshiva: Higher Education, Orthodoxy, and American Judaism* (New York: Columbia University Press, 1988), pp. 18–20.

25. Almost inexplicably, the association's most famous employee, the chief rabbi himself, was listed twice in JTS's *Proceedings* as a subscriber. See *Proceedings, 1890*, p. 58; *Proceedings of the Sixth Biennial Convention of the Jewish Theological Seminary Association of America* (New York: Philip Cowen, 1892), p. 50; noted first in Fierstien, *A Different Spirit*, p. 126. One possible explanation for Rabbi Jacob Joseph's clearly uncharacteristic move is that it was an act of gratitude toward seminary founders Rabbis H. P. Mendes and B. Drachman, who had significant influence over the owners of wholesale butcheries, for their assistance to the chief rabbi in his unending battles to regulate kashruth in New York. Unfortunately, the chief rabbi did not articulate the grounds for his linkage at that moment with that institution. See Karp, "New York Chooses a Chief Rabbi," p. 169.

26. Mordecai Kaplan, "Journals," 21:51 (November 25, 1961). See also Mordecai Kaplan, "The Way I Have Come," in Ira Eisenstein and Eugene Kohn, eds., *Mordecai M. Kaplan: An Evaluation* (New York: Jewish Reconstructionist Foundation, 1952), p. 288. For a picture of Kaplan's Bar Mitzvah invitation, where he is referred to as Max, see "A Pictorial Chronology: The Career of Rabbi Mordecai M. Kaplan," in Ronald A. Brauner, ed., *Jewish Civilization: Essays and Studies*, 3 vols. (Philadelphia: Reconstructionist Rabbinical College, 1981), 2:1. On Israel Kaplan's long-term relationship with the synagogue, see Kaplan, "Journals," 1:258 (February 1, 1917), 4:95 (October 15, 1928).

27. For a brief biography of Abelson, see Philip R. Alstat, "Rabbi Alter Abelson z"l," *Proceedings of the Rabbinical Assembly of America, Sixty-Fifth Annual Convention* (New York: Rabbinical Assembly, 1965), 29:139.

28. For a biographical sketch of Alexander Basel, see Max Drob, "Rabbi Alexander Basel," *Proceedings of the Rabbinical Assembly of America, Forty-Second Annual Convention* (New York: Antin, n.d.), 8:116–18. Additional information on Basel, Eichler, Speaker, Greenstone, and the some fifty-five other men who attended the old seminary (1887–1902) but did not always finish their studies, during the time Kaplan studied there is made very difficult by the absence of complete student files at JTS. Indeed, our very knowledge of most of their names is derived not from seminary records but from the *Proceedings* of the seminary association meetings between 1887–1902. In these published sources, students are listed by the class they are in (Preparatory, Junior, Senior, etc.). Through these reports we are able to trace the movement of a given student, like Greenstone, Eichler, or Speaker, through the school and ascertain when they were classmates of Kaplan. We might infer from the quick mobility of some students through the ranks that "advanced standing" may have been granted to older, yeshiva-trained students. As far as the birthplace, age, and previous schooling of seminary students of that era, we have to rely on the information they themselves provided the *American Jewish Year Book* (hereinafter *AJYB*) in its "Biographical Sketches of Rabbis and Cantors Officiating in the United States," published in 1903–1904 (5664) with additions in 1904–1905 (5665). Unfortunately, many of the respondents did not indicate which East European yeshiva they attended. Beyond the *AJYB*, we have sought to use necrologies printed by members of the Rabbinical Assembly of their late colleagues. But relatively few of these early seminary men were favored with such testimonials. For a contemporary compendium that relies on these sources and follows some of these rabbis throughout their careers, see Pamela S. Nadell, *Conservative Judaism in America: A Biographical Dictionary and Sourcebook* (New York: Greenwood, 1988).

29. Kaplan, "Journals," 12:30 (June 1, 1954), 19:228 (January 11, 1959).

30. Kaplan, "Journals," 5:181 (October 4, 1929), 15:59 (June 29, 1951), 21:73 (January 9, 1962). See also Kaplan's interview with the *Intermountain Jewish News* (note 10 above).

For other references in Kaplan's diaries to his classmate Kauvar, see "Journals," 5:189 (October 10, 1929), 7:57 (February 6, 1933), 9:131 (April 8, 1940), 18:188 (December 22, 1956), 21:231 (November 20, 1962).

31. See Kaplan, "Journals," 18:188–90 (December 22, 1956). For a reference to Abramowitz as Kaplan's classmate, see "Journals," 7:69 (January 1, 1936). On Kaplan's relationship with Solomon, see "Journals," 18:188–90 (December 22, 1956). For Kaplan's relationship with and thoughts about Israeli, see "Journals," 1:261–62 (February 2, 1917).

32. For this aspect of Israeli's later relationship with Kaplan, see chapter 4.

33. Kaplan, "Journals," 5:181 (October 4, 1929), 6:97 (May 9, 1931), 18:188 (December 22, 1956), 19:232 (January 14, 1959). Kaplan received his M.A. from Columbia in 1902.

34. Kaplan, "Journals," 19:232 (January 14, 1959).

35. Kaplan, "Journals," 10:227 (December 2, 1941), 18:188–90 (December 22, 1956), 19:232 (January 14, 1959).

36. Both Kaplan's memoir sketches and journal entries on the subject of his education at JTS, composed and written intermittently over several decades, consistently depict him as unhappy with the level of traditional learning offered to him at the seminary. If anything, in all the sources, Kaplan projected himself as a budding student of the Talmud, and uniquely so within his closest circle of seminary colleagues, whose progress was stymied by poor instruction. Of course, it is impossible to ascertain for certain the quality of Joffe's pedagogy. And, as far as Kaplan's views of where he stood as a talmudic scholar in comparison with others in his class, we know that he won prizes for excellence in his studies, but we cannot gauge how well his friends compared to him. In any event, it appears that while Kaplan may have been somewhat hyperbolic about his own classmates, even as he was characteristically acerbic and dismissive about their abilities, it is perfectly conceivable that the young Kaplan had a penchant for talmudic studies that was not sufficiently addressed at JTS. In other words, it is possible that, shortly before his bar mitzvah, when he came to the seminary, his greatest Jewish educational interests did not center around the wider worlds of modern Jewish disciplines his parents hoped would enable him to be an effective rabbi but with the traditional study of Talmud that he had learned at Etz Chaim and from his father. Unfortunately, it is not possible to specify a point in time when Talmud study became less important and other disciplines emerged as his greatest interest. Indeed, as we will see in chapter 3, it is, likewise, not easy to determine at what precise moment—during or after his days at JTS—Kaplan began to have questions about his Orthodoxy.

37. William Berkowitz, *Let Us Reason Together* (New York: Crown, 1970), p. 72. See also Kaplan, "Journals," 18:189 (December 22, 1956); Mordecai Kaplan, "The Influences That Have Shaped My Life," *Reconstructionist* 8, no. 10 (June 26,

1942):29; Stephen H. Pinsky, "The Society for the Advancement of Judaism (1922–1945)," master's thesis, Hebrew Union College-Jewish Institute for Religion, 1971, p. 9. Indeed, the entrance requirements for the preparatory department of the seminary were not rigorous at all. See *American Hebrew* 29, no. 2 (November 19, 1886):9 and 36, no. 4 (August 31, 1888):8.

38. Kaplan, "Journals," 13:99 (December 31, 1944). See also the Kaplan interview with the *Intermountain Jewish News*, 24; "Journals," 1:293 (April 29, 1917), 3:162 (August 9, 1926), 3:261–62 (December 15, 1927).

39. Kaplan, "Journals," 13:99 (December 31, 1944). For Kaplan's attitudes toward Joffe, see "Journals," 3:162 (August 9, 1926), 18:188–90 (December 22, 1956). For Kaplan's overall negative assessment of his JTS experience, see Kaplan, " The Influences," p. 29; Kaplan, "The Way I Have Come," p. 289.

Notwithstanding Kaplan's harsh views of Joffe's abilities, the young rabbinical student was not put off from asking his teacher to help him secure his first pulpit appointment in 1902. Indeed, it may well have been a somewhat disingenuous Kaplan who, in the salutation of a letter to a man whose "efforts on my behalf have already begun to show results," closed with, "Your loving pupil." See Kaplan to Dr. Joffe, November 26, 1903; MKA.

40. C. Kauvar, "Joshua A. Joffe," *Proceedings of the Rabbinical Assembly of America, Thirty-Sixth Annual Convention* (New York: Rabbinical Assembly of America, 1939), 5:275.

41. There is a variance in Kaplan's own writings as to the nature of the teachings offered him by Sossnitz. The diary indicates, as we have noted in the text, that Sossnitz was hired to supplement the seminary's studies. See Kaplan, "Journals," 14:157 (October 16, 1948); and Kaplan, "The Way I Have Come," p. 290. In "The Influences," p. 30, Kaplan credits Sossnitz as being one of the teachers who contributed to his "intellectual and spiritual development." Sossnitz, as this Kaplan reminiscence tells it, taught him "to synthesize the spirit of religion with that of science and to become aware of ethics as the indispensible prerequisite to worship." What is suggested here is that Sossnitz performed several functions for the Kaplan family. He supplemented young Mordecai's talmudic studies, taught him philosophy, and served as an intellectual antidote to Ehrlich. However, we do not know precisely when Sossnitz worked with Kaplan during the latter's period of study at JTS and whether Sossnitz performed the multiple functions mentioned in the sources at the same time or in different periods. Finally, it is not clear even from the statement in "The Influences," whether Kaplan is suggesting that Sossnitz moved him along the road out of Orthodoxy. See also chapter 3, note 3.

42. Kaplan, "Journals," 3:162 (August 9, 1926), 3:261 (December 15, 1927).

43. Kaplan, "Journals," 18:189 (December 22, 1956).

44. Kaplan, "Journals," 18:188–90. For Drachman's outspokenness against Kaplan in the 1920s, see chapters 5 and 6 in this volume.

It should be noted, using Kaplan as a source, that, as time went on, Drachman undoubtedly came to look more appreciatively at his student's qualities of mind and commitment even as Kaplan undeniably became more Americanized in speech and manner. It was Drachman, according to Kaplan, who recommended him for his first pulpit job at age nineteen when this teacher of his apparently argued that Kaplan had talent beyond his years. Kaplan recorded this event in his diary without comment or retrospective thanks to his former professor. See Kaplan, "Journals," 23:289 (September 26, 1966). Equally important, years later—long after the two had split on more compelling and enduring theological questions—Drachman would recall his early experiences with the young Kaplan in the most positive terms. As a seminary neophyte, he described his students as part of "a splendid group of . . . [early seminary] students, not very numerous, but of outstanding quality . . . almost entirely of European birth . . . [who] would become in later years respected and valued leaders of Jewish congregations." Abramowitz, Kauvar, Eichler, Greenstone, and Solomon were also recalled so favorably by their teacher. See Bernard Drachman, *The Unfailing Light* (New York: Rabbinical Council of America, 1948), p. 184. For his part, however, Kaplan never reevaluated and mellowed in his negative thoughts about Drachman.

45. For a discussion of such efforts on the part of Kehal Adath Jeshurun, including the issues of cantors, itinerant preachers, decorum, and the like, see Gurock, "A Stage," pp. 22–25.

46. Drachman, *The Unfailing Light*, pp. 225–26.

47. On the history of the Endeavorers and Drachman's involvement with them, including some discussion of the nature of their services, see Jeffrey S. Gurock, " The Jewish Endeavor Society (JES)," in Michael N. Dobkowski, ed., *Jewish American Voluntary Organizations* (New York: Greenwood, 1986), pp. 228–31; Jeffrey S. Gurock, "From Exception to Role Model: Bernard Drachman and the Evolution of Jewish Religious Life in America, 1880–1920," *American Jewish History* 76, no. 4 (June 1987):456–84. For references to Kaplan's involvement with the society, see "Prospectus of Lectures Offered to the Public by the Jewish Endeavor Society, 1900–1901, 1902–1903," Library of the American Jewish Historical Society. See also Kaplan, "Journals," 15:159 (June 29, 1951), where Kaplan wrote that "in my 19th year I took part in organizing the Jewish Endeavor Society which my fellow students hoped would become the replica of the Christian Endeavor Society."

48. On the founding of the Orthodox Union, see Gurock, "From Exception to Role Model," p. 475 and n. 39. See also Jeffrey S. Gurock, "Why Albert Lucas Did Not Serve in the New York Kehillah," *Proceedings of the American Academy for Jewish Research* 51 (1983): 55–56 for information on the background of Orthodox Union leaders.

49. Kaplan, "Journals," 15:61 (September 17, 1950). The Endeavorers also had

difficulties with downtown itinerant preachers, who competed with them for space in downtown synagogues. See Gurock, "From Exception to Role Model," p. 480, n. 48.

3. Promoting American Orthodoxy While Beset by Doubts in a Yorkville Pulpit

1. For an identification of the multiplicty of ideas and thinkers that impacted upon Kaplan during his school days and formed his heretical worldview, see Mel Scult, *Judaism Faces the Twentieth Century: A Biography of Mordecai M. Kaplan* (Detroit: Wayne State University Press, 1994), pp. 77–87; see also note 7 below.

2. Mordecai Kaplan, "The Way I Have Come," in Ira Eisenstein and Eugene Kohn, eds., *Mordecai M. Kaplan: An Evaluation* (New York: Jewish Reconstructionist Foundation, 1952), pp. 289–90.

3. Mordecai Kaplan, "The Influences That Have Shaped My Life," *Reconstructionist* 8, no. 10 (June 26, 1942):30–31; Mordecai Kaplan, "A Heart of Wisdom," *Reconstructionist* 17, no. 6 (May 4, 1951):13. Since both the 1951 and 1952 sources mention Kaplan's reading of medieval Jewish philosophical writings as either being useless in stopping his defection from Orthodoxy or, alternately, as having had the power of temporarily solving his theological problems, one must consider again (see above chapter 2, note 41) the function Rabbi Sossnitz played in Kaplan's theological development. To be sure, one account, noted in the previous chapter, has Sossnitz teaching Kaplan some philosophy as a supplement to tutoring him in Talmud. Another source, already discussed as well, has him studying with Kaplan as a balance to Ehrlich's influence, although, in that latter account, there is no mention of a curriculum per se. Here, in Kaplan's memoirs, the mention of his study of medieval Jewish philosophy makes us wonder whether he studied it within his seminary classrooms or, rather, at the feet of Rabbi Sossnitz. If the latter possibility is really the case, then it is conceivable that Sossnitz was himself not only hired to help Kaplan with Talmud but also as a medium through which the Kaplan elders hoped to bring their wavering son back to tradition. Unfortunately, all these references to Sossnitz and the study of philosophy are not synchronized chronologically, making it difficult to ascertain when he was actually engaged to work with Kaplan. We will also presently see that a similar problem exists with reference to when precisely Ehrlich's influence impacted on Kaplan.

4. Mordecai Kaplan, "Preface," *Judaism as a Civilization* (New York: Macmillan, 1934), p. xiv.

5. Kaplan, "The Way I Have Come," p. 31.

6. Mordecai Kaplan, "Journals," 18:232–33 (March 19, 1957).

7. M. Kaplan, "A Founding Father Recounts," *Alumni Association Bulletin*, Teachers Institute and Seminary College of Jewish Studies, Jewish Theological Seminary of America (1959), p. 6; Kaplan, "Journals," 19:254 (February 7, 1959). Once

again, Kaplan's memoir account does not note precisely when Ehrlich's influence turned his worldview around.

Kaplan elaborated on the significance of Matthew Arnold's work for his changing conception of the Bible and Judaism in "The Way I Have Come," pp. 296–99. For an analysis of the impact of Kaplan's "post-graduate studies in philosophy, sociology and education," especially the influence of the works of Emile Durkheim, William James and John Dewey, as well as those of Matthew Arnold and Ahad Ha-Am, see Ira Eisenstein, "Mordecai M. Kaplan and His Teachers," in Ira Eisenstein and Eugene Kohn, eds., *Mordecai M. Kaplan: An Evaluation* (New York: Jewish Reconstructionist Foundation, 1952), pp. 17–25; Richard Libowitz, *Mordecai M. Kaplan and the Development of Reconstructionism* (New York and Toronto: Mellen, 1983), pp. 17–54; Allan Lazaroff, "Kaplan and John Dewey," pp. 173–96, and Meir Ben-Horin, "Ahad Ha-Am in Kaplan: Roads Crossing and Parting," pp. 221–33, both in Emanuel S. Goldsmith, Mel Scult, and Robert M. Seltzer, eds., *The American Judaism of Mordecai Kaplan* (New York: New York University Press, 1990).

8. Mordecai Kaplan, "Response," *Proceedings of the Rabbinical Assembly of America* 15 (1952), pp. 216–17.

9. For the earliest examples of Kaplan's questionings, see "Communings with the Spirit," October 24, 1904, December 7, 1904, December 20, 1904, March 16, 1905, May 7, 1905, August 1, 1905, August 17, 1905, and August 23, 1905. On December 7, 1904, he wrote of "purging the Shulchan Aruch [Code of Jewish Law] of Orthodoxy's antiquated legal religion." This handwritten notebook is in MKA.

10. See Kaplan, "Untitled Diary," May 11, 1906, pp. 4–5; see also "Untitled Diary," May 9, 1906, p. 4, MKA.

11. Ibid., March 17, 1907, pp. 49–51. See also ibid., May 8, 1906, pp. 1–3; December 5, 1906, pp. 23–26; December 10, 1906, p. 31; December 31, 1906, p. 45; n.d., p. 60. For terminology that will become significant for Kaplan some fifteen to twenty years later, see ibid., November 23, 1906, p. 10: "The great problem for us Jews therefore is how to *reconstruct* (emphasis added) our past experience"; May 23, 1907, p. 55: "The Jews were to *reconstruct* their past history and their future course in the world in the light of absolute truth"; December 8, 1904: "a Theology of *Reconstructionion*"; March 24, 1905: "a '*renaissance*' in Judaism"; November 24, 1907: "Judaism *Reconstructed*." See also "Communings with the Spirit," October 24, 1904, December 7, 1904.

12. Kaplan, "Untitled Diary," March 17, 1907, pp. 49–50.

13. Kaplan, "Communings with the Spirit," August 23, 1905.

14. Ibid., August 1, 1905.

15. Ibid., August 17, 1905.

16. Ibid., August 23, 1905.

17. Ibid., May 7, 1905.

18. Kaplan, "Untitled Diary," May 23, 1907, pp. 55–56.

19. It would be useful to determine at what point, before 1907, Kaplan's parents knew of their son's deep disaffection from Orthodoxy. Such an understanding would help us delineate Rabbi Sossnitz's role and permit us to comprehensively describe the reaction to Kaplan from that element of downtown Orthodoxy closest to him, his parents. Unfortunately, we have no sources other than the reference in "Communings with the Spirit" from May 23, 1907, which indicates that Kaplan's parents knew of his thoughts and hoped he would change them.

20. See note 13 above.

21. This quotation, which appeared in "The Advance of Orthodox Judaism," *Hebrew Standard* (June 14, 1907), p. 8, and was first cited in Jenna W. Joselit, "Modern Orthodox Jews and the Ordeal of Civility," *American Jewish History* 84, no. 2 (December 1984):137, n. 22, did not refer specifically to Kehilath Jeshurun but rather to the style of Orthodoxy that, as we will presently see, obtained in a number of Yorkville congregations at the turn of the century.

22. For a brief discussion of migration patterns of Germans from the Lower East Side to Yorkville in the 1870s–1880s, see Stanley Nadel, *Little Germany: Ethnicity, Religion, and Class in New York City, 1845–1880* (Urbana and Chicago: University of Illinois Press, 1990), pp. 161–62.

23. Moses Weinberger, *People Walk on Their Heads: Moses Weinberger's "Jews and Judaism in New York"*, trans. Jonathan D. Sarna (New York: Holmes and Meier, 1982), p. 116. See also *Congregation Orach Chaim Centennial Journal* (New York, 1980), n.p.

24. Joseph H. Lookstein, "Seventy-Five Yesteryears: A Historic Sketch of Kehilath Jeshurun," *Congregation Kehilath Jeshurun Diamond Jubilee, 1872–1946* (New York, 1946), pp. 17, 20–22; "We Remember: Saga of the Baum-Webster Family Tree, 1842–1964," manuscript; document provided courtesy of Rabbi Haskel Lookstein. See also Jenna W. Joselit, *New York's Jewish Jews* (Bloomington: Indiana University Press, 1990), pp. 25–28, 87.

25. Bernard Drachman, *The Unfailing Light* (New York: Rabbinical Council of America, 1948), pp. 197–200.

26. Ibid., 208–9.

27. Kaplan, "Journals," 1:109–10 (October 25, 1914), 16:5–6 (June 20, 1952), 19:253 (February 7, 1959); Mordecai Kaplan, "A Founding Father Recounts," *Alumni Association Bulletin*, Teachers Institute and Seminary College of Jewish Studies, Jewish Theological Seminary of America (1959), p. 5; Lookstein, "Seventy-Five Yesteryears," p. 24; Drachman, *The Unfailing Light*, p. 213. Meyer Jarmulowsky is listed in the centennial journal of Orach Chaim as an officer in 1913.

The cornerstone of Kehilath Jeshurun was laid on May 4, 1902. See *American*

Hebrew 70:25 (May 9, 1902):750; *Hebrew Standard* 43:19 (May 9, 1902):1 (including an artist's rendition of the new building). The last meeting of the board of trustees at the old building took place on March 1, 1903, the first meeting at the new building taking place on March 29, 1903, a few weeks later. See "Minutes of the Members and Board of Trustees Meetings of the Congregation Kehilath Jeshurun, 1903 to 1927" (hereafter "KJ Minutes"), pp. 5, 8, found in the synagogue's archives.

28. Kaplan, "Journals," 1:109 (October 25, 1914), 19:253 (February 7, 1959); Kaplan, "A Founding Father Recounts," p. 5; Mel Scult, "Controversial Beginnings: Kaplan's First Congregation," *Reconstructionist* 50, no. 8 (July-August 1985):21; Joselit, *New York's Jewish Jews*, pp. 29–30; letter from M. Kaplan to Aaron I. Reichel, November 28, 1976. Our thanks to Aaron Reichel for making this letter available to us.

29. The *1903 By-Laws of the Cong. Kehilath Jeshurun* were printed in a separate pamphlet. See article 13, section 4, p. 13. Copies are found in the synagogue's archives. See also "KJ Minutes," April 6, 1903, p. 9. This requirement of application, however, was not included in the bylaws.

30. "KJ Minutes," April 15, 1903, pp. 10–12. A motion to reelect the cantor was also defeated, this time by a vote of nineteen to eighteen. Joseph Lookstein was being charitable when he wrote that "Rabbi Peikes resigned." See his "Seventy-Five Yesteryears," p. 24.

Rabbi Peikes did not leave the scene without difficulty. At the December 7, 1903 trustee meeting, it was "moved and seconded that a letter be sent to Dr Peikes asking him to refrain from interfering in our synagogue matters." See "KJ Minutes," December 7, 1903, p. 29. Nevertheless, eight days later Peikes was invited to the banquet celebrating the completion of the new building and he delivered an address at that event, which took place on December 20. "KJ Minutes," December 15, 1903, p. 30, and December 20, 1903, p. 31. See also note 43 below.

31. "KJ Minutes," April 27, 1903, pp. 13–14.

32. Ibid., April 20, 1903, p. 12.

Dr. Asher (born in Manchester, England in 1872) joined the seminary faculty shortly after Solomon Schechter arrived there in 1902. See *American Hebrew* 71, no. 24 (October 31, 1902):674; *American Jewish Year Book 5664* (Philadelphia: Jewish Publication Society of America, 1903), p. 42; Cyrus Adler, ed., *The Jewish Theological Seminary of America Semi-Centennial Volume* (New York: Jewish Theological Seminary of America, 1939), p. 79. He served as rabbi of New York's Congregation B'nai Jeshurun from 1901–1906 and then, when the congregation wanted to deviate from the traditional ritual, left to serve as rabbi of Congregation Orach Chaim. See Israel Goldstein, *A Century of Judaism in New York: B'nai Jeshurun, 1825–1925* (New York: Congregation B'nai Jeshurun, 1930), pp. 223–26. Asher was a featured speaker at the cornerstone-laying ceremony of Kehilath Jeshurun's new building on May 4, 1902. See *American Hebrew* 70, no. 24 (May 2, 1902):724; *American Hebrew* 70, no. 25 (May 9, 1902):750; *Hebrew Standard* 43, no. 19 (May 9, 1902):4.

33. For a brief discussion of the phenomenon of itinerant rabbis, some of whom were, in fact, possessed of no rabbinical training, see Jeffrey S. Gurock, "Resisters and Accommodators: Varieties of Orthodox Rabbis in America, 1886–1983," *American Jewish Archives* 35, no. 2 (November 1983):111. There is no extant data on Brande as an American rabbi.

34. "KJ Minutes," April 20, 1903, p. 12, May 4, 1903, p. 16, May 26, 1903, p. 17, September 9, 1903, p. 23.

35. "KJ Minutes," June 15, 1903, p. 19, September 9, 1903, p. 23, October 19, 1903, p. 25. For brief biographical data on Levine, see *American Jewish Year Book 5665* (Philadelphia: Jewish Publication Society of America, 1904), p. 220.

36. For mentions of Kaplan's name in the Anglo-Jewish press, see *American Hebrew* 68, no. 5 (December 21, 1900):818; *American Hebrew* 68, no. 8 (January 11, 1901):264; *American Hebrew* 68, no. 18 (March 22, 1901):546; *American Hebrew* 68, no. 19 (March 29, 1901):577; *American Hebrew* 68, no. 20 (April 5, 1901):606; *American Hebrew* 70, no. 5 (December 20, 1901):170; *American Hebrew* 70, no. 8 (January 10, 1902):251; *American Hebrew* 70, no. 11 (January 31, 1902):343; *American Hebrew* 70, no. 15 (March 1, 1902):465; *American Hebrew* 70, no. 16 (March 7, 1902):491; *American Hebrew* 70, no. 16 (March 14, 1902):521; *American Hebrew* 70, no. 18 (March 21, 1902):546; *American Hebrew* 70, no. 23 (April 25, 1902):698. For Kaplan's account of Davis's daughter's activities, see Kaplan, "Journals," 18:165 (October 27, 1956). See Kaplan, "Journals," 5:63 (July 1, 1929) for Kaplan's embarrassment arising from memorizing a sermon as a student.

37. Kaplan, "Journals," 19:28 (December 15, 1957). The contrast may be drawn to the topics of historical or sociological nature that lecturers often gave to Jewish Endeavorer Society groups. See also Kaplan, "The Way I Have Come," p. 292, for a fuller description of this sermon.

38. See above for our discussion of the Bachrach family. Kaplan's journals also include a reference to the Hutkoff family moving up from the Lower East Side and Kehal Adath Jeshurun and affiliating with Kehilath Jeshurun. Nochum Hutkoff, who was president of the downtown synagogue in the first years of this century, moved uptown somewhat later. See Kaplan, "Journals," 1:110 (October 28, 1914).

39. See Philip Cowen, *Memories of an American Jew* (New York: International, 1932), pp. 104–6. Kaplan's name (spelled *Kaplin*) is found in the list of teachers of the first page of the Polonies School roll books of 1900–1901 and 1901–1902. In the 1903–1904 roll book (the 1902–1903 one is missing), his name appears but is crossed out. Presumably he began the school year on the school's staff ("sessions commenced October 18th") but resigned when he was elected superintendent of Kehilath Jeshurun's religious school in November (see below). Our thanks to

Rabbi Marc Angel of Congregation Shearith Israel and to the congregation's archivist, Ms. Susan Tobin, for their assistance. See also Libowitz, *Mordecai M. Kaplan*, p. 216, n. 11.

40. "KJ Minutes," November 24, 1903, p. 28, November 25, 1903, p. 28. Kaplan recorded in his journal that he was invited by the synagogue in 1903–1904 "to organize its religious school and to preach occasionally." Kaplan, "Journals," 1:65 (August 23, 1914). Elsewhere, he was more precise and wrote that "in the fall of 1903, I was given charge of the school at Kehilath Jeshurun and had to preach once a month." Kaplan, "Journals," 9:131 (April 8, 1940). See also Kaplan, "Journals," 19:28 (December 15, 1957): "I was appointed head of the Hebrew School which I was to organize and required to preach once a month." See also Kaplan, "A Founding Father Recounts," p. 5: "Having been found acceptable, I was asked to wait for formal election till the following *Hol-ha-Moed Pesah*, when the congregation would hold its annual meeting. In the meantime I was to organize their first religious school and to preach once a month."

41. "KJ Minutes," January 4, 1904, p. 32, February 1, 1904, p. 34. See also Kaplan's letter to Moses Davis, April 3, 1904, Archives of Congregation Kehilath Jeshurun.

42. "KJ Minutes," April 3, 1904, p. 37. See also Kaplan, "Journals," 27:20 (November 28, 1976); *American Jewish Year Book 5665*, p. 219. Cf. Kaplan, "Journals," 11:294 (November 24, 1942) and 16:6 (June 20, 1952) where Kaplan erroneously writes that he already became minister in 1903. The fact is that while he was appointed superintendent of Kehilath Jeshurun's religious school and was asked to preach occasionally in November of 1903, he was not formally elected minister until April of the following year.

43. It should be noted that the reverend continued to be formally affiliated with the congregation. In September 1903 it decided to invite Peikes to deliver a traditional sermon on the Saturday afternoon between Rosh Hashanah and Yom Kippur (Shabbat Shuvah). See "KJ Minutes," July 1, 1903, p. 20.

44. Kaplan to Moses Davis, April 3, 1904, Archives of Congregation Kehilath Jeshurun.

45. Kaplan, "Journals," 18:165 (October 27, 1956).

46. M. Kaplan to Dr. Joffe, November 26, 1903, MKA.

47. For the beginnings of the Agudath ha-Rabbanim and its connection with Rabbi Jacob Joseph, see Gurock, "Resisters and Accommodators," p. 20.

48. See *American Hebrew* 75, no. 5 (June 17, 1904):130; *American Hebrew* 75, no. 7 (July 1, 1904):174, 180. For a discussion of the evolution of the ideas of Conservative Judaism at the seminary during the early years of this century, see Herbert Parzen, *Architects of Conservative Judaism* (New York: Jonathan David, 1964), pp. 26–78.

49. *American Hebrew* 75, no. 4 (June 17, 1904):130. See also Kaplan, "Journals," 3:126 (March 10, 1926).

50. For references to Kaplan's thinking that the Agudath ha-Rabbanim's campaign was focused against him and that his designation as minister was a result of that campaign, see Kaplan, "Journals," 2:96 (August 31, 1922), 3:126 (March 10, 1926), 11:294 (November 24, 1942), 19:28 (December 15, 1957), 23:240 (April 24, 1966), 27:20–21 (November 28, 1976). Yet, in these journal entries written at different moments in Kaplan's life, different versions of the minister story appear. In the 1926 account Kaplan wrote: "the old man [Levinthal] who then headed the Agudath Harrabonim issued a 'herem' against seminary graduates being taken as rabbis by Orthodox Congregations. I was the occasion of that herem. It was shortly *after I had been engaged as minister* at the 85th St. Congregation" (emphasis added). In the 1957 version Kaplan wrote that "the congregation took fright and elected me minister, with the understanding that I would be given the title rabbi when I would obtain hatarath-horaah from a recognized Orthodox rav," indicating that the Levinthal campaign was a significant factor in his originally being designated only as "minister." Kaplan also tells the story in his "A Founding Father Recounts," p. 5, where he adds, "The trustees of the congregation took fright and asked me to consent to function under the title of 'Minister,' which was considered good enough in Britain for graduates of Jews' College in London." It should also be noted that, in 1951, Kaplan credited Kehilath Jeshurun, "which braved the anathema of the Union of Orthodox Rabbis by calling me to its pulpit while I was in my early twenties." See Mordecai Kaplan, "A Heart of Wisdom," *Reconstructionist* 17, no. 6 (May 4, 1951):10. Here, of course, Levinthal's influence was not mentioned by name. The common factor in all these accounts and also in his other references to the Agudath ha-Rabbanim was Kaplan's antipathy toward those rabbis. That may have moved him to attribute his designation as minister to Levinthal's actions.

51. *American Hebrew* 75, no. 21 (October 7, 1904):549.

52. Aaron Rothkoff, "The American Sojourns of Ridbaz: Religious Problems Within the Immigrant Community," *AJHQ* 57, no. 4 (1968):560. For more information about the Ridbaz, also known as the Slutzker Rav, see Ze'ev Kaplan, *Edut bi-Ya'akov* (Warsaw, 1904); J. D. Eisenstein, *Memoirs* [Hebrew] (New York: J. D. Eisenstein, 1929), pp. 107–8, 356–58; Rothkoff, "The American Sojourns," pp. 557–72; Abraham J. Karp, "The Ridwas: Rabbi Jacob David Wilowsky, 1845–1913," *Perspectives on Jews and Judaism: Essays in Honor of Wolfe Kelman* (New York: Rabbinical Assembly, 1978), pp. 215–37, reprinted in Leo Jung, ed., *Sages and Saints* (Hoboken: Ktav, 1987), pp. 157–79; *Encyclopaedia Judaica*, 16 vols. (Jerusalem: Keter, 1972), 16:518–19. See, most recently, Ridbaz, *The Responsa of Ridbaz* [Hebrew] (Jerusalem: Mosad Harav Kook, 1995) and the biographical sketch by Bezalel Landau in that volume, pp. 5–34.

Regarding the Ridbaz's publishing project, Kaplan wrote, in a letter to Aaron I. Reichel dated November 28, 1976, that "the members of Kehilath Jeshurun happened to be the only Jews in New York who were both learned and rich enough to purchase his commentary. He therefore applied to them first of all."

53. The Ridbaz had already made his opposition to English sermons clear in the introduction to the second volume of his *She'elot u-Teshuvot Bet Ridbaz*, which he later printed (1908) in Jerusalem. In the autobiographical introduction to that work, p. 11, he bemoaned the current state of American Jewry and, in particular, attacked rabbis who delivered sermons in English. Rothkoff, "The American Sojourns," pp. 561–62, wrongly attributes this passage to Ridbaz's first visit to America in 1900–1901. It is clearly related to his second visit in 1903–1905 and is obviously a reference to his experience with Kaplan at Kehilath Jeshurun.

In general, Ridbaz railed against Jewish life in America. At a convention of the recently founded Union of Orthodox Congregations at the turn of the century, he deplored the state of Judaism in this country: "He exclaimed that whoever comes to America is Poshé Yisrael [a sinner in Israel], for here, Judaism, the Torah Shel [*sic*] Bal Pe [the Oral Law], is trodden under foot." See *American Hebrew* 68, no. 7 (January 4, 1901):236.

54. "KJ Minutes," October 3, 1904, p. 47. See also Mordecai Kaplan to Aaron I. Reichel, November 28, 1976: "When I learned what happened, I made it a point to mimeograph letters trying to convince them that preaching in English was in keeping with authoritative Rabbinic Talmudic teaching." For a text of Kaplan's letter to the congregation, see "To the Members of Congregation Kehilath Jeshurun," Ellul 29, 5664 [1904], Faculty Files, JTS Archives. See also *American Hebrew* 75, no. 20 (September 30, 1904):516; *American Hebrew* 75, no. 21 (October 7, 1904):543, 549; Kaplan, "Journals," 11:294 (November 24, 1942), 4:218 (January 17, 1929), 5:181 (October 4, 1929), where Kaplan refers to his "unpleasantness" with the Ridbaz. Also, when he wanted an example of an ultratraditionalist, Kaplan referred to the Slutzker Rav on more than one occasion. See, for example, Kaplan, "Untitled Diary," December 2, 1906, p. 18, December 4, 1906, p. 22.

55. *American Hebrew* 76, no. 2 (December 9, 1904):93; Kaplan, "Journals," 4:218 (January 17, 1929). See also *American Hebrew* 75, no. 28 (November 25, 1904):750.

56. *American Hebrew*, 76, no. 5 (December 30, 1904):192–93. See too Joselit, *New York's Jewish Jews*, pp. 30–31.

57. "KJ Minutes," September 7, 1904, p. 46; Kaplan, "The Influences," p. 30. For biographical sketches of Ramaz, see Gurock, "Resisters and Accommodators," p. 122, and Joselit, *New York's Jewish Jews*, pp. 62–63, 91.

58. "KJ Minutes," September 7, 1904, p. 46, September 25, 1905, p. 63, October 31, 1905, p. 64, November 15, 1905, p. 65, December 26, 1905, p. 66; Kaplan, "Journals," 17:21 (November 28, 1976). A *hadran* is the ritual formula recited upon the completion of a talmudic tractate. In his letter to Aaron I. Reichel, November 28, 1976, Kaplan wrote, "While I was teaching the Mishnah group, Ramaz was on the other side of the Ark studying the book (?) of the Talmud by himself." For

references to Ramaz as Kaplan's associate, see, e.g., "KJ Minutes," September 25, 1905, p. 63, October 31, 1905, p. 64, November 15, 1905, p. 65. See also Kaplan, "Journals," 11:286 (June 18, 1963).

59. "KJ Minutes," April 14, 1906, p. 71 and April 2, 1907, pp. 93–94.

60. In his "Journals," 11:294 (November 24, 1942), Kaplan explicitly noted that "the Slutzker rabbi *Ridbaz* was agitating for the late Rabbi M. Z. Margolies to have him elected as rabbi of the congregation." In Kaplan, "Journals," 27:20 (November 28, 1976), Kaplan went even further and wrote that the Ridbaz recommended Ramaz "as Rabbi of Congregation Kehilath Jeshurun instead of me." Whatever were Ridbaz's intentions and role in the Ramaz appointment, the congregational record clearly shows that he was never intended to replace Kaplan.

61. Kaplan to Aaron Reichel, November 28, 1976.

62. For a further discussion of Margolies's support for Americanization activities, see Gurock, "Resisters and Accommodators," pp. 30–37.

63. On one occasion Ramaz and Kaplan addressed the congregation together to raise money on behalf of the victims of the San Francisco earthquake in May 1906 and, on another, Ramaz readily accepted the communal call with Kaplan to "unite with other ministers and protest against the College of the City of New York for having the students who did not attend to their studies during the High Holidays [of 1906] fined 10 points." See Kaplan, "Journals," 17:191 (July 20, 1955); "KJ Minutes," May 2, 1906, p. 74, October 30, 1906, p. 81.

64. Kaplan, "Journals," 18:49 (May 8, 1956).

65. "Remarks of Harry Fischel on the Fortieth Anniversary of His Membership in Congregation Kehilath Jeshurun," "KJ Minutes," April 25, 1944, cited in J. Joselit, "Of Manners, Morals, and Orthodox Judaism: Decorum Within the Orthodox Synagogue," in Jeffrey S. Gurock, ed., *Ramaz: School, Community, Scholarship and Orthodoxy* (Hoboken: Ktav, 1989), pp. 29–30 and 37–38, n. 53. The question of how much English might be used in the American Orthodox services was an issue of discussion during this time period within and without JES circles.

66. "KJ Minutes," May 2, 1904, pp. 39–40, September 18, 1905, p. 61, October 30, 1906, p. 80, November 27, 1906, pp. 83–84; Joselit, *New York's Jewish Jews*, p. 42.

67. "KJ Minutes," December 3, 1906, p. 85. A copy of the committee's report is appended to page 85 of the "KJ Minutes."

However, the problem of decorum was still not fully resolved. See "KJ Minutes," March 12, 1907, p. 91: "Moved . . . that we appoint young men to keep order among the women (carried)." Indeed, the question of whether to completely end "schnoddering," continued to be debated at the congregation for two more generations. See Joselit, *New York's Jewish Jews*, p. 40.

68. On Rabbi Ebin, see Kaplan, "Journals," 18:23 (January 21, 1956). Kehilath Jeshurun archives also contain a 1907 letter from Kaplan to Mr. Jacob Hecht, the congregation's president at the time, requesting that his summer vacation be

extended until September 25, 1907, in order "to devote myself entirely in study. It may be that I shall go to Hamburg to study with Rabbi Cohen, a Dayan of that city."

69. Kaplan, "Journals," 2:96 (August 31, 1922), 7:121 (June 4, 1933), 15:295 (June 1, 1952), 18:23 (January 21, 1956), 19:28 (December 15, 1957), 22:136 (October 29, 1963), 27:20 (November 28, 1976); "KJ Minutes," April 18, 1908, p. 118, October 18, 1908, p. 125. See also Mordecai Kaplan, "Response," p. 217; Kaplan, "The Influences," p. 30; Kaplan, "A Founding Father Recounts," p. 5; Eisenstein, "Mordecai M. Kaplan," p. 255. For a complete analysis of Kaplan receiving semichah from Reines, see Jacob J. Schacter, "Mordecai M. Kaplan's Orthodox Ordination," *American Jewish Archives* 46, no. 1 (Spring/Summer 1994):1–11.

70. Kaplan, "Untitled Diary," December 31, 1906, pp. 45–46. See also Kaplan, "The Way I Have Come," pp. 294, 299; Kaplan, "Journals," 18:233 (March 19, 1957); Kaplan, "The Influences," p. 31: "I soon began to realize that I could not remain in the Kehilath Jeshurun pulpit. . . . Every sermon I preached made me keenly aware of my anomalous position. The more I succeeded in avoiding controversial issues the unhappier I was, because I felt I was sailing under false colors." See also Kaplan, "Preface," *Judaism as a Civilization*, p. xiv.

71. Kaplan, "A Founding Father Recounts," p. 6; Kaplan, "Journals," 19:254 (February 7, 1959). See also Kaplan, "The Influences," p. 31; Kaplan, "The Way I Have Come," p. 295; Kaplan, "Solomon Schechter and Ethical Nationhood: A Personal Memoir," *Proceedings of the Rabbinical Assembly of America* 37 (1975):350; Kaplan, "Journals," 5:181–82 (October 7, 1929) and 9:131 (April 8, 1940), where Kaplan added: "At one time I wanted to take up farming and join an agricultural school." See also Stephen H. Pinsky, "The Society for the Advancement of Judaism (1922–1945)," master's thesis, Hebrew Union College-Jewish Institute for Religion, 1971, p. 12; Kaplan interview with Hillel Goldberg, *Intermountain Jewish News* 63, no. 21 (May 21, 1976):24.

As early as August 17, 1905, Kaplan wrote in his diary: "I find that time is doing little to move me from my determination to take up the study of law this fall. When I told that to mother she of course made a rueful face, but I will never allow this to influence me any." See Kaplan, "Communings with the Spirit."

On Kaplan's appointment to the seminary, see Kaplan, "Journals," 8:86 (April 16, 1936), 6:119 (June 10, 1931), 19:28 (December 15, 1957), 22:136 (October 29, 1963); Kaplan, "The Influences," p. 31. For a description of the event that apparently spurred Schechter to offer Kaplan the position, see Kaplan, "A Founding Father Recounts," p. 6; Kaplan, "The Influences," p. 31; Kaplan, "A Heart of Wisdom," p. 13; Kaplan, "Journals," 27:39 (February 27, 1977); Kaplan, "Solomon Schechter and Ethical Nationhood," p. 350. For the significance of this speech in Kaplan's developing theology, see Kaplan, *Judaism as a Civilization*, p. xiv; Libowitz, *Mordecai M. Kaplan*, pp. 54–58. Kaplan's letter of resignation was read at a Kehilath Jeshurun membership meeting on October 4, 1909, and his resignation was "accepted with deep regret." See "KJ Minutes," October 4, 1909, p. 145.

72. *American Hebrew* 85, no. 11 (July 16, 1909):284.

4. An Unrecognized Opponent

1. Mordecai Kaplan, "Judaism and Nationality," *Maccabaean* 17 (August 1909):59–64, especially p. 60. See also Mordecai Kaplan, "A Heart of Wisdom," *Reconstructionist* 17, no. 6 (May 4, 1951):13.

2. Mordecai Kaplan, "Journals" 1:40–42 (January 25, 1914) contains the abstract of the speech from which these quotes are borrowed. Again it should be noted, as did the newspaper accounts of the speech, that Kaplan was equally unsparing of Reform Judaism. See *American Hebrew* 94, no. 14 (January 30, 1914):401 for an account of the speech and of other society activities. See also *American Jewish Year Book 5674* (1913–1914), p. 407 for the briefest of descriptions of the organization.

3. Mel Scult, "Halakhah and Authority in Early Kaplan," in Ronald A. Brauner, ed., *Jewish Civilization: Essays and Studies*, 3 vols. (Philadelphia: Reconstructionist Rabbinical College, 1981), 2:102–3.

4. In reporting on the speech in 1912, the *American Hebrew* 91, no. 11 (July 12, 1912):293 stated that its title was "Tradition and the Bible."

5. Mordecai Kaplan, "The Supremacy of the Torah," *Jewish Theological Seminary Students Annual* (May 1914), pp. 180–92.

6. Mordecai Kaplan, "How May Judaism Be Saved?" *Menorah Journal* 2, no. 1 (February 1916):38. To be sure, in these articles, as in *Judaism as a Civilization*, Kaplan was also highly critical of Reform Judaism, noting its inadequacies to the challenge faced by modern Judaism. In one telling remark ("How May Judaism Be Saved?" p. 40), which attacked Reform's overly rationalized Judaism, Kaplan noted that while "Judaism bristles with irrationalities which do violence to our established modes of thinking—on the other hand, Judaism dare not be so rational as to be indistinguishable from mere copy-book morality."

7. Mordecai Kaplan, "The Future of Judaism," *Menorah Journal* 2, no. 3 (June, 1916):165.

8. Kaplan, "How May Judaism Be Saved?" pp. 38–39. For more on Kaplan's thought as articulated in these journal articles, see Richard Libowitz, *Mordecai M. Kaplan and the Development of Reconstructionism* (New York and Toronto: Mellen, 1983), pp. 60–79.

For additional examples of Kaplan's public statements critical of Orthodoxy during this period, see his "Remarks Made at the Menorah Society on Friday November 17th, 1911," file no. CXXI-A; Mordecai Kaplan, "Minutes of Study

Group," file no. CXXI-B, January 10, 1912, February 7, 1912, February 21, 1912; Mordecai Kaplan "Jewish Orientation in Life," lecture delivered to the Collegiate Zionist League, January 10, 1915, file no. CXXI-A, p. 10; Mordecai Kaplan, "Address to the Harvard and Boston University Menorah Societies," March 15, 1915, pp. 4, 6; Mordecai Kaplan, "Outline of Course Given at Teachers College During Academic Year 1915–1916," file no. LXXVI-B; all in MKA.

9. Mordecai Kaplan, "Minutes of Sabbath Afternoon Study Group," file no. CXX, April 1, 1916, p. 2, MKA.

10. Kaplan, "Journals," 1:32–37 (January 4, 1914); Kaplan, "Minutes of Study Group," file no. CXXI-B, January 10, 1912, MKA.

11. Kaplan, "Journals," 1:230 (July 30, 1916), 1:244 (August 23, 1916).

12. For an overview of Schechter's basic articulation of Conservative Jewish ideology and its embodiment in the seminary that he led, see Marc Lee Raphael, *Profiles in American Judaism: The Reform, Conservative, Orthodox, and Reconstructionist Traditions in Historical Perspective* (San Francisco: Harper and Row, 1985), pp. 89–91. See Bernard Drachman, *The Unfailing Light* (New York: Rabbinical Council of America, 1948), p. 261, for his discussion of the difficulties with Schechter that led to his leaving JTS.

13. See Mordecai Kaplan, "Solomon Schechter and Ethical Nationhood: A Personal Memoir," *Proceedings of the Rabbinical Assembly of America* 37 (1975):350; Kaplan, "Journals" 20:104–5 (February 5, 1960).

14. Raphael, *Profiles in American Judaism*, p. 90. Raphael argues that the founding of the United Synagogue "represented . . . perhaps the clearest beginning of Conservative Judaism in North America." See also on the beginnings of the USA, *United Synagogue of America, Report* (1913); Jack Wertheimer, "The Conservative Synagogue," in Jack Wertheimer, ed., *The American Synagogue: A Sanctuary Transformed* (New York: Cambridge University Press, 1987), pp. 115–16; Herman Rubenovitz, "The Birth of the United Synagogue," *USA Review* 16, no. 2 (Summer 1963):10–11; *USA Review* 16, no. 3 (Autumn 1962):8–9. See also Herbert Rosenblum, "The Founding of the United Synagogue of America, 1913," Ph.D. diss., Brandeis University, 1970, pp. 163–64, 166, 175, 221–44.

15. Kaplan, "A Heart of Wisdom," p. 13. Kaplan made references to the "Copernican" nature of his statements in two other places as well. See Kaplan, "Preface," *Judaism as a Civilization* (New York: Macmillan, 1934), p. xiv; Mordecai Kaplan, "The Influences That Have Shaped My Life," *Reconstructionist* 8, no. 10 (June 26, 1942):13. On the "walking on eggs" turn of phrase, see Libowitz, *Mordecai M. Kaplan*, p. 58; Schacter interview with Rabbi Alan W. Miller, November 22, 1991. This phrase has been attributed to Schechter in several other contexts as his reaction to Kaplan's expression of his beliefs. See, for example, Kaplan, "Solomon Schechter and Ethical Nationhood," p. 351; Kaplan, "Journals," 9:131–32 (April 8, 1940); Stephen H. Pinsky, "The Society for the Advancement of Judaism (1922–1945)," master's thesis, Hebrew Union College-Jewish Institute for Religion, 1971, p. 13.

16. "The Alumni of the Seminary," *American Hebrew*, 85, no. 6 (June 11, 1909):143.

17. "Alumni Association of the Jewish Theological Seminary," *American Hebrew* 91, no. 11 (July 12, 1912):293.

18. Julius Greenstone to Mordecai Kaplan, July 8, 1914; MKA.

19. Mordecai Kaplan to Julius Greenstone, July 14, 1914; MKA.

20. Rev. Dr. H. Pereira Mendes to Mordecai Kaplan, October 20, 1915; MKA.

21. Rev. Dr. H. Pereira Mendes to Mordecai Kaplan, February 21, 1916; MKA.

22. See Bernard Revel, "Restoring the Ideals of the Messianic Age," *Menorah Journal* 4, no. 4 (August, 1918):238–41.

23. Harry Fischel to Mordecai Kaplan, November 12, 1915; MKA.

24. On the transformation of the Yeshiva Rabbi Isaac Elchanan, see Jeffrey S. Gurock, *The Men and Women of Yeshiva: Higher Education, Orthodoxy, and American Judaism* (New York: Columbia University Press, 1988), chapter 3.

25. Gilbert Klaperman, *The Story of Yeshiva University* (London: Macmillan, 1969), p. 133.

26. Gurock, *The Men and Women of Yeshiva*, p. 34.

27. Ibid., p. 51.

28. Mordecai Kaplan to Harry Fischel, November 14, 1915; MKA.

29. "Journals" 2:326 (November 9, 1917). For background on Travis, Revel, and Yeshiva, see Aaron Rothkoff, *Bernard Revel: Builder of American Jewish Orthodoxy* (Philadelphia: Jewish Publication Society of America, 1972), pp. 56–57.

30. Proverbs 26:5, *The Writings* (Philadelphia: Jewish Publication Society of America, 1982), p. 246.

31. "Journals" 1:244–45 (August 23, 1916).

32. For the history of this ephemeral organization, see Ira Robinson, "Cyrus Adler, Bernard Revel, and the Prehistory of Organized Jewish Scholarship in the United States," *American Jewish History* 69, no. 4 (June, 1980):497–505.

33. "Journals," 1:243 (August 23, 1916).

34. Ibid.

35. On the early history of the Yeshiva Rabbi Jacob Joseph, see Alexander Dushkin, *Jewish Education in New York City* (New York: Bureau of Jewish Education, 1917), pp. 75–77.

36. "Journals," 1:217–19 (January 23, 1916).

37. Kaplan was invited to occupy the pulpit on Kol Nidre night, the first day of Sukkot, and Shemini Atzeret, 1910; the first day of Pesach, both days of Shavuot, Rosh Hashanah, and Kol Nidre night, 1911; and the first day of Shavuot, Rosh Hashanah, and Kol Nidre night, 1912. See "KJ Minutes," September 29, 1910, p. 167, November 2, 1910, p. 172, March 20, 1911, p. 183, May 24, 1911, pp. 188–89, October 11, 1911, p. 190, May 7, 1912, p. 204, October 14, 1912, p. 208. On negotiations between Kehilath Jeshurun and Kaplan (and other candidates), see,

"KJ Minutes," April 15, 1911, p. 186, January 6, 1913, p. 216, January 15, 1913, p. 217, February 20, 1913, p. 219, May 12, 1913, p. 231. For the offer to Hyamson, see also "KJ Minutes," April 24, 1913, p. 229. MKA file no. CXXI-A contains a two-page typewritten text, "Spoken from 85th St. Pulpit the Sabbath After Pesah of the year (5773) [5673]" (= May 3, 1913). On that occasion Kaplan installed the new officers of the congregation. See also note 40 below.

38. Kaplan, "Journals" 1:67 (August 23, 1914), 1:97 (October 10, 1914).

39. For information on Goldstein's education, see Aaron I. Reichel, *The Maverick Rabbi: Rabbi Herbert S. Goldstein and the Institutional Synagogue: A New Organization Form* (Norfolk and Virginia Beach, Va.: Donning, 1984), pp. 28–32; Kaplan, "Journals" 1:98–99 (October 4, 1914).

40. We can deduce from Kaplan's diary that he was offered the pulpit sometime in 1913. See Kaplan, "Journals," 1:97 (October 4, 1914), which makes reference to an offer tendered "last year." Goldstein, according to Reichel, *The Maverick Rabbi*, p. 59, was called to Kehilath Jeshurun at the end of November 1913. Hence, it may be possible that Hyman, who played a major role in Goldstein's activities at the synagogue, might have turned first to Kaplan before hiring his student. This impression is confirmed by Kaplan's diary, where he claims that "in order to make sure that I would not be tempted to accept the pulpit once again, I forced myself to urge upon them to appoint Herbert S. Goldstein." See Kaplan, "Journals," 1:98 (October 4, 1914).

41. Kaplan, "Journals," 1:98 (October 4, 1914).

42. Reichel, *The Maverick Rabbi*, pp. 47–49. Reichel's account also details the circumstances that led up to this speech and notes the efforts of Schechter to tone it down.

43. Goldstein claimed that this speech criticizing Kaplan, albeit not by name, led him to be appointed at Kehilath Jeshurun. Apparently his staunch stance for Orthodoxy impressed the synagogue's leaders. It should also be noted that, at his graduation, Goldstein spoke as valedictorian and was critical of the theological teachings of some of his teachers, which obviously included Kaplan. And although the *New York Journal* picked up Goldstein's criticism of "disruptive perils" in Judaism, Kaplan was not the named focus of these criticisms. See Reichel, *The Maverick Rabbi*, pp. 50, 52.

44. Kaplan, "Journals," 1:98–99 (October 4, 1914).

45. Ibid.

46. Ibid.

47. Ibid., 1:255–56 (January 6, 1917).

48. "Arverne Synagogue Service," *Hebrew Standard* 59, no. 25 (July 19, 1912):6.

49. Privately, however, he did have some misgivings about the ostentatiousness of some the members of that community. See Kaplan, "Journals," 1:70 (August 23, 1914).

50. Kaplan, "Journals," 1:69–70 (August 23, 1914). The biblical quotation is

from Deuteronomy 16:16, *The Torah* (Jewish Publication Society of America, 1962), p. 355.

51. "Journals," 1:80–81 (September 13, 1914).

It is not clear in which synagogue in Long Branch Kaplan served as rabbi from 1914 to 1916. In correspondence with Kaplan Aaron Garfunkel refers to himself as head of the "Long Branch Synagogue." See Aaron Garfunkel to Mordecai Kaplan, August 9, 1915; MKA. This seems to be a different synagogue from the older, apparently more permanant, congregation Brothers of Israel, which dated back to 1898. The latter synagogue's commemorative journals make no references either to Garfunkel or to Kaplan. See *Sixty-Fifth Anniversary Journal of Congregation Brothers of Israel* (Long Branch, N.J., 1963).

52. Garfunkel to Kaplan, August 9, 1915, September 7, 1915; MKA.

53. Kaplan, "Journals," 1:247 (August 26, 1916).

54. Kaplan, "Journals," 1:211 (January 19, 1916), 1:317 (October 17, 1917).

55. Mordecai Kaplan, "Outline of Serman Preached at Orach Chaim Synagog [*sic*] Sabbath Hanukkah, 12/4/15; at the invitation of Dr. Hyamson"; file no. CXVIII, MKA.

56. *American Hebrew* 92, no. 11 (January 10, 1913):303; *Hebrew Standard* 60, no. 25 (January 12, 1913):9; *Morgen Zhurnal* (January 10, 1913):4. Rosenthal, the Young Israel's first president, was in the JTS class of 1913. See *Jewish Theological Seminary of America Student Annual* (1914):50–51. All of these sources are quoted from and utilized by Shulamith Berger, "The Early History of the Young Israel Movement," seminar paper, YIVO Institute, Fall 1982. For a reference to Sachs, see Kaplan, "Journals," 1:45 (January 27, 1914).

57. For a comprehensive history of the New York Kehillah, see Arthur A. Goren, *New York Jews and the Quest for Community, The Kehillah Experiment, 1908–1922* (New York: Columbia University Press, 1970).

58. *Y.I.S. Reporter* (March 3, 1962):1–2; undated circular, "Young Israel, 270 Broadway" (circa 1912–1914), found in the Judah L. Magnes Collection, file P3/538, Central Archives for the History of the Jewish People, Jerusalem (hereafter JLM).

59. Transcript of Arthur A. Goren interview with Benjamin Koenigsberg, December 1, 1964. William E. Wiener Oral History Library of the American Jewish Committee, New York City.

60. See "Young Israel, 270 Broadway"; undated circular "Young Israel, New York City" (circa 1914); Moses Rosenthal to Judah Magnes, 6 Heshvan 5674 (1914); JLM.

61. "Minutes of Meeting of the Executive Committee of Young Israel," March 9, 1916, p. 87, March 14, 1916, p. 88. Photocopies of these minutes are in the possession of Ms. Regina Stein, New York City. The Dr. Krass to whom the minutes refer was probably Nathan Krass who was, in 1917, a member of the [Reform] Central Conference of American Rabbis. See the listing of him as a

member in the *Jewish Communal Register of New York City, 1917–1918* (New York: Jewish Community of New York City, 1918), p. 1175.

62. See undated flyer (circa 1914) from Young Israel noting that Kaplan would be speaking in their lecture series; JLM. See also "Minutes of Regular Meeting of the Young Israel," October 17, 1917, p. 148, where Kaplan is listed as a projected speaker along with Rabbis Goldstein, Morais, and Solomon, among others.

63. *Y.I.S. Reporter*, March 3, 1962, pp. 4–6; *Hebrew Standard* 68, no. 8 (September 19, 1916):11.

64. "Journals," 4:95–97 (October 15, 1928), 7:263 (January 20, 1935). On the early disputes within the Young Israel groups, see also *Y.I.S. Reporter*, March 3, 1962, p. 6. Herbert Parzen contends that while Kaplan, along with Israel Friedlaender, "frequently preached in their synagogue [the Young Israel] on the East Side," Kaplan was "eased out" because of his "shock methods of pedagogy and frank speaking." However, Parzen's footnote to that remark does not evidence any conflict over Kaplan. See Parzen, *Architects of Conservative Judaism* (New York: Jonathan David, 1964), pp. 170, 231.

65. See Max Drob to Mordecai Kaplan, October 29, 1913, MKA, for an example of an invitation to Kaplan to speak at a synagogue, in this case Temple Beth El of Buffalo, New York, where, according to the rabbi, "family pews [are] its only departure from the path of Orthodoxy."

66. This information on the evolution of the Roxbury synagogue is derived from David Kaufman, "Shul with a Pool: The Synagogue-Center in American Jewish Life, 1875–1925," Ph.D. diss., Brandeis University, 1993, pp. 310–14, which, in turn, relies heavily on contemporary Boston general and Jewish newspaper accounts of that synagogue's activities. See also Kaplan, "Journals," 1:126 (December 29, 1914).

67. Kaplan, "Journals," 1:126–27 (December 14, 1914), 1:144 (March 16, 1915).

68. Ibid., 1:126–28 (December 14, 1914).

69. Ibid., 1:261–62 (February 2, 1917).

For information on Konvitz and his relationship with the Ridbaz, see B. Landau, "Rabbi Joseph Konvitz" [Hebrew], in *The Responsa of Ridbaz* [Hebrew] (Jerusalem: Mosad Harav Kook, 1995), pp. 35–43.

70. "Minutes of Directors' Meeting," April 27, 1911; file P3/468, JLM.

71. See "Minutes of Directors' Meeting," May 8, 1911; file P3/468, JLM. Harry Fischel to Mordecai Kaplan, May 15, 1911; Harry Fischel papers, Agudath Israel Orthodox Jewish Archives (hereafter AI), New York City, for a discussion of the use of space in the Uptown Talmud Torah by the Teachers Institute. See Herbert S. Goldstein, *Forty Years of Struggle for a Principle: The Biography of Harry Fischel* (New York: Bloch, 1928), p. 144, for information on Rebecca Fischel.

72. Harry Fischel to Louis Marshall, June 7, 1911; AI. See the *Register, Teachers Insti-*

tute, Jewish Theological Seminary, 1910–1911, which lists the members of the Teachers Institute board of directors, an enumeration that did not include Fischel's name.

73. Goren, *New York Jews,* pp. 88–96; Mordecai Kaplan and Bernard Cronson, "First Community Survey of Jewish Education in New York City—1909, Presented at the First Annual Convention of the New York Kehillah, February 27, 1910," *Jewish Education* 20, no. 3 (Summer 1949):113–16; Mordecai M. Kaplan, "The Impact of Dr. Benderly's Personality," *Jewish Education* 20, no. 3 (Summer 1949):16–20, 26.

74. Goren, *New York Jews,* pp. 127–34.

75. See the listing of members of the board of directors of the Bureau of Education from February 1917, which lists twenty-four directors, including Dukas, Fischel, William Fischman, Hyman, Leon Kamaiky, Joseph H. Cohen, Otto Rosalsky, and Bernard Semel, all important Yorkville Orthodox lay leaders. See file P3/1680, JLM.

76. For references to Fischel's activities in support of Kaplan's Kehillah activities, see "Minutes of the Executive Committee of the Jewish Community of New York City," October 10, 1911, pp. 3–4, December 12, 1911, p. 5; "Minutes of the Meeting of the Trustees of the Bureau of Education of the Jewish Community (Kehillah) of New York City," September 19, 1912, pp. 1–2; JLM.

5. Hiring a Critic at the Jewish Center

1. Mordecai Kaplan, "Journals," 16:85 (December 14, 1952). The geographical boundaries of the Upper West Side that are social and not legal or political were derived from an account written by a contemporary observer of the scene. See Israel Goldstein, *A Century of Judaism in New York: B'nai Jeshurun, 1825–1925* (New York: Congregation B'nai Jeshurun, 1930), p. 258. The population estimates for the area were extrapolated from Alexander M. Dushkin, "A Statistical Study of the Jewish Population of New York," *Jewish Communal Register of New York City, 1917–1918* (New York: Jewish Community of New York City, 1918), p. 84. See also Aaron M. Frankel, "Back to Eighty-Sixth Street," *Commentary* 2, no. 2 (August, 1946):169.

2. Goldstein, *A Century of Judaism in New York,* p. 258. For a discussion of the nature of Upper West Side housing as opposed to Yorkville's, see James Trager, *West of Fifth: The Rise and Fall and Rise of Manhattan's West Side* (New York: Atheneum, 1987), pp. 60–61. For statistics on Yorkville's population and population density as opposed to that of the Upper West Side, see the *Jewish Communal Register,* p. 84ff. For a contrast between Yorkville's ecological conditions and those of neighboring East Harlem, see Jeffrey S. Gurock, *When Harlem Was Jewish, 1870–1930* (New York: Columbia University Press, 1979), chapter 2.

3. Peter Salwen, *Upper West Side Story: A History and Guide* (New York: Abbeville, 1989), pp. 68, 82, 92.

4. David de Sola Pool, *An Old Faith in the New World* (New York: Columbia University Press, 1955), p. 465.

5. See the *Jewish Communal Register*, pp. 148, 227, for brief descriptions of these two synagogues.

6. Mordecai Kaplan, "The Influences That Have Shaped My Life," *Reconstructionist* 8, no. 10 (June 26, 1942):34; Isaac B. Berkson, *Theories of Americanization: A Critical Study* (New York: Columbia University Teachers College, 1920), p. 183, n. 1.

7. "KJ Minutes," April 23, 1905, p. 56, May 1, 1905, p. 58, September 25, 1905, pp. 62–63, April 14, 1906, p. 72, November 27, 1906, p. 84, December 3, 1906, p. 85, April 2, 1907, p. 95, October 7, 1907, p. 102, November 5, 1908, p. 127 (appointed as member of "the finance commission"), January 6, 1909, p. 130 (chairman of that committee), April 8, 1909, p. 133, April 18, 1912, p. 199, April 20, 1915, p. 259.

8. For basic biographical information about Cohen, see the *Hebrew Standard* 68, no. 14 (October 27, 1916):10B; *Jewish Communal Register*, pp. 1014–15; Jacob Pfeffer, ed., *Distinguished Jews of America*, 2 vols. (New York: Distinguished Jews of America, 1917), 1:82–83; and his obituary in the *New York Times*, March 28, 1934. Our thanks to Dr. Malcolm Cohen, Joseph H. Cohen's nephew, and to Mr. Elias S. Cohen, his grandson, for their gracious assistance and encouragement.

9. Schacter interview with Malcolm Cohen, November 24, 1991. For examples of other modern Orthodox synagogues in the 1910s, see the previous chapter.

10. See *Jewish Communal Register*, pp. 72, 73, 373, for a brief biographical description of Fischman. Our thanks also to Mrs. Virginia Slifka, great-granddaughter of Fischman, Rabbi Samuel Geffen, and Mr. Peter Geffen for sharing information and memorabilia about Fischman. See also Kaplan, "Journals," 1:365 (September 17, 1918).

11. Kaplan, "Journals," 1:165 (April 17, 1915).

12. Ibid., 1:158–59 (April 10, 1915); Kaplan, "A Heart of Wisdom," p. 14.

13. See chapters 3 and 4 of this volume for the details of Kaplan's many activities along these lines, which surely were known to Cohen and Fischman.

14. Kaplan, "Journals," 1:104 (October 24, 1914).

15. Ibid., 1:133 (February 15, 1915).

16. Kaplan's letter to Warburg was published in Moshe Davis, "Jewish Religious Life and Institutions in America," in Louis Finkelstein, ed., *The Jews: Their Religion and Culture* (New York: Schocken, 1971), p. 331. See also Mel Scult's reference to this letter in his *Judaism Faces the Twentieth Century: A Biography of Mordecai M. Kaplan* (Detroit: Wayne State University Press, 1994), p. 132.

17. Scult, *Judaism Faces the Twentieth Century*, pp. 199–200, 400, n. 42. In that note Scult argues extensively that Kaplan should not be credited with the founding of the CJI, that designation more properly belonging to Goldstein. Still, from Berkson's writing on, Kaplan did loom large in the popular mind as a force behind the CJI, and his activities, ceremonial or otherwise, would have

been known to former Kehilath Jeshurun people like Cohen and Fischman. See also Aaron I. Reichel, *The Maverick Rabbi: Rabbi Herbert S. Goldstein and the Institutional Synagogue: A New Organization Form* (Norfolk and Virginia Beach, Va.: Donning, 1984), p. 65.

18. Kaplan, "Journals," 1:160–61 (April 10, 1915).

19. Ibid., 1:154–55, 159 (March 15, 1915).

20. Ibid., 1:160 (April 10, 1915).

21. Ibid., 1:160–61 (April 10, 1915).

22. Ibid.

23. Ibid., 1:223–25 (June 12, 1916).

24. Ibid., 1:223–25 (June 12, 1916), 1:300 (August 17, 1917).

25. Ibid., 1:204 (October 31, 1915). See the discussion of this comment of Kaplan in chapter 3 of this study.

26. Ibid., 1:304 (August 29, 1917).

27. Ibid., 1:245 (August 24, 1916); 1:304 (August 29, 1917).

28. Ibid., 1:305 (August 29, 1917).

29. For a discussion of this incident at the Waldorf Astoria, including the suggestion that fish was served at this otherwise obviously nonkosher restaurant, see Jenna W. Joselit, *New York's Jewish Jews* (Bloomington: Indiana University Press, 1990), p. 21.

30. Schacter interview with Rabbi Alan W. Miller, November 22, 1991.

31. See, for example, Myer S. Kripke, "The Synagogue Center and the Jewish Center," *Conservative Judaism* 2, no. 3 (April, 1946):10; Abraham J. Karp, "Ideology and Identity in Jewish Group Survival in America," *American Jewish Historical Quarterly* 65, no. 4 (June 1976): 327; Deborah Dash Moore, *At Home in America: Second Generation New York Jews* (New York: Columbia University Press, 1981), p. 131; Marshall Sklare, *Conservative Judaism: An American Religious Movement* (Lanham, Md.: University Press of America, 1985), pp. 135–36. See also Louis L. Kraft, "Mordecai M. Kaplan's Contribution to the Jewish Center Movement," in Ira Eisenstein and Eugene Kohn, eds., *Mordecai M. Kaplan: An Evaluation* (New York: Jewish Reconstructionist Foundation, 1952), pp. 121–22; Herbert Millman, "Kaplan's Influence on the Jewish Community Center Movement," *Judaism* 30, no. 1 (Winter 1981):96–97.

32. Moshe Davis, "Israel Friedlaender's Minute Book of the *Achavah* Club (1909–1912)," in Gerson D. Cohen, ed., *Mordecai M. Kaplan Jubilee Volume* (New York: Jewish Theological Seminary of America, 1953), pp. 163, 185–86. Davis suggested, p. 163, without citing any sources, that "Magnes' presentation was based on a suggestion made to him by Dr. Kaplan." Ironically, Kaplan did not attend the session where Magnes made this suggestion. See also Sklare, *Conservative Judaism*, p. 305, n. 9, where it is suggested that the role played by Kaplan and his group "was confined chiefly to reflecting some of the contemporary developments."

33. Judah L. Magnes to Solomon Lowenstein, November 9, 1912, cited in Deborah Dash Moore, "A New American Judaism," in William A. Brinner and Moses Rischin, eds., *Like All the Nations? The Life and Legacy of Judah L. Magnes* (Albany: SUNY Press, 1987), pp. 44–45.

34. Kaplan, "Journals," 1:31 (December 15, 1913).

35. Abraham M. Hershman to Kaplan, October 26, 1914; MKA.

36. Herbert S. Goldstein, "The Institutional Synagogue," *Hebrew Standard* 68, no. 8 (September 15, 1916):1. See also Reichel, *The Maverick Rabbi*, pp. 92–94.

37. Kaplan, "Journals," 1:98–99 (October 4, 1914).

38. Ibid., 1:333 (January 20, 1918). The boy's name was Walter Weinstein. In an interview (December 2, 1991), Weinstein told Schacter that he was born on January 5, 1905, and that, since 1914, had been attending the Franklin School on West 89th Street. A Hebrew teacher came to his home to give him private lessons for his bar mitzvah. He also told Schacter that Kaplan "was a rather distinguished gentleman. I don't think he was innately the Orthodox type of rabbi. He wasn't what you would call particularly worrisome over any slight deviations. I don't remember him propounding strict Orthodoxy."

39. Kaplan, "Journals," 1:337–38 (March 2, 1918).

40. Ibid.

41. Ibid., 1:338–39 (March 3, 1918).

42. Ibid., 1:339 (March 3, 1918); 1:342 (April 5, 1918). See also Kaplan, "The Influences," p. 34. For another reference to Kauvar's visit, see the letter of Rabbi Jacob Kohn to Rabbi Herman H. Rubenovitz, May 21, 1918. In the letter Kohn wrote, "Kauvar was in New York last week to try for the Jewish Center but, though he preached a very fine sermon, I hear that he has not met with success. I am sure that the Center will finally ask to be taken to the bosom of our friend Kaplan and, in the end, he will consent." See Herman H. Rubenovitz and Mignon L. Rubenovitz, *The Waking Heart* (Cambridge: N. Dame, 1967), p. 140.

43. Kaplan, "Journals," 1:350–51 (April 21, 1918).

44. Ibid., 1:378 (December 26, 1918). See above, p. 95 for Kaplan's remark about his agreement to be "tactful and circumspect."

45. For more information on this aspect of Kaplan's thought, see Rebecca Trachtenberg Alpert, "The Quest for Economic Justice: Kaplan's Response to the Challenge of Communism, 1929–1940," in Emanuel S. Goldsmith, Mel Scult, and Robert M. Seltzer, eds., *The American Judaism of Mordecai Kaplan* (New York: New York University Press, 1990), pp. 385–87.

46. See, for example, Kaplan, "Journals," 1:386–89 (July 28, 1919). Mr. Jay Harold Garfunkel, who attended services at the center every Shabbat during those years, remembered (interview with Schacter, December 18, 1991) how "Kaplan would preach against the labor practices of some of the outstanding leaders of the congregation, and this upset them." Mr. Clarence Horwitz remembered simi-

larly (interview with Schacter, December 19, 1991) how Kaplan would berate his congregants for being hypocrites, attending services on Saturday morning and then going to work in the afternoon where they employed Jewish workers. Mrs. Selma Jaffee Goldman, Kaplan's daughter, recalled (interview with Schacter, November 24, 1991) how "the disagreements were ethical as much as they were religious." Her father "did not approve of his congregants' business ethics. He preached about it and for this he was criticized. He was very socially aware." Rabbi Ira Eisenstein recalled (interview with Schacter, November 24, 1991) that his father-in-law "began to publicly take sides in union-management struggles in favor of the workers, which also displeased his congregants." See also Ira Eisenstein, "Mordecai M. Kaplan," *Great Jewish Thinkers of the Twentieth Century* (Clinton: Colonial, 1963), p. 258. See also Kaplan's "Judaism as a Living Civilization," the address he gave at the center's dedication ceremony, published in *The American Jewish Chronicle* 4, no. 24 (April 19, 1918):678–79.

47. Kaplan, "Journals," 1:390 (July 28, 1919). See also "Journals," 2:20 (July 27, 1920): "The preaching which I kept up regularly was good. Now and then I would touch upon the economic problem, especially around Pesah time. Every time I did so I rubbed the fur the wrong way."

For another example of his position, see "Journals," 1:379 (December 26, 1918). In this later journal entry Kaplan wrote, "How can they, if they belong to the self-satisfied bourgeois class, and are still too intoxicated with the joy of their newly acquired wealth, to take notice even of the gathering storm that will break upon the heads of the capitalistic classes everywhere?" See also Stephen H. Pinsky, "The Society for the Advancement of Judaism (1922–1945)," master's thesis, Hebrew Union College-Jewish Institute for Religion, 1971, pp. 25–27; Marc Lee Raphael, *Profiles in American Judaism: The Reform, Conservative, Orthodox, and Reconstructionist Traditions in Historical Perspective* (San Francisco: Harper and Row, 1985), p. 180.

For a larger context for the charge of "Bolshevism" at this time, see John Higham, *Strangers in the Land: Patterns of American Nativism, 1860–1925* (New Brunswick: Rutgers University Press, 1955), pp. 254–63. See also "Bolshevism and the Public Schools," *American Hebrew and Jewish Messenger* 106, no. 7 (January 2, 1920):216.

48. Kaplan, "Journals," 1:333 (January 20, 1918), 1:346–47 (April 9, 1918).

49. Ibid., 1:390 (July 28, 1919).

50. Ibid., 1:280–81 (February 22, 1917).

51. Ibid., 2:21 (July 21, 1920).

52. See ibid., 1:367 (September 17, 1918), where Kaplan referred to some of his members as "a vulgar crew"; "Journals," 1:386 (July 28, 1919), 1:398 (July 29, 1919), and 2:19 (October 28, 1919), where he described a member as being "mountainously fat and inordinately vulgar." See also "Journals," 2:3 (December 8, 1919): "There is very little promise of developing any kind of spiritual power. They

have money and that money makes it impossible for them to care for other things in life besides their immediate and personal welfare. They wear their religion very lightly." Later (2:107 [October 2, 1922]), Kaplan described his members' "ingrowing bourgeoisie hypocritical religiosity that is devoid of the least idealistic aspiration" and went on to say that "they are unfortunate spiritually in having come from homes where religion and morality were treated as two radically different domains."

See also "Journals," 1:384 (July 28, 1919): "I am really surprised at myself that I have held on to the Center so long"; and 1:378 (December 26, 1918): "My contact with the Center has not meant anything for my mental or spiritual development"; see also "Journals," 1:391 (July 28, 1919), 2:21 (July 21, 1920).

53. Kaplan, "Journals," 1:385–86 (July 28, 1919).

54. Rev. Dr. H. Pereira Mendes to Mordecai Kaplan, January 5, 1919 (1920); MKA.

55. Mordecai Kaplan to Rev. Dr. H. Pereira Mendes, January 8, 1920; MKA.

56. See Kaplan, "Journals," 1:352 (May 7, 1918), 2:3 (December 8, 1919). See also the *Journal of the Jewish Center* 1, no. 1 (April 18, 1918):4; *Journal of the Jewish Center* 4, no. 40 (June 10, 1921):2–3. In December 1918 seventy families were affiliated with the center. See "Journals," 1:376 (December 26, 1918). For a description of the founding and early years of the center, see Jacob J. Schacter, "'A Rich Man's Club': The Founding of the Jewish Center, in *Hazon Nahum: Essays in Honor of Dr. Norman Lamm on the Occasion of His Seventieth Birthday,* ed. Yaakov Elman and Jeffrey S. Gurock (New York: Yeshiva University Press, forthcoming).

6. The Struggle for Control of the Jewish Center

1. *Hebrew Standard* 76, no. 26 (December 24, 1920):8.

2. *Jewish Forum* 4, no. 1 (January 21, 1921):645–46.

3. Edwin Kaufman to Cyrus Adler, December 27, 1920; Library of the Jewish Theological Seminary of America (hereafter JTSA).

4. See the front page article in *Der Morgen Zhurnal* 20 (January 12, 1921). See also J. D. Eisenstein, *Memoirs* [Hebrew] (New York: J. D. Eisenstein, 1929), p. 144.

5. See "The Society of the Jewish Renascence," *Maccabaean* 34, no. 4 (November, 1920):111. This essay was reprinted as a separate pamphlet as part of the Zionist Publications series of the Zionist Organization of America (New York, 1920). See pp. 6–7.

6. Much information about this short-lived society, the first meeting of which took place on June 18, 1919, is available in MKA, file no. CXXIV-B, and in the correspondence between Kaplan and Rubenovitz, a member of its administrative committee, also in MKA, in the Rubenovitz papers in the Jewish Theological Seminary of America, and in Herman H. Rubenovitz and Mignon L. Rubenovitz, *The Waking Heart* (Cambridge: N. Dame, 1967), pp. 57–60, 140–47. See also Herbert

Rosenblum, "The Founding of the United Synagogue of America, 1913," Ph.D. diss., Brandeis University, 1970, pp. 247–48; Herbert Rosenblum, "The Emergence of the Reconstructionist Movement," *Reconstructionist* 41, no. 4 (May 1975):9–10, 15; Herbert Parzen, *Architects of Conservative Judaism* (New York: Jonathan David, 1964), pp. 202–04; Richard Libowitz, *Mordecai M. Kaplan and the Development of Reconstructionism* (New York and Toronto: Mellen, 1983), pp. 98–100.

7. Kaplan's talk was entitled "Reconstruction of Judaism from the Zionist Standpoint." The original typescript is in file no. XXXI, MKA.

8. *Menorah Journal* 6, no. 4 (August 1920):195. See Libowitz, *Mordecai M. Kaplan*, pp. 93–98.

Although this article is not explicitly identified as the written version of the paper Kaplan delivered before the Society of the Jewish Renascence, we assume that it is. See the editor's note in the *Menorah Journal* introducing the article:

> The paper here presented was read before an informal conference of rabbis and laymen in New York, called recently to consider the state of Judaism in view of the world upheaval and the changes in Jewish life. An organization has since been formed to promote the interpretation and advancement of Judaism along the "historical and progressive" lines formulated in this paper.

This is a clear reference to the society. In addition, see Mordecai Kaplan, "The Influences That Have Shaped My Life," *Reconstructionist* 8, no. 10 (June 26, 1942):34, where Kaplan writes, "I finally succeeded in organizing *The Society for the Jewish Renascence*. It was then that I publicly stressed the need for reconstructing the organization and ideology of Jewish life," using the same terminology as used in the title of this essay.

9. *Hebrew Standard* 77, no. 1 (January 7, 1921):8; *Hebrew Standard* 77, no. 3 (January 21, 1921):8. Kaplan made reference to Morais's criticism in a letter to Rabbi Herman Rubenovitz dated January 11, 1921. See Rubenovitz and Rubenovitz, *The Waking Heart*, p. 59.

10. Edwin Kaufman to Cyrus Adler, December 27, 1920; JTSA.

11. Cyrus Adler to Edwin Kaufman, December 31, 1920; JTSA. From this point on the issue of whether Kaplan was an appropriate faculty member of JTS would be a continuing problem for Adler and his successors. For an enlightening discussion of a subsequent JTS president's handling of this concern, see Jack Wertheimer, "Kaplan vs. 'The Great Do-Nothings': The Inconclusive Battle over *The New Haggadah*," *Conservative Judaism* 45, no. 4 (Summer 1993):20–37.

12. Rubenovitz and Rubenovitz, *The Waking Heart*, p. 59.

13. Ibid., pp. 146–47; Mel Scult, *Judaism Faces the Twentieth Century: A Biography of Mordecai M. Kaplan* (Detroit: Wayne State University Press, 1994), p. 194.

14. Herman H. Rubenovitz to Mordecai Kaplan, January 7, 1921; MKA.

15. *Der Morgen Zhurnal* 20 (January 16, 1921):8. His letter was reprinted in *Ha-Toren* 7, no. 43 (January 21, 1921):10–11.

16. Bernard Drachman, "An Examination of Prof. Mordecai M. Kaplan's Views on Judaism," *Jewish Forum* 4, no. 2 (February 1921):724–31; *Hebrew Standard* 77, no. 8 (Februaray 25, 1921):8.

17. Letter of Mordecai M. Kaplan to the Jewish Center membership, February 4, 1921; Jewish Center Archives.

This statement about what Kaplan actually said at the meeting is derived from Mel Scult's summary of Kaplan's remarks contained in a document entitled "The Jewish Center Convention-February 9, 1921," which represents professionally recorded minutes of that gathering. Scult's description first appeared in his "Becoming Centered: Community and Spirituality in the Early Kaplan," in Emanuel S. Goldsmith, Mel Scult, and Robert M. Seltzer, eds., *The American Judaism of Mordecai Kaplan* (New York: New York University Press, 1990), pp. 84–85. Unfortunately, that important document, onced housed in the Reconstructionist Rabbinical College, is no longer extant. We have relied on Scult's rendering of Kaplan's remarks. The Kaplan speech is also quoted in Scult, *Judaism Faces the Twentieth Century*, pp. 194–95.

18. Copies of these sermons (and others) can be found in MKA. See file no. CVII-A, p. 144, file no. CVII-B, pp. 159–60, file no. CXVIII, pp. 223, 228.

19. Bernard Drachman, *The Unfailing Light* (New York: Rabbinical Council of America, 1948), p. 374.

20. Rubenovitz and Rubenovitz, *The Waking Heart*, p. 59.

21. Mordecai Kaplan, "Journals," 1:355–57 (May 8, 1918), 1:367 (September 17, 1918), 2:3–4 (December 8, 1919).

22. Both letters were printed in Drachman's, *The Unfailing Light*, pp. 376–77. Drachman claimed the credit for galvanizing Orthodox support against Kaplan, which led to his resigning from the center. See ibid., pp. 372–78. As we shall see, this is an oversimplification of the facts.

23. William Fischman to Mordecai Kaplan, April 7, 1921; MKA.

24. Kaplan, "Journals," 2:30–31 (April 25, 1921).

25. Ibid.

26. Mordecai Kaplan to William Fischman, April 28, 1921; Jewish Center Archives. See also Kaplan, "Journals," 2:36 (May 6, 1921).

27. William Fischman to Mordecai Kaplan, April 7, 1921; MKA.

28. Kaplan, "Journals," 2:34–35 (May 3, 1921). See also *Journal of the Jewish Center* 4, no. 34 (May 2, 1921):4.

29. Kaplan, "Journals," 2:35–36 (May 5, 1921).

30. Ibid., 2:36–37 (May 6, 1921).

31. Ibid., 2:39–41 (May 9, 1921).

32. Ibid.

33. Ibid., 2:35–36 (May 5, 1921). This story is important in light of the widely accepted tradition among old-timers at the Jewish Center that it was Kaplan who once told a prospective bar mitzvah boy either that God does not exist or that the Adam and Eve story in the Bible was a myth, and that it was this that aroused the storm of opposition against him. In his memoirs, Rabbi Leo Jung, Kaplan's successor at the center, has another version of this story:

> A curious incident brought the matter out into the public and to a speedy decision. A teacher, appointed by Dr. K. and at that time his faithful disciple, prepared the son of one of the trustees for the *Bar Mitzvah*. The portion of the *Torah* dealt with the miracles in Egypt. The teacher instructed the boy that there were no miracles, that what the *Torah* taught were fables, legends. The parent was not a *Torah*-true Jew, but he had sentimental attachment to Judaism, and he felt that teaching a lad of twelve denial of the faith to which the Center had proclaimed its fealty was a breach of trust. Kaplan was forced to reveal his attitude. When the boy's father (Arthur M. Lamport) questioned him: "Would you say, Doctor, that God cannot perform any miracles?," he remained silent. To him Mr. Lamport offered a lesson, which, coming from the mouth of an honoured trustee, had profound effect on some who were still on the fence: "Well, Sir," he said, "if you as rabbi of my congregation tell me that the faith of my parents is nothing but a collection of folktales, I may or may not be overwhelmed by this denial of the cause for which we appointed you our rabbi. But surely I am not going to accept your substitute. If I should break with Orthodox Judaism, I would go shopping and not substitute for faith in God a faith in Mordecai Kaplan.

See Leo Jung, *The Path of a Pioneer* (London and New York: Soncino, 1980), pp. 75–76. This story was also repeated by Erna Villa, daughter of Rabbi Jung; interview with Schacter, December 22, 1991.

There is, however, no independent evidence that any version of this story ever took place, although it is conceivable that Kaplan could have said what he allegedly did in the second one. The event described by Kaplan regarding Max Kadushin, Kaplan's disciple and teacher in the center's school, is the closest we find to such a story in the historical record, but it is entirely possible that the repercussions of that event alone were strong enough to lead eventually to Kaplan's leaving the center.

34. Kaplan, "Journals," 2:39–41 (May 9, 1921).

35. Ibid., 2:41–45 (May 11–12, 1921). See also 2:47–48 (May 16–17, 1921).

36. This entire description is based on entries in Kaplan's "Journals," cited in note 35 above.

37. Kaplan, "Journals," 2:45 (May 12, 1921).

38. Ibid., 2:50 (May 17, 1921).

39. Ibid., 2:57–60 (May 27, 1921).

40. Mordecai Kaplan to Moses P. Epstein, April 7, 1960; MKA. On Kaplan's Long Beach stay, see Kaplan, "Journals," 2:65–66 (September 21, 1921). For an identification of Garfunkel as vice president of Ohab Zedek, see Samuel Rosenblatt, *Yossele Rosenblatt: The Story of His Life as Told to His Son* (New York: Farrar, Straus and Young, 1954), p. 95, and Schacter interview with Jay Harold Garfunkel (December 7, 1995).

41. Kaplan, "Journals," 2:66–68 (September 21, 1921).

42. Ibid.

43. Mordecai Kaplan to William Fischman, September 20, 1922; MKA; Jewish Center Archives.

44. The Society for the Advancement of Judaism, "Minutes" (hereafter SAJ "Minutes") January 11, 1922, pp. 1–4. They are found in the archives of that institution on West 86th Street.

45. Ibid., pp. 4–5. Did the beleaguered rabbi personally take the fight to the very end? Kaplan family tradition has it that, when all was said and done, "Kaplan was just not a fighter. He just did not want to, and couldn't, put up with all the *narishkeit* (foolishness)." He was, rather, "by temperment," more prone to compromise than to fight and was "more interested in his ideas, in writing and working out his theories." Their claim that, when faced "with a vocal minority in opposition," Kaplan "simply and finally left" may well be true. It may also be possible that a more determined Cohen built sufficient strength to turn the majority of center members against the rabbi. The Kaplan family's and supporters' side of the story is based on Schacter's interviews with Rabbi Alan Miller, November 22, 1991, and Dr. Ira Eisenstein, November 24, 1991.

46. Kaplan, "Journals," 1:385 (July 28, 1919). In an interview with Schacter (December 19, 1991), Clarence Horwitz recalled that membership dues varied according to the size of the family. His father had four children and paid annual dues of $750. See also SAJ "Minutes," p. 6.

47. Kaplan, "Journals," 2:69 (May 10, 1922); Mordecai Kaplan to William Fischman, January 16, 1922, and William Fischman to Mordecai Kaplan, January 19, 1922; Jewish Center Archives.

It is interesting to note that Kaplan indicated, many years later, that his tenure as rabbi of the center ended in 1921. See Mordecai Kaplan to Evelyn Shafner, October 11, 1945, and Mordecai Kaplan to Carl Hermann Voss, January 20, 1955; MKA. In the letter to Voss he wrote: "In 1921 I broke with the group which, at my suggestion, had built the first Jewish Center on 131 West 86th St., because the board of directors objected to my having published in the Menorah Journal of 1920 the fact that Judaism is in need of reconstruction." He also made reference there to "the 31 families that followed me from the Jewish Center." Kaplan's daughter, Judith Kaplan Eisenstein, recalled in an interview with Schacter (November 24, 1991) that "our family left the Jewish Center in the fall [of 1921], after the High Holidays, and we were in limbo until the SAJ was founded in January of 1922." In an interview with Schacter (December 19, 1991), Clarence Horwitz recalls coming home from summer camp at the end of the summer of 1921 and finding Kaplan sitting in the front row of the pews in the synagogue rather than on the *bimah* (podium). He was told that a dispute took place "and Kaplan was not permitted to speak any more." See also SAJ "Minutes," p. 19.

48. Marc Lee Raphael, "Rabbi Leo Jung and the Americanization of Orthodox Judaism," in Jacob J. Schacter, ed., *Reverence, Righteousness, and Rahamanut: Essays in Memory of Rabbi Dr. Leo Jung,* (Northvale: Jason Aronson, 1992), pp. 30–40; Leo Jung, "Orthodoxy, Reform and Kaplanism," *Jewish Forum* 4, no. 4 (April, 1921):778–79.

49. Samuel M. Cohen to Cyrus Adler, June 15, 1923; JTSA.

50. S. A. Israel to Cyrus Adler, December 13, 1921; JTSA.

51. S. A. Israel to Cyrus Adler, May 19, 1922; JTSA. See also S. A. Israel to Cyrus Adler, April 21, 1922; JTSA.

52. S. A. Israel to Cyrus Adler, May 19, 1922; JTSA. See also S. A. Israel to Cyrus Adler, April 21, 1992, and June 29, 1922; JTSA.

53. S. A. Israel to Cyrus Adler, July 17, 1922; JTSA. See also S. A. Israel to Cyrus Adler, December 21, 1922; Cyrus Adler to S. A. Israel, January 4, 1923; Cyrus Adler to S. A. Israel, January 12, 1923; JTSA.

54. Samuel M. Cohen to Cyrus Adler, June 15, 1923; JTSA.

55. For an example of a discussion within JTS precincts about the possibility that Kaplan could be dismissed because of the difficulties he caused the institution in its relations with American Orthodox Jews, see Rabbi Max Drob's discussion with Cyrus Adler, noted in Aaron Rakeffet-Rothkoff, "The Attempt to Merge the Jewish Theological Seminary and Yeshiva College, 1926–11927," *Michael* 3 (1975):269.

56. See Mordecai Kaplan to Cyrus Adler, September 16, 1923, JTSA, where reference is made by Kaplan to correspondence between Adler and Israel where the former reportedly made these comments about Kaplan's role at the seminary.

57. Mordecai Kaplan to Cyrus Adler, September 16, 1923; JTSA.

58. Cyrus Adler to Mordecai Kaplan, September 21, 1923; JTSA.

59. Kaplan, "Journals," 4:71–72 (September 18, 1928).

60. "Minutes of Meetings of the Jewish Center Membership and Board of Trustees Meetings," December 31, 1931, December 13, 1931, December 20, 1931, December 27, 1931, and January 1, 1932; Jewish Center Archives.

61. Kaplan, "Journals," 6:186 (October 8, 1931), 6:264–65 (May 21, 1932).

62. See Legislative Act No. 2920, State of New York, which became law on April 22, 1931. See chapter 572 of the Laws of 1931, State of New York. Mrs. Sylvia Baris, a prominent old-time Jewish Center member, referred to these gentlemen as the "elder statesmen" of the center; interview with Schacter (January 29, 1992). Dr. Malcolm Cohen, nephew of Joseph H. Cohen and son of Louis

Cohen, who was then serving as president of the center, told Schacter that "they were leaders of the Jewish Center—part of the leadership"; interview (November 21, 1991). Martin Schwarzschild, long-time Jewish Center leader, and president from 1980–1987, said, "They were leaders, there is no question about it" (interview with Schacter, November 13, 1991). For Rabbi Jung's views of these men, see his *The Path of a Pioneer*, p. 76. See also SAJ "Minutes," pp. 554–56 (May 23, 1932).

63. SAJ "Minutes," pp. 557–58 (May 28, 1932). For Kaplan's description of this meeting, see Kaplan, "Journals" 6:269–70 (May 28, 1932).

64. Kaplan, "Journals," 6:269–70 (May 28, 1932).

65. Ibid., 6:559 (June 6, 1932). See also Stephen H. Pinsky, "The Society for the Advancement of Judaism (1922–1945)," master's thesis, Hebrew Union College-Jewish Institute for Religion, 1971, pp. 105–7. In a series of conversations with prominent center members active at the time and with subsequent leaders of the synagogue, all informed Schacter that they never heard of this story. Their reactions ranged from simple dismissal to utter incredulity that a merger with the SAJ could ever have even been contemplated by center leaders in 1932. Mortimer J. Propp, a prominent long-time center leader, said, "I was there in 1932 and never heard of it. It was an impossible thing!"; interview (January 30, 1992). Clarence Horwitz said, "It is strange to me, I can't imagine it could've happened. The people at SAJ maybe thought it was a good idea but the center leadership certainly could not have"; interview (January 29, 1992). Rabbi Jung's daughter, Erna Villa, told Schacter that she and her mother never heard of this story and they denied that Rabbi Jung ever contemplated leaving the center to return to England; interviews (December 22 and 23, 1991). Only Raphael Courland and Nehama Courland recalled that once, during the Depression, while Rabbi Jung was summering in Switzerland, a faction of the center cabled him to stay there and not return for the High Holidays. Their parents, Maurice and Rebecca Courland, formed an ad-hoc committee to fight this and they prevailed by a small margin. The issue, they stressed, was not that this faction personally opposed Rabbi Jung, it was felt, rather, that they could no longer afford his services; interview (January 28, 1992). It is also quite intriguing to note that the minutes of the Jewish Center board meetings are missing from January to October 1932, precisely the time when this merger was being discussed. It is tempting to speculate that perhaps later center leaders wanted to erase what they considered to be an embarrassing chapter from their history.

7. Learning from a Heretic?

1. Mel Scult, *Judaism Faces the Twentieth Century: A Biography of Mordecai M. Kaplan* (Detroit: Wayne State University Press, 1994), p. 367.

2. William Cutter, "Kaplan and Jewish Education: Reflections on His Influence," in Emanuel S. Goldsmith, Mel Scult, and Robert M. Seltzer, eds., *The*

American Judaism of Mordecai Kaplan (New York: New York University Press, 1990), p. 376.

3. Israel Chipkin, "Kaplan and Jewish Education," in Ira Eisenstein and Eugene Kohn, eds., *Mordecai M. Kaplan: An Evaluation* (New York: Jewish Reconstructionist Foundation, 1952), pp. 111–12.

4. Louis Kraft, "Kaplan's Contribution to the Jewish Center Movement," in Eisenstein and Kohn, *Mordecai M. Kaplan: An Evaluation*, pp. 119–20.

5. Samuel S. Kohs, "Mordecai M. Kaplan's Contribution to Jewish Social Work," in Eisenstein and Kohn, *Mordecai M. Kaplan: An Evaluation*, pp. 65–85; Harriet Feiner, "Kaplan's Influence on Jewish Social Work," in Goldsmith, Scult, Seltzer, *The American Judaism of Mordecai M. Kaplan*, pp. 357–69. See also Samuel S. Kohs, "Current Fallacies Regarding Jewish Social Work: Is It Drifting Towards Extinction?" *Jewish Social Service Quarterly* 9, no. 3 (June 1933):296–304, quoted in Feiner, "Kaplan's Influence on Jewish Social Work," p. 359.

6. See Arnold M. Eisen, *The Chosen People in America* (Bloomington: Indiana University Press, 1983), p. 17. For more on this idea in Judaism, see H. H. Ben-Sasson, "The Uniqueness of Israel in the Opinion of Those Who Lived in the Twelfth Century" [Hebrew], *Chapters in the Study of Jewish History* [Hebrew] 2 (Jerusalem, 1971):145–218; Shmuel Almog and Michael Heyd, ed., *Chosen People, Elect Nation, and Universal Mission* [Hebrew] (Jerusalem, 1991); Amos Funkenstein, *Perceptions of Jewish History* (Berkeley: University of California Press, 1993), 52–53, 202–8, 293–94; David Novak, *The Election of Israel: The Idea of the Chosen People* (Cambridge: Cambridge University Press, 1995); "Chosen People," *Encyclopaedia Judaica*, 16 vols. (1971), 5:498–502.

7. Mordecai Kaplan, *Judaism as a Civilization* (New York: Macmillan, 1934), passim.

8. Ira Eisenstein, Eugene Kohn, Milton Steinberg, "Preface to the Second Edition," in Mordecai M. Kaplan, *Judaism in Transition* (New York: Covici, Friede, 1936), pp. viii–ix.

9. For a complete bibliography, year by year, of Kaplan's works, see "Complete Bibliography of the Writings of Mordecai M. Kaplan," in Goldsmith, Scult, Seltzer, *The American Judaism of Mordecai M. Kaplan*, pp. 415–52.

10. Alexander J. Burstein, "Mordecai M. Kaplan's Contribution to Conservative Judaism," in Eisenstein and Kohn, *Mordecai M. Kaplan: An Evaluation*, pp. 223–32; Roland B. Gittelson, "Mordecai M. Kaplan and Reform Judaism: A Study in Reciprocity," in Eisenstein and Kohn, *Mordecai M. Kaplan: An Evaluation*, pp. 233–42. See also Scult, *Judaism Faces the Twentieth Century*, pp. 301–2, on Judith Kaplan's bat mitzvah, and p. 362, on Reconstructionism as a "school of thought."

11. On Kaplan's flirtation with this change of status, see Scult, *Judaism Faces the Twentieth Century*, pp. 269–71.

12. A. Rakeffet-Rothkoff, "The Attempt to Merge," p. 269.

13. There is every reason to believe that the Agudath ha-Rabbanim took this excoriation seriously, as opposed to it being merely a symbolic act. For the text of the excommunication decree, see *Hapardes* 19, no. 4 (July 1945):2–3. For the laws regarding excommunication, see the *Shulchan Aruch, Yoreh De'ah*, no. 334 (New York: E. Grossman), pp. 162–66. See also J. D. Eisenstein, *Ozar Yisrael* [Hebrew], 10 vols. (New York: Pardes, 1910), 4:313–14.

14. See *Hapardes*, 19, no. 4 (July 1945):2; *Hapardes*, 19, no. 8 (November 1945):23–24; *Der Morgen Zhurnal* (June 13, 1945):3. Scult, *Judaism Faces the Twentieth Century*, p. 420, n. 38, suggests that the act of book burning was unintentional and not directed by the rabbinic leaders themselves, but all evidence cited above points to the contrary. This was clearly an official act, sanctioned by all those assembled as a fitting and appropriate conclusion to a most serious and solemn deliberation.

15. *Sabbath Prayer Book* (New York: Jewish Reconstructionist Foundation, 1945), v, xvii–xxx, and passim.

16. See *Hapardes* 19, no. 4 (July 1945):2–4; 19, *Hapardes* 19, no. 8 (November 1945):23–24; *Der Morgen Zhurnal* (June 13, 1945):1, 3; "Editorial," *Der Morgen Zhurnal* (June 14, 1945):4; *Der Morgen Zhurnal* (June 18, 1945):4; "Orthodox Rabbis 'Excommunicate' Author of Prayer Book Though He is Not a Member," *New York Times* (June 15, 1945).

17. See *Der Morgen Zhurnal* (April 6, 1941):6; Mordecai M. Kaplan, Eugene Kohn, and Ira Eisenstein, eds., *The New Haggadah* (New York: Behrman's Jewish Book House, 1941); *Hapardes* 19, no. 4 (July 1945):2.

It is interesting to note that Kaplan's colleagues at the Jewish Theological Seminary also considered the appearance of the siddur to be a much greater offense than that of the Haggadah. While the first elicited only a private letter of criticism, the latter elicited a public attack. See Jack Wertheimer, "Kaplan vs. 'The Great Do-Nothings': The Inconclusive Battle over *The New Haggadah*," *Conservative Judaism* 45:4 (Summer 1993):20–37; Louis Ginzberg, Saul Lieberman, Alexander Marx, "Publicizing an Opinion" [Hebrew], in *Hado'ar* 24, no. 39 (October 5, 1945), trans. as "A Declaration About Dr. Kaplan's Siddur," *Jewish Forum* 19, no. 1 (January 1946):7–8, 16; see note 20 below.

18. Alexander Dushkin, *Jewish Education in New York City* (New York: Bureau of Jewish Education, 1918), p. 96; *Jewish Communal Register of New York City, 1917–1918* (New York: Jewish Community of New York City, 1918), pp. 454–55; Israel Chipkin, "The Jewish Teacher in New York and the Remuneration for His Services," *Jewish Education* 1, no. 3 (October, 1930):171.

19. Kaplan, "Journals," 3:93–94 (October 11, 1925). The correct phrase is "meisis u-maydi'ach."

20. Aaron Rosmarin, "Wither the Jewish Theological Seminary?" *Jewish Forum* 17, no. 8 (September, 1934):242, 246. Years later, when Kaplan published his con-

troversial Haggadah and, ultimately, the prayer book that evoked the excommunication of the Agudath ha-Rabbanim, calls for silencing his influential voice
within the seminary and beyond were again heard, this time emanating from colleagues within JTS itself. Interestingly enough, those who publicly distanced themselves from Kaplan included Rabbi Saul Lieberman, the renowned talmudist who
was well respected within Orthodox circles, and Professor Louis Ginzberg, a
longtime subject of old-line Orthodox attack. These two men, along with historian Alexander Marx, proclaimed in an article first published in the Hebrew *Ha-
Doar* and then reprinted in the *Jewish Forum* (see note 17 above), that while the
Agudath ha-Rabbanim was ill-advised in imposing its excommunication, since it
may "cause a 'hillul Hashem' and bring disgrace on the Torah and its culture
bearers," nonetheless, "an alarm should have been sounded against the profana-
tion of the sanctities of our people." They averred further that just a few years
earlier they themselves had "protested against his aberrations and deviations from
tradition when Kaplan published his controversial new Haggadah for Passover.
We gave him a hint, but he disregarded it; we pricked him; but he ignored the
stinging." Rabbi Yitzchak Gersh's recollection was that many seminary students
believed that Lieberman was the driving force behind this article; Gurock interview (January 27, 1994). Kaplan himself claimed that Lieberman seemed to
support the ostracism that the excommunication prescribed. Reportedly, in the
days after the special conference, Lieberman who "always was antagonistic to
[Kaplan's] work" gave Kaplan the cold shoulder. Kaplan told his diary, "Journals," 12:146 (June 16, 1945), "As soon as he noticed me, he lowered his eyes and
hastened his step. 'Why are you angry at me,' I said in all innocence. 'I am not
angry,' he replied and ran on. . . . He regarded it as his duty to obey the herem of
the rabbis."

21. Leo Jung, "Reconstructionism," in *Modern Trends in American Judaism* (New
York, 1936), p. 15.

22. In 1935 Kaplan would confide to his diary that "Leo Jung, my successor at
the Jewish Center, representative of the Agudah [is] a violent opponent of mine.
When we meet in the street I feel embarrassed, for as a colleague I ought to greet
him, but as the object of frequent attacks on his part I ought to ignore him. He
probably feels the same way about me."

See Kaplan, "Journals," 8:48 (September 11, 1935). There is also some evidence
that during those days, and thereafter, Kaplan would cross the street when he saw
his antagonist approaching; Schacter interview with Rabbi Alan W. Miller
(November 22, 1991).

23. On this issue, see Louis Bernstein, *Challenge and Mission: The Emergence of the
English-Speaking Orthodox Rabbinate* (New York: Shengold, 1982), pp. 141–56. See also
Jeffrey S. Gurock, "Resisters and Accommodators: Varieties of Orthodox Rabbis
in America, 1886–1983," *American Jewish Archives* 35, no. 2 (November 1983):154–55.

24. Kaplan, "Journals," 10:98–99 (May 24, 1941).

25. Ibid., 16:73 (November 15, 1952). At the very end of Kaplan's life there was a final contact between these two rabbis where Jung apparently reached out to the Reconstructionist in the spirit of personal reconciliation. Sometime around 1981, when Jung was close to ninety and Kaplan was one hundred years old, Jung visited a congregant in the Hebrew Home for the Aged in Riverdale. On his way out of the building, he stopped off to pay a visit to Kaplan, who was then a resident there. In telling about the visit, Jung informed a different congregant that he said to Kaplan, "I hope God gives you a speedy *refuah shelemah* and may God be with you." To yet another he said, "the past is past. I felt I wanted to visit him." And Jung's congregant intuited that "in Rabbi Jung's mind you got a sense that at the end of these people's lives he was effecting a reconciliation." Schacter interviews with Martin Schwarzschild (November 13, 1991) and Avery Neumark (November 20, 1991).

26. Alexander Dushkin, "Kalman Whiteman," *Jewish Education* 18, no. 1 (November 1946):2; Gurock interview with Sylvia Ettenberg (January 6, 1994). For more on the history of the Agudath ha-Morim, see Zevi Scharfstein, ed., *Jubilee Book of the Hebrew Teachers' Union of New York City and Vicinity* (New York: Hebrew Teachers Union, 1944); Kaplan, "Journals," 3:93–94 (October 31, 1925).

27. Kaplan, "Journals," 2:131–32 (October 30, 1922). See also Scult, *Judaism Faces the Twentieth Century*, p. 111, for background on the Friedlaender classes.

28. Rev. Dr. H. Pereira Mendes to Mordecai Kaplan, January 5, 1919; Mordecai Kaplan to Rev. Dr. H. Pereira Mendes, January 8, 1920; Rev. Dr. H. Pereira Mendes to Mordecai Kaplan, January 4, 1927; JTSA.

It should also be noted that in 1929 an Orthodox rabbi approached Kaplan for help of a different type. Rabbi Menachem M. Kasher, editor of the *Torah Shelemah* commentary on the Bible, approached the rabbi for assistance in convincing seminary supporters—particularly lay people—of the importance of his work, undoubtedly for fundraising motives. See Kaplan, "Journals," 5:218 (December 4, 1929).

29. David de Sola Pool, "To the Editor," *Jewish Forum*, 17, no. 9 (October, 1934):290. That same year de Sola Pool sent a draft article on "State and Church in Education" to Kaplan for his comments and assistance, thereby giving them an additional professional connection. See Kaplan, "Journals," 6:237 (January 16, 1932).

30. Aaron Rosmarin, "To The Editor," *Jewish Forum* 17, no. 10 (November, 1934):315–16.

31. Rev. Dr. H. Pereira Mendes to Mordecai Kaplan, May 28, 1935; JTSA.

32. See Kaplan, "Journals," 7:242 (September 25, 1934); the descriptions of Rabbi Lookstein's "Sociology of the Jews" course at Yeshiva College in the catalogues of Yeshiva University, 1937–1958, and Gurock interview with Rabbi Her-

schel Schacter, February 16, 1994. For the best biographical study of Lookstein, his orientation toward American Judaism, and the congregation that he led, see Jenna W. Joselit, *New York's Jewish Jews* (Bloomington: Indiana University Press, 1990), pp. 71–73, and passim. See also Kaplan, *Judaism as a Civilization*, p. 441.

33. See Kaplan, "Journals," 18:204 (January 21, 1957); and Gurock interview with Joseph Tabachnik (February 5, 1994). Tabachnik would have a distinguished career as a Conservtive rabbi, occupying pulpits in New Haven and Chicago.

See also Kaplan, "Journals," 16:23 (August 25, 1952), for a reference to Kaplan's works being read by Yeshiva College students outside the classroom setting.

34. Kaplan, "Journals," 18:61–62 (June 1, 1956); *Intermarriage and the Future of the American Jew* (New York: Federation of Jewish Philanthropies, 1964).

35. Kaplan, "Journals," 18:61–62 (June 1, 1956).

36. *Intermarriage and the Future of the American Jew*, pp. 1–18.

37. "The Nature of the Zionist Movement: Working Paper for the AZC Committe on Fundamental Zionist Ideology (1957–58)"; "A Proposed Platform for the Greater Zionism: Report to the Commission on Zionist Ideology, October 23–26, 1958"; "Minutes of American Zionist Council Committee on Ideology, March 26, 1959," p. 1. These documents are available in the Zionist Archives, Jerusalem.

38. "Minutes of the Committee on Zionist Ideology, May 7, 1959," p. 1, including "Statement by Dr. Mordecai Kaplan and Rabbi Irving Miller" and "Statement by Rabbi Emanuel Rackman"; Rabbi Emanuel Rackman to Rabbi Jerome Unger, June 22, 1959; Rabbi Jerome Unger to Rabbi Emanuel Rackman, June 24, 1959; "Minutes of American Zionist Council Committee on Ideology, October 7, 1959," p. 1, November 19, 1959, pp. 1–2, December 10, 1959, p. 1, April 25, 1960, p. 1; Zionist Archives, Jerusalem.

In addition, in 1956 Rackman would serve with Kaplan and others on a B'nai Brith–sponsored committee that planned a conference on the "Foundations of Jewish Spiritual and Cultural Unity." And, later that year, Rackman and Kaplan were both speakers at a New York Board of Rabbis' symposium on "The Reported Upsurge of Religion and its Relevance to the Program of the Synagogue." See Kaplan, "Journals," 18:51–53 (May 10, 1956), 19:63 (February 25, 1959), 20:77 (October 8, 1959).

39. Kaplan, "Journals," 4:201–03 (January 7, 1929).

40. Ibid.

41. Ibid., 15:15 (March 16, 1950), 15:21 (March 26, 1950).

42. Ibid., 15:261 (March 29, 1952).

43. Ibid., 20:101 (February 28, 1960); Gurock interview with Arthur Kahn, November 21, 1994. Tulsa's Orthodox synagogue was on the liberal fringe of Orthodoxy. As Rabbi Kahn himself indicated, although he was a member of the Rabbinical Council of America and the synagogue maintained the traditional liturgy, it did not have, to some minds, a "fully kosher" mechitzah.

44. Kaplan, "Journals," 23:243–44 (May 7, 1966). Other examples of Kaplan being warmly and respectfully greeted in Orthodox or Orthodox-leaning congregations in the 1920s–1940s include his visit to Pittsburgh, described in "Journals," 3:101–02 (November 24, 1925), to Kansas City, described "Journals," 3:272–73 (February 4, 1928), and to Gary, Indiana, described in "Journals," 10:271–74 (January 1, 1942). See also the description of his appearances during these decades in East Coast Orthodox or very traditional Conservative synagogues in "Journals," 2:161 (June 26, 1923), for his stay in Far Rockaway, New York, and "Journals," 8:77–78 (February 1, 1936), for his trip to Boston.

45. Scult, *Judaism Faces the Twentieth Century*, p. 362.

46. *New York Times*, November 10, 1983, p. D25.

47. Mordecai Cohen, "The Sukkah," *Hamevaser* 24, no. 1 (September, 1985):4–6. See also Kaplan, *Judaism as a Civilization*, pp. 206–21.

48. Shlomo Riskin, "Why Are We So Demanding of Would-Be Converts When Our Own Jews Hardly Maintain Such an Exacting Lifestyle Themselves?" *Moment* 18, no. 2 (April 1993):18–19.

Conclusion

1. This view of Rabbi Joseph's American career was first forcefully argued in Abraham J. Karp, "New York Chooses a Chief Rabbi," *PAJHS* 44, no 3 (March 1955). A similar perspective is also offered by Gilbert Klaperman, *The Story of Yeshiva University* (London: Macmillan, 1969); and Aaron Rothkoff, *Bernard Revel: Builder of American Jewish Orthodoxy* (Philadelphia: Jewish Publication Society of America, 1972).

2. For a fuller analysis of the differing degrees of resistance to modernity and Americanization harbored by members of Rabbi Jacob Joseph's circle, see Jeffrey S. Gurock, "How 'Frum' Was Rabbi Jacob Joseph's Court: Americanization Within the Lower East Side's Orthodox Elite, 1886–1902," *Jewish History* 8, no. 1–2 (1994):255–68.

3. For a discussion of the Agudath ha-Rabbanim's attitudes toward the Orthodox Union, see Jeffrey S. Gurock, "Resisters and Accommodators: Varieties of Orthodox Rabbis in America, 1886–1983," *American Jewish Archives* 35, no. 2 (November 1983):112, 168. On Kaplan's characterization of the Agudath ha-Rabbanim, see Mordecai M. Kaplan, "Journals," 6:237 (January 16, 1932).

INDEX •